CYBERSECURITY FOR SMALL NETWORKS

CYBERSECURITY FOR SMALL NETWORKS

A No-Nonsense Guide for the Reasonably Paranoid

by Seth Enoka

San Francisco

Printed in the United States of America

Third printing

27 26 25 24 23   3 4 5 6 7

ISBN-13: 978-1-7185-0148-5 (print)
ISBN-13: 978-1-7185-0149-2 (ebook)

Published by No Starch Press®, Inc.
245 8th Street, San Francisco, CA 94103
phone: +1.415.863.9900
www.nostarch.com; info@nostarch.com

Publisher: William Pollock
Managing Editor: Jill Franklin
Production Editors: Paula Williamson and Katrina Horlbeck Olsen
Developmental Editors: Jill Franklin and Eva Morrow
Cover Illustrator: Gina Redman
Interior Design: Octopod Studios
Technical Reviewer: Kyle Rankin
Copyeditor: Kim Wimpsett
Compositor: Scribe Inc.
Proofreader: Scribe Inc.
Indexer: BIM Creatives, LLC

Library of Congress Cataloging-in-Publication Data

Names: Enoka, Seth, author.
Title: Cybersecurity for small networks / by Seth Enoka.
Description: San Francisco, CA : No Starch Press, Inc., [2022] | Includes index.
Identifiers: LCCN 2022021005 (print) | LCCN 2022021006 (ebook) | ISBN 9781718501485 (print) | ISBN 9781718501492 (ebook)
Subjects: LCSH: Local area networks (Computer networks)—Security measures.
Classification: LCC TK5105.7 .E56 2022 (print) | LCC TK5105.7 (ebook) | DDC 004.6/8—dc23/eng/20220707
LC record available at https://lccn.loc.gov/2022021005
LC ebook record available at https://lccn.loc.gov/2022021006

For customer service inquiries, please contact info@nostarch.com. For information on distribution, bulk sales, corporate sales, or translations: sales@nostarch.com. For permission to translate this work: rights@nostarch.com. To report counterfeit copies or piracy: counterfeit@nostarch.com.

To my darling wife, without whom I would surely be unable to do all the things

About the Author

Seth Enoka is an IT and cybersecurity veteran, having worked on large and complex cybersecurity incidents and investigations all over the world. When he's not helping organizations kick and keep adversaries out of their networks, you can find him teaching digital forensics and incident response, mentoring and being mentored by others in the security community, working through some degree or certification, or preparing for his next powerlifting competition (whenever that might be . . .).

About the Technical Reviewer

Kyle Rankin is the chief security officer at Purism and the author of *Linux Hardening in Hostile Networks* and *DevOps Troubleshooting*, among other books. Rankin was an award-winning columnist for *Linux Journal*. He speaks frequently on open source software and has given keynotes at SCALE and FOSDEM.

BRIEF CONTENTS

CONTENTS IN DETAIL

2
ARCHITECTING AND SEGMENTING YOUR NETWORK 25

3
FILTERING NETWORK TRAFFIC WITH FIREWALLS 33

4
SECURING WIRELESS NETWORKS 53

5
CREATING A VIRTUAL PRIVATE NETWORK 67

11
TIPS FOR MANAGING USER SECURITY ON YOUR NETWORK 177

INDEX 185

ACKNOWLEDGMENTS

There are altogether too many individuals I should thank, and I'm all too likely to leave out an important name or two, so I'd like to acknowledge the cybersecurity community as a whole. Thank you for being as open and generous with your time and expertise as I aspire to be.

INTRODUCTION

This book is an introduction to cybersecurity, written to help system and network administrators and owners understand the fundamentals of securing a network. Your personal cybersecurity is critical in protecting yourself from fraud and other harmful events attempted by adversaries. It's easy to tell yourself that you can't be a target, that you have nothing an adversary would want to use or exploit. However, your personal identifiable information (PII), protected health information (PHI), intellectual property, and government information and identification all have value. Failing to protect those things can lead to consequences such as identify theft, which can have a serious impact on your life.

For our purposes, a small network consists of 100 or fewer *endpoints*. An endpoint, or *host*, is any system or device that connects to or is part of a network, such as a desktop or laptop computer or a mobile device like a phone or tablet. Larger networks, approaching the size of an enterprise network, use similar tools and techniques that are covered in this book to provide security to their users and systems, just on a much larger scale and often at a much higher cost.

The drawback to securing small networks is that you have to maintain and administer everything yourself, with limited support and likely a limited budget. Securing your network will require constant care, and we'll cover some ways that you can do this cheaply when the need arises. Ultimately, the goal of this book is to arm you with the tools and knowledge to secure your network with whatever resources you have available, in terms of both time and money.

How to Use This Book: What to Expect

This book is written so that if you follow it logically from chapter to chapter, you'll progress through several levels of security maturity, ending with a network that has a *defense-in-depth* architecture. Defense-in-depth is an approach to cybersecurity where several defensive solutions are layered to protect valuable data and information. Chapters 1 to 4 cover how to design and architect your network to better enable your defenses and network monitoring capabilities. Then, Chapters 5 to 8 discuss low-cost, high-impact passive defense strategies to prevent adversaries from gaining access to your network or endpoints. Finally, Chapters 9 to 11 focus on the value of regular backups and active defenses, whereby you receive and respond to alerts to suspicious or malicious activity in your network, enabling cyber incident response.

Most chapters contain stand-alone projects. You can choose to complete each project in order, or you can pick and choose which projects you want to complete. However, the concepts covered in earlier chapters on network architecture provide the best return on investment, in terms of both time and money, and require less ongoing support and maintenance. The later chapters that cover active defenses require constant monitoring and are made more efficient with the completion of earlier projects. In some cases, working through the projects in earlier chapters also provides baseline knowledge that may be useful in later projects, such as familiarity with the command line. Essentially, you should complete each chapter in whichever order makes the most sense for you and your environment; for example, if you already have host and network firewalls in place, you can probably skip Chapter 3.

I recommend starting with Chapter 1 before setting off on your own adventure. It covers two fundamental topics: setting up the servers you'll use throughout the book and creating a network map and asset list. Before you can secure your network, you need to understand its *topology*: which hosts are connected to it and how they connect to each other. Mapping the topology will help you keep track of your devices and recognize unusual activity on the network. It's expected that the vast majority of readers will implement the projects contained in this book as virtual machines (VMs). *Virtual machines* (which are also endpoints!) let you run multiple computers using one physical computer. Using VMs is a cheaper and easier way to achieve the same results with fewer hardware requirements. (I'll describe the remaining hardware recommendations in the section "Recommended Hardware.")

Recommended (But Not Required) Knowledge

In this book, you'll learn the fundamentals of cybersecurity as it relates to securing small networks. The book will guide you through all of the necessary steps to complete each chapter and project at a very low level. Having previous experience working with virtual machines, using the command line, and generally managing or administering a network of any size will prove beneficial. Having said that, you should be able to follow along regardless of experience, as you'll learn the necessary skills as you progress.

Recommended Hardware

Some of the projects in this book may require hardware or a device or system that you may not currently have on hand. Wherever possible, alternatives will be provided to purchasing new hardware, but in some cases, you might find the best or only way forward is to buy something new. What follows is a list of the hardware used in each chapter.

Virtual Machine Host System

You can use a computer you already have to run your virtual machines, so long as that physical computer has enough memory (RAM) and processor (CPU) resources. As a general rule, you'll need 2GB of memory and one CPU core for each VM you plan to run, plus at least 4GB of memory and one CPU core for the host operating system. Therefore, to complete every chapter of this book, you should plan to use a physical system with at least 16GB of RAM and eight CPU cores.

Most modern systems come with specifications of this level, and you can also use network attached storage (NAS) or another system capable of running virtual machines, or a small computing unit such as an Intel NUC, in the same way. A NAS is a device connected to your network that allows storage and retrieval of data from a central location and in most cases will offer additional network services and capabilities, like the ability to host virtual machines. If you have spare resources on your computer, start there. You can always move your virtual machines to a new system if they outgrow their original host and its hardware.

Firewall

In Chapter 3, you'll be led through the installation and configuration of a pfSense firewall. This firewall can be purchased cheaply, and it will go a long way in increasing the security of any network very quickly and with minimal effort. The recommended device is the Netgate SG-3100 as it's cost-effective and easy to set up and maintain. It is possible to build your own, but the Netgate will likely be more secure and have a better cost.

NOTE *Netgate's pfSense SG-3100 has been discontinued. We recommend using the Netgate 2100 or 4100 instead. The configuration options will still be equivalent.*

Wireless Router

If you plan to use wireless in your small network (it's expected that the majority of your devices will be wirelessly connected), you'll need a wireless router or access point. We'll use the ASUS RT-AC5300 for most of the relevant examples in this book. This router is a mid-range device in terms of price and features. It provides enterprise-grade functionality without the premium price tag.

NOTE *The ASUS RT-AC5300 has been discontinued. For best value, we recommend using the ASUS RT-AX55 or ASUS RT-AC86U, but any AC/AX series ASUS router should have the same interface and configuration options.*

Managed Switch

A *managed switch* is a device that can be configured to monitor and control network traffic. This is another relatively low-cost device that will provide you with very useful capabilities, like the ability to keep vulnerable and valuable devices separate. We'll mostly be discussing and using the Netgear GS308E.

Network TAP

A *network tap* is a monitoring device that mirrors traffic passing between two points on a network, allowing you to collect network traffic as it travels between devices as well as networks. You can analyze captured traffic to identify suspicious or malicious behavior and then tailor your defenses to prevent or alert on that activity, providing the best chance to prevent cybersecurity incidents. Dualcomm offers several TAPs with varying capabilities, capacities, and price points. For most small networks, the ETAP-2003 will be sufficient; this is the device we'll focus on.

Alternatives

While the step-by-step instructions will be tailored to these recommended devices, the processes are generalized enough that you should be able to follow them with any other similar devices. Alternatives to all the devices recommended in this introduction are devices available from Ubiquiti. While Ubiquiti devices will be more expensive, they provide greater functionality and ease of administration, and they offer commercial support.

Summary

If you want to begin your security journey in the most cost-effective way possible, complete Chapters 1 to 4 on creating a defensible network architecture. If your interests lie more in the network monitoring, detection, and incident prevention domains, dive into Chapters 5 to 8 to learn high-impact defense strategies for mitigating cyber vulnerabilities and preventing adversary access to your endpoints. If your network and defense capabilities are somewhat mature already, investigate Chapters 9 to 11 for more active strategies to protect your network, endpoints, and users from adversaries that might be targeting your personal information or business data.

1

GETTING STARTED WITH A BASE LINUX SYSTEM AND NETWORK MAP

This chapter presents two fundamental projects: setting up a basic Ubuntu system that you'll use throughout the book and creating a network map. You'll use this system as a base on top of which you will install and run various security tools, and the network map will provide a visual overview of all the devices in your network and how they interrelate and communicate.

We'll start with a definition and overview of common Linux operating systems and then go through the steps to install a version of Linux (specifically, Ubuntu) in a virtual machine (VM), on a physical computer, and in the cloud. Regardless of where it's installed, I'll show you how to make Ubuntu more secure and then add it to your network map. Every time a new endpoint is added to your network, you must update your network map to ensure it's always up-to-date. An out-of-date network map is no use to anyone.

Linux Operating Systems

Linux is the operating system of choice, as Linux systems are open source and therefore very extensible, especially when compared to Windows or macOS. The level of control you have over the operating system and the applications that run on top of it is very granular, enabling you to have far better control over the security of your endpoints and your network.

Several Linux operating systems (or *distributions*) are available. Each distribution uses a different set of basic utilities and graphical user interfaces (GUIs), and each one looks and functions in a slightly different way. For example, Kali Linux is a distribution geared toward offensive operations and is commonly used by penetration testers to perform network assessments. Red Hat Linux is probably the most used enterprise distribution, and several other distributions are based on Red Hat, such as Fedora and CentOS. If you're interested in Linux, try various distributions to find the one you like the most.

In this book, we'll primarily use Ubuntu, which is one of the most user-friendly and among the easiest to use for beginners or those new to Linux in general. Ubuntu is available in three editions: Desktop, Server, and Core. For our purposes, the Desktop edition is sufficient. If you plan to use your Ubuntu servers for additional network services, such as a file or Dynamic Host Control Protocol (DHCP) server, the Server edition would be appropriate. Ubuntu Core is specifically for resource-limited applications, like internet of things (IoT) implementations.

The most recent versions of the Ubuntu operating system are available from *https://ubuntu.com/download/*. These downloads will be in ISO file format, meaning the file extension will be *.iso*. ISO files are logical images or containers that can be used to emulate physical media such as CDs or DVDs.

The following sections walk through installing Ubuntu, either as a physical device or as a virtual machine on either macOS or Windows, as well as in the cloud. Using a physical device allows you to take advantage of all of a system's resources, such as CPU and RAM, but it requires that you have a physical system available onto which you can install Ubuntu. Using virtual machines provides several useful features, like the ability to take snapshots (this will be discussed later in this chapter). Creating a virtual machine in the cloud provides additional capabilities, like easy access to your system from any location, but often comes with additional security considerations. Once you're finished with the platform-specific instructions for your setup, jump to "Finalizing the Linux Installation" on page 8.

#1: Creating an Ubuntu Virtual Machine

Throughout this book, you'll create Ubuntu systems for various purposes. Each of them will be based on the system we'll create now, which will act as a standard base operating system, on top of which you can add tools and applications necessary for securing your network.

Hypervisor Options

A *hypervisor* is software that allows you to create and run virtual machines using a guest operating system. For this initial project, you can create an Ubuntu VM using an inexpensive commercial hypervisor from VMware. Multiple editions of VMware Workstation are available from *https://www.vmware.com/*. VMware Player (for Windows) and VMware Fusion Player (for Mac) are free for personal use, but they don't have some of the more advanced features we'll want to take advantage of in later chapters. I recommend using VMware Workstation Pro and VMware Fusion Pro. The commercial license for either of these is relatively inexpensive. An alternative solution is to use the free Workstation Player to begin with and then upgrade to the commercial license if you need to. The step-by-step instructions for Workstation and Player editions are mostly the same, with some slight differences between Workstation and Fusion.

Another option is to use VirtualBox, a free solution for creating and managing VMs maintained by Oracle. VirtualBox is available for all major operating systems, and you can download it from *https://www.virtualbox.org/wiki/Downloads/*.

VMware Workstation and VMware Player for Windows

To create your VM in VMware Workstation or VMware Player, follow these steps:

1. Click **File ▸ New Virtual Machine** in VMware.
2. On the New Virtual Machine screen that opens, choose **Typical (recommended)** and click **Next**.
3. Select **Installer Disc Image File (iso)**.
4. Using the **Browse** button, navigate to and select the Ubuntu ISO you downloaded earlier; then click **Next**.
5. The Easy Install wizard will ask for the user details for your VM; fill out the Full Name, User Name, and Password fields, and click **Next**.
6. Give your VM a meaningful name indicating its role on your network when asked.
7. Save the VM to the default location (or anywhere you desire) and click **Next**.
8. Set the virtual disk size to 40GB if your host machine has enough disk space; otherwise, accept the default 20GB.
9. Store the virtual disk as a single file, rather than split into multiple files and click **Next**.
10. Click **Customize Hardware**.
11. If your host has enough RAM, increase the RAM of the VM from 2GB to 4GB.
12. Set Processors to 1.

13. Under Network Adapter, select **Bridged** mode to give your VM its own independent IP address and network connection.
14. Click **Sound Card ▸ Remove**.
15. Click **Printer ▸ Remove**.
16. Click **Finish**.

Your virtual machine will be created, and the operating system will begin installing.

VMware Fusion and VMware Fusion Player for macOS

Once you've installed VMware Fusion or VMware Fusion Player, follow these steps to create your first VM:

1. Click **File ▸ New ▸ Continue** in VMware.
2. Drag and drop your ISO file onto the VMware Fusion window, or click the **Use Another Disc or Disc Image** button to locate the file in your filesystem; then click **Continue**.
3. The Easy Install wizard will ask you for the user details for your VM; fill out the Display Name, Account Name, and Password fields.
4. Ensure the Make your home folder accessible to the virtual machine checkbox is not ticked and click **Continue**.
5. Click **Customize Settings**.
6. Save the VM to the default location (or anywhere you desire).
7. Set the virtual disk size to 40GB if your host machine has enough disk space; otherwise, accept the default 20GB.
8. In the **Processors and Memory** menu, if your host has enough RAM, increase the RAM of the VM from 2GB to 4GB, and set Processors to 1.
9. Untick the **Connect** checkbox to either add or disconnect the following peripherals within their context menus: sound card, floppy, printer, and camera. (Disconnecting unused or superfluous peripherals from your virtual machines removes potential attack vectors.)

Click the **Play** button to start your VM, and the operating system installation will begin.

VirtualBox

The steps for creating a VM in VirtualBox are the same whether you're using a Windows PC or Mac as the host system. Once you've downloaded and installed VirtualBox, follow these steps to create a VM:

1. Click the **New** button at the top of the VirtualBox window.
2. Provide a relevant name for your VM, specify the location to save the files (the default folder is usually fine), and select the correct operating system from the drop-down menus: **Linux ▸ Ubuntu (64-bit)**; then click **Continue**.

3. If your host has enough RAM, increase the RAM of the VM from 2GB to 4GB, and click **Continue**.
4. Select **Create a New Virtual Hard Disk Now** and then click **Create**.
5. Select **VMDK** as the hard disk format and click **Continue**.
6. Select **Dynamically Allocated** and click **Continue** or **Next** (depending on your OS).
7. Set the virtual disk size to 40GB if your host machine has enough disk space; otherwise, accept the default 32GB and click **Create**.
8. Select the VM in VirtualBox and click **Settings**.
9. Go to **Settings ▸ System ▸ Motherboard**.
10. Under Boot Order, untick the **Floppy** checkbox.
11. Go to **Settings ▸ System ▸ Storage**.
12. Select the CD drive (it'll be listed as **Controller: IDE** and have a CD icon next to it).
13. In the attributes pane, click the **CD icon** to choose a disk file, and point it at your Ubuntu ISO file.
14. Under **Settings ▸ Audio**, untick the **Enable Audio** checkbox.
15. Under **Settings ▸ Network ▸ Adapter 1**, switch the **Attached to** drop-down to **Bridged Adapter** so your VM will be assigned its own IP address and be logically separate from the host system's network settings.
16. Click **OK**.

NOTE *The options for hard disk format are VDI, VHD, or VMDK. VDI is VirtualBox's proprietary format. VHD was developed by Microsoft, is compatible with Windows, and can be easily mounted under the Windows operating system as a virtual disk. VMware originally developed VMDK, but it's now an open file format. VMDK is compatible with both VirtualBox and VMware, so if you choose to switch from one to the other, your virtual hard disks shouldn't cause any challenges.*

#2: Creating a Physical Linux System

Instead of creating a virtual machine, you might want to use a physical computer and install Ubuntu the same way you'd install Windows or macOS directly onto the hardware. Using a physical system has benefits like increased performance or reduced resource requirements in terms of memory and processing power. The main drawback is that physical systems usually aren't as flexible as virtual machines. As you progress through this book, you'll be asked to create multiple Linux systems, so we'll assume that you'll use mostly virtual machines. However, should you choose to use physical systems for each of these projects, you should still be able to follow along.

To create a physical Ubuntu system, you need a *bootable USB drive*, which means you'll install Ubuntu on a USB that you can plug into any computer and install it from there.

Bootable USB on Windows

On a Windows computer, the simplest way to create a bootable Ubuntu USB is with Rufus, a small utility specifically for creating bootable media. Download the latest version from *https://rufus.ie/*. Rufus is a *portable executable*, which means you don't need to install it; just download and run it. Once downloaded, follow these steps:

1. Plug in a USB thumb drive at least 16GB in size. Rufus will format this USB drive, so make sure it doesn't contain anything you want to keep.
2. Run the Rufus executable.
3. Once Rufus is open, ensure the Device drop-down menu indicates that the correct USB drive is selected. It's often easiest to plug in only your target USB device and unplug any others.
4. Under Boot Selection, choose **Disk or ISO Image**.
5. Click **Select**.
6. Navigate to your Ubuntu ISO file and select it.
7. Once selected, Rufus will load a set of default settings for the bootable USB; accept them and click **Start**.
8. Rufus might display a pop-up asking whether you want to write the media in ISO or DD image mode; choose **ISO Mode** and click **OK**. When installing Ubuntu later, if you aren't able to proceed with the installation or it seems to hang, repeat this process and select **DD Mode** instead.
9. Rufus will display a pop-up to inform you that it will format the USB drive; click **OK** to proceed.

Bootable USB on macOS

Etcher is an open source utility for macOS used for writing operating system images to removable media such as USB drives and SD cards. Download the latest version from *https://www.balena.io/etcher/*. Once it's downloaded and installed, follow these steps:

1. Plug in a USB thumb drive at least 16GB in size. Etcher will format your USB drive, so make sure it doesn't contain anything you want to keep.
2. Run Etcher.
3. Once Etcher is open, click **Flash from File**, and select your Ubuntu ISO file.
4. Click **Select Target** and select your USB drive.
5. Click **Flash** to create your bootable Ubuntu USB (you might be asked to enter your computer password to allow Etcher to make changes to the USB).

6. The flashing process will begin, and a progress bar will appear. Once the process completes, you may be informed that "The disk you inserted was not readable by this computer." If so, just eject the USB; don't choose Initialize.

Using the Bootable USB

When the process completes, you'll have a bootable Ubuntu Linux USB drive. Plug it into the computer on which you want to install Ubuntu and boot or reboot it. You might have to change the system's boot order so it boots from the USB instead of the internal hard drive. To do that, you need to interrupt the boot sequence, which is typically done by pressing ESC, F8, F10, or F12. Do an internet search to find the correct interrupt key for your computer, or reboot the system and press each of those keys until you successfully enter the computer's basic input/output system (BIOS).

NOTE *Technically, most modern computers use the Unified Extensible Firmware Interface (UEFI), which has improved features over the outdated BIOS. We'll use the terms BIOS and UEFI interchangeably.*

From the BIOS, which is responsible for hardware management outside your operating system, change the boot order so that the computer boots from the USB first. Then restart the computer, and it will boot into the Ubuntu installation environment. On a Mac, just hold the OPTION key while the system boots and then choose to boot from USB.

#3: Creating a Cloud-Based Linux System

It's common to move network infrastructure to the cloud, which just means running our services on someone else's computer(s). Websites and the web servers that run them are often easier to access (from anywhere in the world) and manage in the cloud than they would be on our private networks and VPN servers. (We'll cover VPNs in greater detail in Chapter 5.) In this section, we'll explain how to create your Linux computer using a cloud service provider. We'll use Vultr for this project as it's relatively inexpensive, it's reliable, and it presents an easy learning curve if you haven't used a cloud provider before. The steps should be similar regardless of provider, whether you're using Amazon Web Services, Microsoft Azure, or something else.

1. Create an account at *https://www.vultr.com/*.
2. On the account dashboard, click **+ ▸ Deploy New Server**.
3. Choose **Cloud Compute**. The other options (High Frequency, Bare Metal, and so on) are for specialist applications, not suitable for our purposes.

4. Choose a location for your server. Choosing a location geographically close to you can improve access speeds to your VM; however, if you want to obfuscate your location, choose a location in a different country.
5. For Server Type, choose the latest available version of Ubuntu.
6. Choose a server size. The cheapest option is a good place to start; you can always upgrade your VM later if necessary.
7. Supply a hostname for your server.
8. Click **Deploy**.

The service provider will now instantiate your Ubuntu VM, which is the same as creating a VM in VMware or VirtualBox. This process can take some time. Once your VM is confirmed to be up and running, your service provider will supply the IP address, username, and password to access your VM. You'll then be able to complete the steps in the following sections to set up and secure your VM.

Finalizing the Linux Installation

If you created your Linux system in the cloud or using VMware and Easy Install, booting the VM will automatically install Ubuntu, create your user account, and present you with the Ubuntu desktop environment, which will be similar to a Windows or Mac desktop. If you used VirtualBox or are creating a physical Linux system, you'll need to complete some additional steps to get to that stage.

In VirtualBox, follow these steps:

1. Click the **Start** button to boot the VM.
2. Using the Ubuntu installation wizard, select your desired language and click **Install Ubuntu**.
3. Select your keyboard layout and click **Continue**.
4. On the Updates and Software screen, select **Minimal Installation** as you won't need a lot of the additional software that would otherwise be installed with the operating system.
5. Tick both checkboxes to allow software updates to be installed from various sources.
6. Click **Continue**.
7. On the next screen, the wizard will ask if you want to erase the disk and install Ubuntu, with a warning, as shown in Figure 1-1. Click the **Advanced Features** button and select **Use LVM with the New Ubuntu Installation**. Using LVM provides greater flexibility and control over your disks and their partitioning. LVM allows for advanced features such as naming logical volumes and dynamically resizing partitions and virtual hard disks when required.

Figure 1-1: Ubuntu installation type prompt

Keep in mind that this installation wizard is referring only to the virtual machine and the virtual hard disk that is attached to it (which we created earlier). It does not affect the physical hard drive of your host system. There is no risk of losing your files or data by proceeding with the installation inside the VM.

8. Click **OK ▸ Install Now**.
9. You'll be asked to write the changes to disk (meaning the virtual hard disk of the VM). Click **Continue** to accept the configuration you just set for this VM.

As Ubuntu installs, you'll be asked for certain settings for the operating system, such as your location (for time zone settings), your name, your computer or hostname, and your user details such as username and password. Set those as appropriate and continue the installation. Eventually, the operating system installation will complete, and you'll be presented with the Ubuntu desktop environment.

WARNING *Do not set or allow the user to log in automatically, as that configuration isn't secure for any computer. Always use the* ***Require my Password to Log in*** *setting.*

The first time you log in, Ubuntu will ask you to configure online accounts and whether you want to share anonymous statistics with the developer. This system needs to be a secure system and therefore shouldn't be connected to services such as Google or Microsoft cloud services. Skip all of those configuration options and disallow sharing of data wherever possible. This advice is good for life (if you're concerned about privacy), not just the configuration of Ubuntu virtual machines.

You'll follow the same steps to complete Ubuntu installation on a physical system, the only difference being the disk partitioning will affect the physical hard drive within the computer, and not a virtual hard drive. Once you've installed Ubuntu, reset the boot order in the BIOS as you did before so the computer boots from the internal hard drive instead of USB, and also remove the bootable USB from the computer.

Hardening Your Ubuntu System

Now that you've created a base virtual or physical machine, you'll make some initial configuration changes to ensure your system is secure. This process is called *hardening*, which broadly means keeping the system up-to-date with the latest operating system and software patches, installing some additional management software, and altering configuration files to make the system more secure.

#4: Installing System Packages

In Ubuntu, you'll use the Advanced Package Tool (APT) to ensure the system is up-to-date with all of the latest patches. In Linux, people use the term *packages* to refer to software, and APT is a package management utility used to install, uninstall, update, or otherwise manage the tools and software on your system.

APT is a command line interface (CLI) utility, which means you'll use the Linux Terminal to interact with it, rather than a GUI tool like Windows Update.

NOTE *Most operating systems have a CLI; Windows has Command Prompt and PowerShell, and macOS has its own Terminal. Essentially, a CLI is a more direct way to interact with the operating system using text commands. A CLI will look like a simple text editor with a prompt for your input. Command Prompt, Linux Terminal, and macOS Terminal are all black with white text by default. PowerShell is blue.*

In a cloud deployment, you might have access only to the Linux Terminal by default, with no access to a GUI. If that's the case, you'll be presented with a terminal window immediately upon logging in. Otherwise, to access the terminal in Ubuntu, click the **Activities** menu at the top-left side of the screen in Ubuntu, type **Terminal**, and click it when it appears, the same way you'd search for and open an application in the Windows Start menu.

By default, even as an administrator, you can't run certain commands or perform some actions on a Linux system because you don't have the necessary permissions (called *privileges* in Linux). A lot of commands and actions are reserved for *superusers*, or the *root* user account in Linux. As a non-root (that is, a nonsuperuser) user in Linux, you need the `sudo` command, which stands for *superuser do*. For example, to use APT to update all the installed packages in your Ubuntu system, use the following commands, pressing ENTER after each command to execute them:

```
$ sudo apt update
$ sudo apt upgrade
```

The first command, `sudo apt update`, retrieves the list of available updates for each application currently installed. The second command, `sudo apt upgrade`, downloads and installs those updates. When prompted, enter your password; making you authenticate to run privileged commands is a `sudo` security feature. Every time you run a command with `sudo`, the action is logged in the */var/log/auth.log* file, so all administrative actions can be audited after the fact. When asked to continue installing packages, enter **Y** (for yes) and press ENTER.

WARNING *On the command line in Linux and macOS, when your prompt displays a dollar sign ($), this means you're currently in the context of (that is, operating as) a normal, non-administrative user. If your prompt displays a hash mark (#), you're in the context of the root user and have full system access to make changes, move files, and delete files. Be careful if you're operating in the context of root, as it's easy to make mistakes and cause problems with your operating system. It's always best to work primarily in the context of a normal user and use* `sudo` *when using the command line.*

When you install new packages, APT often also installs any dependencies required for those packages (otherwise, your software would look for things it depends on, not find them, and fail to run successfully). However, when you remove or uninstall software, those dependencies might be left behind. Having unnecessary applications on your systems is insecure, as an attacker might exploit a vulnerability in those leftover packages to gain access to your network or use them to perform other nefarious activities. Run `sudo apt autoremove` and `sudo apt clean` as shown here to remove any no longer needed dependencies and delete previously downloaded packages, respectively:

```
$ sudo apt autoremove
$ sudo apt clean
```

To install new packages, use `sudo apt install`. A useful package that allows you to access and administer your system remotely via the command line is SSH (for *secure shell*). Run `sudo apt install openssh-server` to install SSH (to install a different package, you would substitute `openssh-server` for the package name).

You can install multiple packages with `apt` at the same time like this:

```
$ sudo apt install openssh-server package_name1 package_name2
```

Again, type your password and enter **`Y`** if prompted. With SSH installed, you'll be able to configure remote access to your system.

#5: Managing Linux Users

Part of managing your network security is managing the user accounts and hosts within your network. You may need to add new users to your Ubuntu machines, such as a new user account for a new service or application, or to allow others to administer your systems. Adding new users is an administrative function and requires the `sudo` command. Use the `adduser` command to add new users:

```
$ sudo adduser username
```

You'll be asked to specify a password for the user, but using passphrases is better, because they're easier to remember, tend to be longer, and are harder to crack. (We'll discuss passphrases and creating strong passwords in more detail in Chapter 11.)

You also can set names, phone numbers, and other information for your users if you want; otherwise, press ENTER to leave these fields blank.

Deleting a user is just as easy:

```
$ sudo deluser username
```

In addition, you may want to give your new user `sudo` privileges to allow them to administer your system, which you can do with the `usermod` command:

```
$ sudo usermod -aG sudo username
```

The `-aG` (add group) parameter will add the user to the *sudo* group. User groups in Linux are a collection of user accounts, and they're used to assign privileges and permissions to specific user accounts, such as the ability to read and write certain files. Keep in mind, however, that the fewer users with sudo privileges the better. Always practice the principle of least privilege and allow users only as much control as they require on a day-to-day basis. Providing administrator credentials and privileges to more people than necessary will lead to a far less secure network configuration.

Finally, you can reset the password for a given user with the `passwd` command:

```
$ sudo passwd username
```

Managing the users in your network is an important part of keeping your network secure. Having superfluous user accounts, especially if they have more privileges than they require, provides an easy way for adversaries to compromise and gain a foothold inside your network. This is easily preventable, so always be aware of the risks of additional or unnecessary user accounts.

Besides managing the users in your environment, each of your endpoints has a hostname, which is a friendly name or human-readable name used to identify the host. Often, these are configured as some default value by the operating system when it's installed (like `ubuntu` for Ubuntu systems). It can be beneficial to choose a naming scheme for your hosts and to ensure each host has a different name. In Windows networks, for example, multiple hosts cannot have the same hostname, because this results in conflicts that create administrative problems within the network.

You can check the hostname of your Linux system with the `hostname` command:

```
$ hostname
ubuntu
```

To change the hostname, use the `hostname` command again, but this time use `sudo` and specify the desired hostname:

```
$ sudo hostname your_hostname
```

Run the `hostname` command again to confirm the change has occurred. Reboot your server to make the change permanent.

#6: Securing Remote Access

Now that you've made it possible to access the system remotely with SSH, you need to lock down that capability so only authorized users can log in to this host. Several settings are involved in this process. You'll disable password login in favor of SSH keys, as well as disallow the root account from logging in directly via SSH. Allowing superusers such as root to log in interactively using utilities like SSH is bad practice because it allows attackers to perform attacks such as brute-forcing (continually guessing potential passwords until they find the one that works) and then be able to log in with complete access to your system. Likewise, with your other user accounts, using SSH keys to log in instead of passwords eliminates an entire class of potential attacks (username and password guessing) against your systems.

Generating SSH Keys

SSH key pairs are generally accepted to be more secure than passwords or passphrases. SSH keys are cryptographically secure keys that can be used to authenticate a client computer (your local host) to an SSH server (your Ubuntu system). The first part of a key pair is your private key, which is held by and identifies your client, and must remain absolutely secret, just like a password. The other half is the public key, which can be freely shared. The public key is provided to your SSH server and is capable of decrypting your private key, thereby allowing authentication between the two endpoints. Each local user account that you want to use to log in to your Ubuntu system will need its own set of public and private keys.

To create an SSH key pair, open a terminal window on the computer you plan to use as your SSH client (the computer that will connect to your Ubuntu system via SSH). Enter `ssh-keygen` and press ENTER. Press ENTER again to accept the default file in which to save the keys. The default location of this file will be:

- Windows: *C:\Users\<user>\.ssh\id_rsa*
- macOS: */Users/<user>/.ssh/id_rsa*
- Linux: */home/<user>/.ssh/id_rsa*

Next, you'll be asked for a passphrase for your private key, which is optional but recommended. By using a passphrase in addition to your SSH keys, your private key is never exposed on the network, meaning that to get access to your private key, attackers need access to your computer (if they have that, it's probably already game over). Once you've entered your passphrase (or not), press ENTER, and your key pair will be created.

To provide the public key file to your Ubuntu system (or any other server you want to use your key pair to connect with), enter the following command:

```
$ ssh-copy-id user@your_ubuntu_ip
The authenticity of host '192.168.1.10' can't be established.
ECDSA key fingerprint is aa:aa:aa:aa:aa:aa:aa:aa:aa:aa:aa:aa:aa:aa:aa:aa.
Are you sure you want to continue connecting (yes/no)? yes
```

The prompt about an ECDSA key fingerprint might be shown, which just means that the remote computer wasn't able to identify your local computer (because it hasn't connected to it in this way before). If you receive this prompt, type **yes** and press ENTER. Your Ubuntu system will ask you for the password of the user account you're trying to use to connect (that is, the password for the remote user account). Enter the password, and the process is complete. At this point, you can use **ssh *user@your_ubuntu_ip*** to log in to your Ubuntu system, and you'll be prompted for the SSH key passphrase (not the passphrase for the user on the Ubuntu system) if you set one.

Disallowing Password Authentication

Next, change the SSH configuration on your Ubuntu system to disallow password authentication, forcing the use of your SSH keys to log in. Log in to your Ubuntu system as a standard, non-root user, and open the SSH configuration file in the terminal using Nano, the text editor installed by default on many Linux distributions, with the following command:

```
$ sudo nano /etc/ssh/sshd_config
```

Find the line with the setting: `# PasswordAuthentication yes`. To search for text in Nano, press CTRL-W and then type your search term and press ENTER. The setting is currently commented out (the `#` at the start of the line tells SSH to ignore that line) because `yes` is the default configuration and doesn't need to be set explicitly. Remove the `#` from the beginning of the line, and change `yes` to **no**. For every system you create (and on which you enable SSH), you must change this setting.

Disabling Root Login

It's also prudent to disable the ability for the root user to log in remotely. As mentioned earlier, on Linux, the root user has the highest level of permissions or privileges on the system. By disabling its ability to log in, you remove the capability of any would-be attackers to gain privileged access to the system. Technically, the root account on the most recent versions of Ubuntu can't log in because it's locked by default, but it's always good to ensure it's unable to log in anyway. Find the line:

```
PermitRootLogin prohibit-password
```

and change `prohibit-password` to **no**. With that done, save the changes you've made to the file. Press CTRL-O and then press ENTER to overwrite the file you're editing. Press CTRL-X to exit the file and return to the terminal.

Restart the SSH service so that it's reloaded with the new configuration, using the following command:

```
$ sudo systemctl restart ssh
```

There's one more thing left to test. Earlier, you disabled the ability to log in via SSH using password authentication by modifying the configuration file in */etc/ssh/sshd_config*. From any computer in your network, try to SSH into your Ubuntu system using an account on that computer, with the password you configured (not the user account you provided with your SSH key):

```
$ ssh user@your_ubuntu_ip
user@your_ubuntu_ip: Permission denied (publickey).
```

Here, ***user*** is the username you use to log in to the system, and ***your_ubuntu_ip*** is the IP address of your Linux system. If you're able to log in successfully, go back to the "Disallowing Password Authentication" section and make sure your configuration is correct, or reboot Ubuntu. Leaving access open would create a vulnerability in your network, which is easy to fix but potentially a big problem if left unchecked.

Remote Login with SSH

Both macOS and Windows have SSH built in. Using the computer for which you generated an SSH key and copied to your Ubuntu system, connect to your new Linux system by entering the following command:

```
  $ ssh user@your_ubuntu_ip
  Enter passphrase for key '/Users/user/.ssh/id_rsa':
❶ Welcome to Ubuntu (GNU/Linux 5.8.0-44-generic x86_6)
❷ * Documentation:   https://help.ubuntu.com
  * Management:      https://landscape.canonical.com
  * Support:         https://ubuntu.com/advantage

❸ 6 updates can be installed immediately.
  5 of these updates are security updates.
  To see these additional updates run: apt list --upgradable

  Your Hardware Enablement Stack (HWE) is supported until ❹ April 2025.
❺ Last login: Mon Mar  8 17:02:46 from 192.168.1.12
```

When you log in via SSH to Ubuntu, the operating system outputs a lot of useful information. The first line indicates which version of the operating system is currently installed ❶. There are links to documentation and how to get help ❷, followed by a list of any available updates for the system or installed packages ❸. This useful list indicates when you need to run the update commands described earlier in "Installing System Packages." Next, Ubuntu shows when support for your operating system expires ❹, at which point you'll need to upgrade your distribution with the `sudo apt dist-upgrade` command or build a new system with the latest operating system. Finally, the last successful login to the system is shown ❺, which can be useful for identifying suspicious activity. If the last login was at 3 AM or from an unfamiliar IP address, you might want to investigate that activity (unless you're in the habit of administering your network and systems in the early hours).

#7: Capturing VM Configurations

At this point, if you're using a VM, your virtual machine is at a known-good state; you've finished configuring and hardening it, and it's ready to be used in your network. It's a good idea to save this state so that if something goes wrong, you can return to it without completely rebuilding the system. One of the benefits of using virtual machines is the ability to take *snapshots*. Snapshots save the current state of a virtual machine, including its power state (on, off, suspended, and so on), so that you can quickly return to a saved state if necessary. You can't do that with a traditional, physical system, although we've all been in situations where we wish we could. You might choose to take a snapshot before installing a new program, for example, or before changing a VM's network settings or before adding or deleting a new user.

Taking Snapshots in VMware

Regardless of the version of VMware you're using, simply right-click the virtual machine for which you want to create a snapshot, click **Snapshots ▸ Snapshot**, name your snapshot, and wait for the process to complete. That's it. Now, if something happens to your VM, right-click the VM and then click **Snapshots ▸ Restore Snapshot** to revert to this known-good state. It's that simple.

Taking Snapshots in VirtualBox

In VirtualBox, click the menu button (three bullets and three lines) on the VM in the virtual machine panel on the left of the VirtualBox window and then click **Snapshots**. To create a snapshot, click **Take**. Name your snapshot, click **OK**, and wait for the process to complete. To revert to a snapshot, click the snapshot and then click **Restore**.

NOTE *Every snapshot you create will effectively make a duplicate of your virtual machine. Multiple snapshots can take up a large amount of space on your host computer. Keep this in mind when creating snapshots, and remove old snapshots when they're no longer needed. Some cloud providers charge for snapshot storage as well, so keep that in mind when creating snapshots in your cloud dashboard. Snapshots are also not a good long-term backup method. (We'll discuss backups at length in Chapter 9.)*

Network Topology

Understanding how your systems and devices connect to and communicate with each other is critical when it comes to cybersecurity. With that in mind, let's take a crash course on the *Internet Protocol (IP)* and IP addressing. IP is a standard protocol that defines the format of data sent over a network allowing computers and other network-connected devices to communicate with each other.

Each of your computers and other network-connected devices requires an *IP address*. An IP address is comparable to a street address or a post office box; computer A sends network traffic to computer B by embedding computer B's IP address in the data it sends. It's the same as writing an address on an envelope. Any intermediate devices between the two computers can interpret this address from the data and pass it along until it reaches its destination, just like the postal service.

Two commonly used versions of the internet protocol currently exist, version 4 and version 6, which means we have two types of IP addresses, IPv4 and IPv6. While IPv6 has been around since the 1990s, it still isn't used often today. We won't cover it in detail in later chapters as it's largely outside the scope of this book, but it's important to be aware of what it is and why it exists. IPv4 addresses are written in what is known as *dotted quad notation*, which is a fancy way of saying they're composed of four numbers separated by periods, such as 192.168.1.1. Each of the four numbers can range from 0 to 255, meaning that IPv4 addresses range from 0.0.0.0 to 255.255.255.255, or a total of 4,294,967,296 possible addresses.

So many network-connected devices now exist in the world that there aren't enough IPv4 addresses to go around, which is one of the reasons IPv6 was created. IPv6 has a larger address space, with a total of more than 340 trillion, trillion, trillion addresses. To put that in perspective, that's 100 times more addresses than there are atoms on the surface of Earth, which is convenient as more and more internet-connected devices come online. Eventually, IPv6 will be in common use, and every device will be able to have its own public IPv6 address, until we run out of those (probably not in my lifetime).

As there aren't enough IPv4 addresses for everyone, we've had to come up with clever workarounds to connect all of our devices to the internet. One of those solutions is *network address translation (NAT)*. Using NAT, several devices can be contacted via one IP address.

When you connect your home or office to the internet through your router, your internet service provider assigns you (and your network) a public IP address. You can find your IP address using services like *https://www.whatismyip.com/*. IP addresses are usually *dynamic*, meaning that when you disconnect from and reconnect to the internet, you will often receive a different IP address.

Your internet router is responsible for routing traffic from your private, internal network, to the public internet, and vice versa, which is how you're able to access services and browse the internet generally. At a high level, NAT takes the public IP address assigned to your router and translates the traffic it receives so that traffic bound from the internet to one of your internal computers or devices receives the traffic destined for that specific device. It's similar to the way letters and packages are delivered to office buildings at their street address, and then a clerk or mail department determines where that package needs to go internally, forwarding it to the right recipient. It also works in the reverse; traffic outbound from your computer to the internet must be translated from the internal IP address of your computer to the public IP address of your router before being forwarded on to reach its intended destination and return a service, like a web page.

Different IP addresses are reserved and available for use on the public internet and your private network. The private address ranges that can be used for private networks are:

10.0.0.0 to 10.255.255.255

172.16.0.0 to 172.31.255.255

192.168.0.0 to 192.168.255.255

All other IP addresses form part of the publicly available IP ranges or are as yet unassigned.

#8: Checking Your IP Address

Addressing is usually handled by a router or server. If you have a wireless router, you can log in to that device, take a look at the client list or DHCP settings, and find out which address range is being used. Alternatively, you can just check the address of your computer(s). Understanding the addressing in your network, in addition to maintaining an asset inventory and network map, also means you can keep account of the addresses assigned to specific devices, the users who are responsible for or assigned to a specific piece of hardware, and where a particular device is physically located, among other metadata. (We discuss asset management further in Chapter 8.)

On Windows

On Windows, click the Start menu, enter cmd, and press ENTER to open the command prompt. Next, enter **ipconfig** and press ENTER:

```
C:\Users\user>ipconfig

Windows IP Configuration
Ethernet adapter Ethernet:
   IPv4 Address. . . . . . . . . . . : 192.168.1.126
   Subnet Mask. . . . . . . . . . . : 255.255.255.0
   Default Gateway. . . . . . . . . : 192.168.1.1
C:\Users\user>
```

The output will show your current IP address, the relevant *subnet mask*, and the *default gateway* your computer is using. The subnet mask indicates to which segment of a network your computer belongs, and the default gateway is the address of the device your computer uses to access other networks, such as the internet. The gateway is probably your router.

On a Mac

Finding the IP address of a Mac is similar. Open a terminal window, type **ifconfig**, and press ENTER:

```
$ ifconfig
--snip--
en0: flags=8863<UP,BROADCAST,SMART,RUNNING,SIMPLEX,MULTICAST> mtu 1500
        options=400<CHANNEL_IO>
        ether 78:8d:43:a4:ce:29
        inet 192.168.1.120 netmask 0xffffff00 broadcast 192.168.1.255
        media: autoselect
        status: active
```

On macOS, the `ifconfig` output is a bit different: `inet` is the internet or IP address, `netmask` is the subnet mask, and `broadcast` is the *broadcast address* of the network. The subnet mask here is displayed in *hexadecimal (hex)* instead of decimal. Hex is another notation used by computers, different from the dotted quad notation. A broadcast address is a reserved address in a network used for sending traffic to all devices in that network segment (we'll cover this more in Chapter 10, which discusses network security monitoring).

On Linux

On a Linux system, open a terminal window, and enter the following:

```
$ ip addr
--snip--
2: ens32: <BROADCAST,MULTICAST,UP,LOWER_UP> mtu 1500 qdisc fq_codel state UP group default qlen
1000
    link/ether 00:0c:29:db:ee:7c brd ff:ff:ff:ff:ff:ff
    altname enp2s0
    inet  192.168.1.30/24 brd 192.168.1.255 scope global dynamic noprefixroute ens32
       valid_lft 4106sec preferred_lft 4106sec
    inet6 fe80::66e:1ae7:861f:9224/64 scope link noprefixroute
       valid_lft forever preferred_lft forever
```

The IP address is listed under `inet` again; the broadcast address is `brd`, and the subnet mask is shown as `/24`, in *CIDR notation*. CIDR is another way of representing the same subnet mask information in a shorter format.

#9: Creating a Network Map

To get a better understanding of your network and see more granular details, like ingress and egress points (that is, the places where traffic enters and leaves your network), creating a *network map* or *network diagram* is beneficial. A network diagram is a graphical representation of your network that allows you to see the overall architecture at a glance and makes it easier to identify potential issues when it comes to securing your network.

draw.io (*https://www.draw.io/*) is a free and easy-to-use cloud editor that allows users to create various types of diagrams, one being the network diagram. Alternatively, Microsoft Visio is a commercial solution that achieves the same objective. If you choose to use draw.io, load the site and open the Citrix drop-down from the menu on the left. You can then drag and drop the relevant representations, as shown in Figure 1-2, from the menu on the left to the canvas on the right.

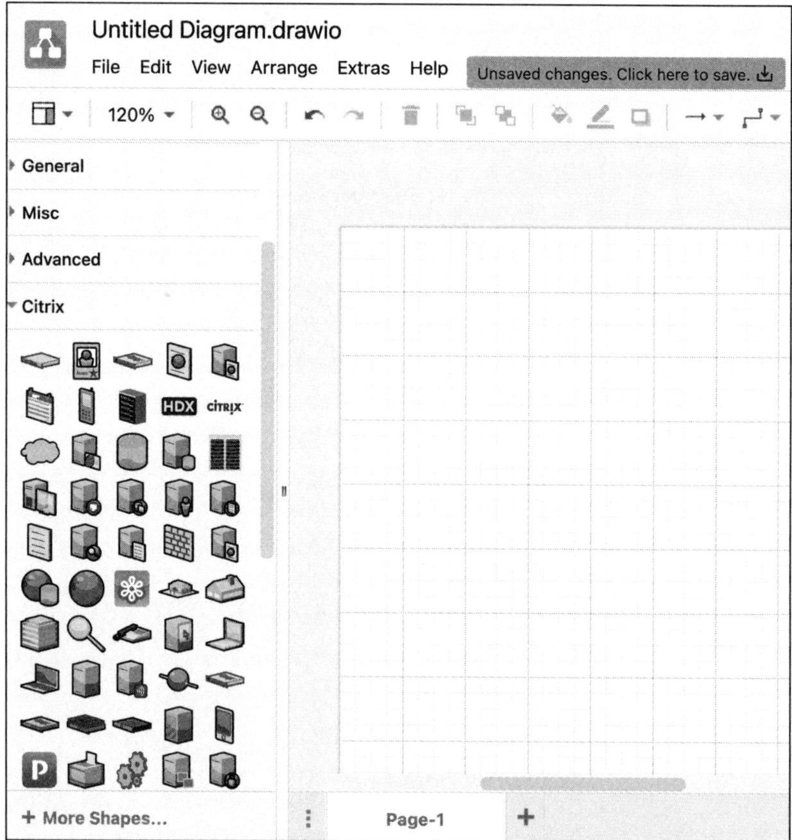

Figure 1-2: draw.io diagramming tool

At its most basic, a small network typically comprises a modem/router, usually provided by your internet service provider, which connects your network and all your devices to the internet, as well as a few devices: computers, laptops, mobile devices, peripherals such as printers, and so on. Keeping track of all the devices on your network better enables you to secure your network, because you know what should be connected and allowed to communicate, both within the network and between your network and the internet.

Always keep your network diagram up-to-date. Whenever you add a new computer, laptop, mobile device, switch, virtual machine, or other system or device to your network (and remove them as well), you should update your network diagram. When it comes to a transient device whose IP addresses aren't static, it might be worth assigning the device a static IP address in your router (see Chapter 4). Otherwise, you can track the IP range that might be assigned to those devices. Even if a device isn't always connected to your network, maintain a record of devices that will be consistently expected to connect (Chapter 4 discusses this in greater detail), and note those IP addresses in your network diagram.

A network diagram also allows you to see where you can implement additional security controls to improve your security posture. For example, Figure 1-3 shows a small, basic network.

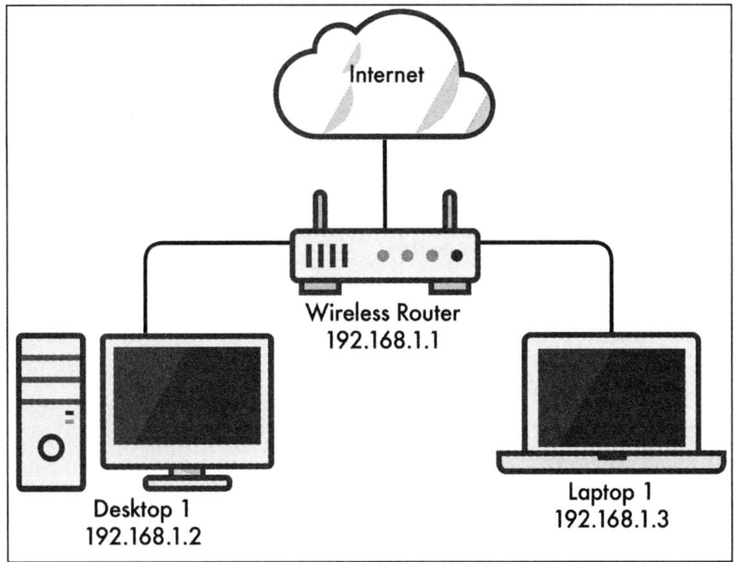

Figure 1-3: A small network

This network layout is typical of most home networks, where a modem/router connects the network to the internet, and all the endpoints use that device as a gateway to the public network. The problem with this network architecture is that it also allows adversaries to use the same network infrastructure to access the private network, without many obstacles in their path. Later in this book, you'll learn how to improve this network's security by adding a firewall between the wireless router and the internet to better manage the ingress and egress traffic and block suspicious traffic entering or leaving the network (see Chapter 3 for more details on firewalls).

When mapping your network, collect as much information as possible about all the devices it includes, such as their IP addresses, MAC addresses, hostnames, purpose, primary user or owner, location, serial numbers, and so on. Start with your computers and move on to mobile devices, such as phones and tablets, and then any IoT devices you might have—if your TV or refrigerator connects to the internet, be sure to capture those as well.

#10: Transferring Files

You may want to transfer files to your Linux machine from another system or from your Linux machine to your local computer. The intuitive rsync tool can synchronize files and folders, either between two locations on one system or between two systems across a network. To transfer specific files from one computer to another, use the following:

```
$ rsync -ruhP --remove-source-files --protect-args "/path/to/source/" \
    "user@computer_ip:/path/to/destination/"
```

Immediately following the rsync command are four flags. The `r` flag stands for *recursive*, meaning that everything inside the source folder will be copied to the destination. The `u` flag stands for *update*, which indicates to rsync that if it finds a copy of a file in the destination location that is newer than the copy in the source directory, skip it. Next, `h` is the typical flag used for *human-readable output*: any numbers (dates, file sizes, and so on) will be shown in an easier-to-read format. The `P` flag is for *progress*, which tells rsync to output the progress of the copy to the screen so you can see how much data has been transferred, how much remains, and how long until the process is expected to complete.

Following this first set of flags, the `--remove-source-files` argument tells rsync to delete the source files once they've been successfully copied, and `--protect-args` tells rsync to interpret the following arguments (the source and destination directories) as one continuous string each, even if they're separated by a space character, which would normally indicate to the terminal that the directories were separate and independent. Without this argument, if your source path has a space in it, the command will interpret each section of the path on either side of the space character as a separate path. The same is true of the destination path. You can exclude one or both of those arguments if you don't want to delete the source files after copying them or if your source and/or destination directories have no space characters in them.

In practice, the following shows how the command might look between two Linux servers (which we'll cover in greater detail in Chapter 5):

```
$ rsync -ruhP --remove-source-files --protect-args test.txt \
    user@192.168.1.30:/tmp
Enter passphrase for key '/Users/user/.ssh/id_rsa':
sending incremental file list
test.txt
              0 100%    0.00kB/s    0:00:00 (xfr#1, to-chk=0/1)
```

As we mentioned in the "Securing Remote Access" section, remember to enter the passphrase for the SSH key pair you created earlier, not the passphrase for the user account you're using for the file transfer. The bottom of this listing contains the progress percentage, the current transfer speed, expected time remaining, and the number of files remaining in the transfer.

NOTE *The best feature of rsync is its ability to resume transfers if they get interrupted. The Secure File Transfer Protocol (SFTP) and Secure Copy Protocol (SCP) are alternatives you could use to transfer files between systems, but neither can stop a transfer and pick it up at the same point so that you don't lose your transfer progress while transferring potentially large files or directories. For these reasons, rsync is superior to SFTP and SCP, so we'll primarily use rsync throughout the remainder of this book.*

Summary

In this chapter, you built and secured your first Linux machine, which you'll need to follow the examples in several chapters of this book. You also learned how to harden your Linux system to increase its security and your overall security posture, including creating a secure SSH configuration by utilizing SSH key pairs, and the fundamentals of how to manage users in your network. You learned about mapping your network topology, how computers and other devices are interrelated, and how they communicate with each other. In Chapter 2, you'll learn how to layout your network to passively increase your overall security.

2

ARCHITECTING AND SEGMENTING YOUR NETWORK

The way you architect and segment your network can provide the most significant security improvement for the least amount of time, effort, and money. A good network segmentation plan allows you to separate high- and low-risk devices and user types, which informs where you implement other security controls in your environment.

For example, your internet of things (IoT) devices are, in all likelihood, less tested, updated, and maintained than your Windows operating system, simply because the technology is newer and less widely adopted. This fact makes them inherently more vulnerable and less secure than other, more widely used technologies. By putting these vulnerable endpoints onto a logically or physically separate network, you lower the risk of an adversary exploiting them and moving laterally across your network to your computer. Once you've separated your devices, you can consider additional controls—such as an intrusion detection or prevention system—or other network security monitoring and alerting solutions, which we'll cover in Chapter 10.

In this chapter, we'll discuss types of network hardware used to segment networks, their strengths and weaknesses, and some recommended solutions and configurations for physically or logically segmenting your network and separating devices utilizing both Ethernet and wireless network devices and settings.

Network Devices

Hubs, switches, and routers can be used to segment a network. Some of these provide more features or are inherently more capable and secure by design. Depending on your needs, you might choose to use one, some, or all of these devices.

Hubs

A *network hub* is the most basic type of device that enables multiple computers to communicate with each another. A hub can be used in small networks relatively safely, whereas in larger networks they would likely cause significant issues. When host A, connected to a hub, communicates with host B, connected to the same hub, the data (packets represented as Ethernet frames) travel from host A to a port on the hub, and the hub then broadcasts that data out through all of its other ports. This means every other endpoint on the network receives the data destined for host B, which isn't very secure. Additionally, because hubs aren't intelligent, all ports are part of the same *collision domain*. This means that if two or more devices attempt to communicate at the same time, the traffic collides, causing network performance problems. When a collision occurs, the sending devices have to stop communicating and wait a randomized amount of time before attempting to communicate again, ideally without causing a second collision, resulting in a further delay.

Because of their limited functionality, hubs are typically cheap to buy and deploy, but they aren't scalable. If you have more than a handful of devices needing to communicate, you're better off getting a switch.

Switches

In contrast to hubs, *switches* forward traffic through a network using the physical hardware (MAC) addresses of the endpoints connected to them. When a host connected to a switch communicates with another host in the network, the data travels from the sender to a port on the switch, and the switch then uses the MAC address for which the data is destined to determine to which port it should forward that data. Switches keep a MAC address table in memory, so they know where each endpoint is located on the network. Each port on a switch has its own distinct collision domain, meaning that if two hosts communicate simultaneously, there won't be a collision—the packets won't meet each other during transmission. This also means that data isn't broadcast to every device on a network, which makes a switch inherently more secure than a hub.

Switches can be used in networks of any size. Small networks rarely need more than a single switch, depending on the number of endpoints.

Routers

A *router* is primarily used for transmitting data between networks or network segments. For example, your local intranet, where all of your endpoints are connected, is a private network. The internet, a very large, publicly accessible computer network, is separate from your private network. A router is the conduit between these two networks, enabling you to access one from the other and browse the internet. Where a switch uses MAC addresses, a router is primarily concerned with IP addresses. All internet-connected networks use a router of some type. In a small network, the border router that connects your network to your internet service provider is likely the only router you'll need.

Creating Trust Zones

Network segmentation is the practice of dividing a network into smaller parts, known as *subnets*, to increase the overall performance and security of that network. You can segment your network by separating devices either physically or logically.

Physical Segmentation

Arguably the simplest way to segment your network is to separate devices using physically discrete hardware (*physical segmentation*). For example, you can use one wireless router for your computers and another for your mobile devices. Or you might use the first router for all your personal devices and the second for all your IoT devices.

Separating your devices and users into classes or categories puts them into *trust zones*, which keep your most critical data and assets separate from more vulnerable devices. Separating devices that require more security and monitoring from those that require less security, and therefore less overhead to maintain, allows you to spend more time focusing on the assets that matter and less time managing those that don't.

By keeping devices of different types separate, your network's security increases, as an attack focusing on one type's vulnerability doesn't allow the attacker to move to other segments of your network. This is becoming more important as household appliances are gradually turning into smart devices.

Physical network segmentation is harder for an attacker to overcome than logical segmentation. The drawbacks associated with physical segmentation are increased administrative overhead, hardware cost, and other infrastructure costs, as you might need a separate internet connection for each physical network.

Logical Segmentation

Logical segmentation is more common than physical segmentation and often less expensive to implement because it doesn't require separate pieces of physical hardware for each network segment. Logical segmentation is usually achieved using *virtual local area networks (VLANs)*: groups of systems that appear to be on the same local area network but are logically separated from systems on other VLANs. Switches capable of creating and managing VLANs are called *managed switches*. Each VLAN acts like a virtual switch that exists within your physical switch. Assigning a physical port on your switch to a particular VLAN is equivalent to plugging a cable into a specific switch.

For example, you can place a switch, like an eight-port Netgear GS308E (or similar), behind your broadband router, allowing the endpoints connected to the switch access to the internet. Then, on the switch itself, you can create VLANs with different purposes, such as a management or administration VLAN, a business or personal VLAN for your primary endpoints, and a guest VLAN for less-secure device types such as mobile and IoT devices.

With the VLANs created, you can specify which of the eight ports on the switch are capable of communicating on each of these VLANs, keeping each of the VLANs and their respective devices logically separated with just one physical device. Of course, this approach works best for networks with more Ethernet or hardwired devices than wireless devices, unless you plan to use multiple wireless access points.

#11: Segmenting Your Network

The recommended approach for network segmentation in small networks is to categorize your endpoints into trust zones based on the type of access and level of security and monitoring they require.

For example, your primary network segment should include your primary devices, which contain or have access to your private data such as your email, contacts, messages, and data stored in cloud services like Google Drive or Dropbox. This network segment is designed to be the most secure, with the strictest security requirements and the most monitoring and detection in place.

Your secondary network segment is for those endpoints that don't need to talk to your primary devices or access the same data, such as your IoT and other connected devices—smart lights, printers, casting devices such as Google Chromecast, and so on. All of those devices should be separated in their own segments because they're inherently less secure than your primary devices; this mitigates the risk of an adversary using them as a stepping-stone into your network. This network segment can afford to have less strict security controls, because it doesn't contain any critical data or information.

Next, you might have one or more tertiary network segments where all other endpoints live, such as your guest network. Again, this segment can have less strict security controls and less monitoring than your primary network segment.

Finally, depending on the types of devices you have in your network (or plan to have), you might want a network segment that has very strict access rules. This network could be for devices that you do not want to connect to the internet under any circumstances, including CCTV or security cameras. With tight network segmentation like this, other considerations need to be made, such as how devices within this network segment will receive updates.

There are various ways to segment your network. Let's go into more detail about how to achieve effective network segmentation, first by using separate wireless networks and then by using Ethernet segmentation with VLANs. It's possible to combine these approaches if your network calls for it.

Ethernet Segmentation

You can use an Ethernet switch capable of assigning specific Ethernet ports to VLANs to logically segment your network and its devices. An inexpensive managed switch such as the Netgear GS308E provides this functionality, and installing it in your small network is quick and easy. This is the device we'll use for the following example network configuration. You can purchase the GS308E directly from Netgear or other online retailers, or second-hand from marketplaces like eBay. Alternatively, I recommend researching the Ubiquiti range of networking equipment, which, while more expensive, is user friendly and highly capable.

VLANs are used for separating trust zones. Ideally, this is done in larger networks by using two different physical switches. If your switch is misconfigured, the higher and lower security networks and devices might be able to communicate, but if two switches are physically separate, this is less likely. However, in small networks, we usually don't have the luxury of buying multiple devices; it's cost prohibitive. So, we do the next best thing and use VLANs to keep our networks virtually separate.

NOTE *Purchasing two unmanaged switches without advanced functionality like VLANs could be cheaper than a single managed switch with VLAN capability. Taking this route will result in two or more physically separate networks, each with one switch. If both networks require internet access, you'll need separate internet connections for each network, or a gateway device capable of keeping the switched networks logically separate. In this case, you'd be better off investing in the slightly more expensive managed switch in the first place. The use of unmanaged switches is not covered in this book because they are plug-and-play with little additional setup required and will result in a less secure architecture than a managed switch.*

Once you have your switch, initial configuration is usually straightforward:

1. Unbox and plug the switch into power.
2. Connect an Ethernet cable from your modem/router (or whichever device provides your internet connection, like the pfSense device we'll cover in Chapter 3).

3. You can find the IP address of the switch in three ways:
    a. The switch will accept an IP address from whichever device in your network provides DHCP. You can find its IP address in your router or other DHCP provider by following the steps in Chapter 1.
    b. Netgear (and most network equipment manufacturers) provides an application to discover its switches on your network. You can download the Netgear Switch Discovery Tool (NSDT) from *https://www.netgear.com/support/product/netgear-switch-discovery-tool.aspx*. Download, install, and run the tool to identify the switch in your network.
    c. The switch is configured with the IP address 192.168.0.239 by default. If either previous method doesn't work, you can use this default IP address to connect to your switch's web interface for configuration.
4. Once you've discovered or configured the IP address for your switch, browse to that IP address in a web browser and log in using the default password (supplied in the switch manual).
5. You'll be prompted to change the admin password. I recommend you do, as default passwords are insecure.

At this point you'll be presented with a summary page that provides the switch information, such as the name, serial number, MAC address, and so on. Add this information to your asset list and network map.

With that done, you're ready to configure the VLANs. The switch will accept and pass through the internet connection to the devices you connect to the switch. Configuring and utilizing VLANs on a Netgear switch is a simple operation, and the method should be similar on any other managed switch:

6. Log in to the switch as an administrator.
7. Along the top of the web interface, locate the VLAN tab, as shown in Figure 2-1.
8. In the menu on the left, click **Advanced** to view the Advanced VLAN options.
9. Toggle Advanced Port-Based VLAN Status from Disable to Enable, as shown in Figure 2-1.

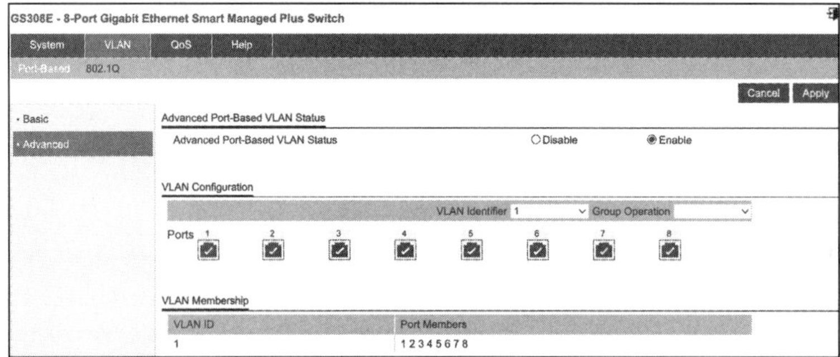

Figure 2-1: VLAN configuration

Next, you need to assign the physical Ethernet ports on the switch to specific VLANs. Configure one VLAN for each trust zone you want in your network. If you want a primary network for your most secure devices, a secondary network for your guest devices, and a tertiary network for your IoT devices, you should configure three separate VLANs. If configuring a new VLAN is equivalent to creating a new physical local network, with a new switch or router, assigning a port to a VLAN is the same as plugging a device into that physical switch. If you think about VLANs as separate networks, assigning each port to a VLAN tells the switch to which logical network that port belongs, and only the ports and endpoints within the same VLAN will be able to communicate.

10. In the VLAN Identifier drop-down menu, select the ID of the VLAN you want to configure.
11. For each physical port you want to add to this VLAN, ensure the port is ticked. Untick the ports that will not be allowed to communicate on this VLAN. Click Apply.
    When you plug devices into these ports, which now have a VLAN assignment, those devices will communicate only within that VLAN.
12. To remove those same ports from VLAN 1 (the default VLAN), select **VLAN 1** from the drop-down menu. Click the relevant ports until their displays are blank. Click **Apply**.

To test your VLAN configuration, connect an endpoint to one of the assigned ports on the switch, and connect another endpoint to any port that still has the default configuration or another VLAN configured. If you're unable to ping between these devices, your VLANs have been correctly configured.

Summary

In this chapter, you've identified and created trust zones for your devices. By doing so, you've been able to segment your network to keep devices of high trust and security separate from those with lower trust. You can create as many or as few network segments as you like by using a switch in this way, helping to keep your network and your users more secure.

3

FILTERING NETWORK TRAFFIC WITH FIREWALLS

A *firewall* monitors and filters incoming and outgoing network traffic. There's a general misconception that the firewall is always the last line of defense; in reality, a perimeter firewall should be the first obstacle adversaries encounter when they try to penetrate any network, large or small. Every time a web browser accesses a website, a messaging program sends a message, or your email client sends and receives email, the traffic generated should pass through at least one firewall along its journey.

In this chapter, you'll explore two firewall solutions: iptables and pfSense. In Linux, iptables is a common firewall often used as a *host firewall* (that is, a firewall that allows or denies traffic on a specific endpoint). pfSense, which can be implemented either as an open source software firewall or as a hardware firewall using the appliances sold by Netgate, is used as a perimeter or boundary firewall responsible for filtering traffic for entire networks or network segments.

Types of Firewalls

A *hardware firewall* can be physically and logically placed in a network. A *software firewall*, installed as an application on an endpoint, requires more configuration of both the firewall and its connected devices to filter traffic effectively. By using one or both of these, you're able to effectively reduce your *attack surface*, which comprises the points where an adversary can try to infiltrate, compromise, or exploit your network. Ideally, attack surfaces should be as small as possible.

A *perimeter firewall*, installed between your private network and other networks like the internet, can be either software- or hardware-based. Perimeter firewalls are placed at the physical and logical border of the network, making it the first thing with which traffic bound for your internal network from the public internet communicates, as well as the last thing in your network that traffic bound for the internet passes through, as shown in Figure 3-1.

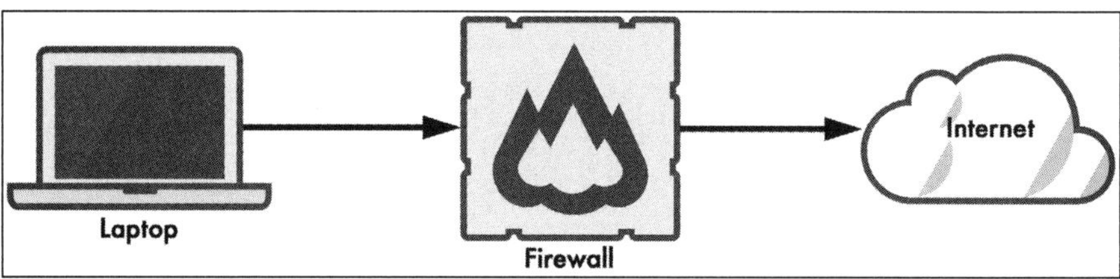

Figure 3-1: A perimeter firewall

Firewalls allow or deny (block) traffic based on a *ruleset* containing a configured list of rules. The way those rules are applied to traffic depends on the type of firewall you're using. The most common type, a *packet-filtering firewall*, inspects each packet of data attempting to make it into (or out of) your internal network and then checks that packet against its ruleset. If the packet contents match a rule in the firewall ruleset, the firewall will either allow or deny that traffic, depending on what that rule indicates it should do.

There are also stateful and stateless firewalls. A *stateful* firewall tracks all inbound and outbound connections and monitors each connection as a unique conversation between two endpoints. This method provides the firewall with context about any given connection and allows more granular control of traffic. By contrast, a *stateless* firewall doesn't record information about each connection. Both iptables and pfSense are stateful firewalls.

Almost all operating systems come with a built-in software firewall, known as a *host-based firewall*, that filters traffic specific to that host. Most Windows and Mac devices ship with an out-of-the-box host-based firewall whose basic ruleset is functional, if not exhaustive. By design, this firewall works as is for ordinary purposes; users don't need to configure their own firewall, lessening confusion as well as the need for technical support from computer manufacturers. On Linux devices, you'll have to configure a firewall—you'll see how to do this in the next section.

It's best to use both a host firewall and a perimeter firewall and to configure them correctly for your network to add multiple layers of defense.

iptables

Linux's iptables utility offers incredible flexibility in filtering traffic entering, traversing, or leaving a network. The firewall organizes its rules in *policy chains*, lists of rules that analyze and match packets based on their contents. Each rule determines what the firewall will do with a packet that matches its definition—it might allow, reject, or drop the packet. When a packet is allowed, it passes through the firewall unhindered. When dropped, the firewall discards the packet and sends no response back to the sender. If a packet is rejected, the firewall discards the packet and sends a rejection message back to the sender, providing context about your network and the firewall you're using.

There are three main types of policy chain: *input chains*, *output chains*, and *forward chains*. Input chains determine whether to allow certain traffic into the network from an external source, such as a *virtual private network (VPN)* connection from a remote location. A VPN is a method for logically—rather than physically—connecting to disparate networks, usually for remote access from one network to the other. VPNs are covered in greater detail in Chapter 5.

Output chains indicate whether the firewall should allow certain outbound traffic to an external network. For example, *Internet Control Message Protocol (ICMP)* is primarily used to diagnose network communication issues. ICMP ping packets are outbound traffic that pass through the output chain. A ping is a query from one device to another, usually to determine whether a connection can be made between the two. You'd need to allow the ping packets to travel from your device, through your firewall, and across several other devices on the public internet, to finally reach their destination. If your output chain blocks ICMP traffic, your device would be unable to ping anything, as the firewall would block or drop those packets.

In most cases, your stateful firewall rules should allow both new and established connections. For example, if you create an output chain to allow your device to ping Google, you need to tell the firewall to allow inbound traffic related to established connections. Otherwise, your device will send a ping out to Google that passes through your firewall, but the response from Google would get blocked by your firewall.

Forward chains forward the traffic your firewall receives to another network. In a small office or home network, host-based firewalls rarely use forward chains, unless the firewall is configured to serve as a router. A perimeter firewall would use the forward chain to route traffic from your internal network to the external network, or from one network segment to another, likely using network address translation (NAT), as discussed in Chapter 1. However, a configuration of this type is more complicated than necessary for small networks and would better fit an enterprise network.

By using these policy chains, you'll be able to control the traffic traversing your network at a very granular level. In the following chapters, you'll create several Linux servers, each of which would benefit from its own host-based firewall. I recommend configuring iptables on each of these servers using the following instructions.

NOTE *iptables isn't capable of securing IPv6 networks and traffic. If you plan to use IPv6 in your network, you'll need to use ip6tables in addition to iptables. Unless you have a strong use case for IPv6 in your network, I recommend disabling IPv6 completely. Disabling IPv6 is covered in Chapter 4.*

#12: Installing iptables

If you've already built a standard Ubuntu server following the steps from Chapter 1, you can start configuring its iptables firewall. Once you've mastered the basics, use that knowledge to configure iptables on all your Linux endpoints. Otherwise, go back and create your Ubuntu system now.

Recent versions of Ubuntu have iptables installed by default, so log in via SSH as a standard, non-root user, and check for iptables by running a version check:

```
$ sudo iptables -V
[sudo] password for user:
iptables v1.8.7 (nf_tables)
```

If iptables is installed, the server should return version information, as shown here. Your version may be different.

If iptables isn't installed, you'll receive an error, in which case, install iptables:

```
$ sudo apt install iptables
```

Once it's installed, run the same version check to confirm that the installation succeeded.

Next, install `iptables-persistent`, a tool that allows you to save your firewall configurations and automatically reload them after a reboot of the server:

```
$ sudo apt install iptables-persistent
```

An installation wizard should take over your terminal window. You'll be shown the file in which your server will save the firewall rules (the default file is */etc/iptables/rules.v4*) and told that rules from this file will load at system startup. Also, you'll need to save any changes to firewall rules manually beyond this installation process. Select **Yes** to save any current firewall rules. If you don't install this component, you'll have to reconfigure your firewall every time you restart the server.

You can now check the current policy chains like so:

```
$ sudo iptables -L
[sudo] password for user:
Chain INPUT (policy ACCEPT)
target     prot opt source               destination
Chain FORWARD (policy ACCEPT)
target     prot opt source               destination
Chain OUTPUT (policy ACCEPT)
target     prot opt source               destination
```

In the output, `policy ACCEPT` indicates that, by default, iptables accepts all traffic for input, output, and forwarding. This default behavior is desirable because it'll work without any user configuration. However, it's an insecure solution, so let's modify it.

iptables Firewall Rules

When creating iptables rules, keep in mind that order matters. As traffic reaches your firewall, iptables checks its rules one after the other *in the order they appear*. If the traffic matches a rule, iptables won't check any further rules—if the first rule in your list of 50 denies all traffic, the firewall will interpret this rule, reject the traffic, and stop processing, which effectively isolates your device entirely. Alternatively, if you have the same 50 rules but the first rule allows all traffic, all traffic will be allowed to pass through the firewall. You should avoid both of those situations.

To understand how to construct an iptables firewall rule, take a look at this example:

```
$ sudo iptables -A INPUT -p tcp --dport 22 -m conntrack \
     --ctstate NEW,ESTABLISHED -j ACCEPT
```

Immediately after `sudo`, iptables is invoked to begin the rule definition. The next argument determines whether the rule will be appended to (`-A`), deleted from (`-D`), or inserted into (`-I`) the specified policy chain. You can also specify `-R` in this position when replacing or updating an existing rule. The `INPUT` indicates that a rule in the input chain is being modified. You also can specify `OUTPUT`, `FORWARD`, or other policy chains.

In most cases, iptables needs to know the protocol and port to which the rules relate. In this example, `-p tcp` indicates the rule will apply only to TCP traffic, and `--dport 22` tells iptables that the rule applies to packets with a destination port of 22. Both of those settings are optional. You can specify multiple ports with this syntax: `--match multiport --dports port1,port2,port3`.

NOTE Transmission Control Protocol (TCP) *is a* reliable *transmission protocol, designed to ensure successful delivery of packets over a network. If a computer* *experiences packet loss during communication that's using TCP, those lost packets will be retransmitted, ensuring all of the data sent is eventually received by the destination host.* User Datagram Protocol (UDP) *is an* unreliable *protocol and does not ensure successful transmission of data or retransmit lost packets. UDP is used when some packet loss is acceptable and usually results in a faster connection. TCP is used when reliability matters, and every packet must be transmitted successfully.*

The iptables firewall offers multiple matching modules, and you can specify the module to use with the `-m` argument. In this example, `conntrack`, a tool that allows stateful packet inspection, is used (also optional). Some other tools include `connbytes`, which creates rules based on the amount of traffic transferred, and `connrate`, which matches on the transfer rate of the traffic. See the iptables man page for more details: *https://linux.die.net/man/8/iptables/*.

Next, `--ctstate` tells iptables to allow and track traffic for the types of connections that follow—in this case, `NEW` and `ESTABLISHED`. Many values are available for connection state, but the most frequently used are `NEW`, `ESTABLISHED`, `RELATED`, and `INVALID`. New and established states are self-explanatory; the packets are part of new or established traffic flows. Related packets don't necessarily match an established connection, but they are expected by the firewall because an existing connection necessitates it (that is, it's expected based on the firewall's existing context). Invalid packets are any packets that don't match the criteria for any other states.

Finally, iptables will interpret `-j` and whatever follows it as the action to jump to (perform) when this rule is matched. Most commonly, it will be either `ACCEPT` to allow traffic matching this rule; `DROP`, or `REJECT`, to deny or block the traffic; or `LOG` to log the traffic to a logfile (more details on that later).

Now that you understand the fundamentals of iptables rules, you'll configure your firewall to allow and deny traffic.

Configuring iptables

When configuring iptables, first add rules to drop invalid traffic:

```
$ sudo iptables -A OUTPUT -m state --state INVALID -j DROP
$ sudo iptables -A INPUT -m state --state INVALID -j DROP
```

Then, add rules to accept traffic related to existing connections, as well as established connections and the loopback address to avoid any issues later (a *loopback address* is an internal address that computers use for testing and diagnosing network issues):

```
$ sudo iptables -A INPUT -m state --state RELATED,ESTABLISHED -j ACCEPT
$ sudo iptables -A OUTPUT -m state --state RELATED,ESTABLISHED -j ACCEPT
$ sudo iptables -A INPUT -i lo -j ACCEPT
```

This allows the firewall to accept traffic matching a known connection or related to a connection in progress and discard any unexpected packets (which can protect your network from unsolicited or malicious network scanning activity).

Once you've run these commands to enter the rules into the policy chains, rerun the list command to ensure they've been accepted:

```
$ sudo iptables -L
Chain INPUT (policy ACCEPT)
target     prot opt source               destination
DROP       all  --  anywhere             anywhere             state INVALID
ACCEPT     all  --  anywhere             anywhere             state RELATED,ESTABLISHED
ACCEPT     all  --  anywhere             anywhere
Chain FORWARD (policy ACCEPT)
target     prot opt source               destination
Chain OUTPUT (policy ACCEPT)
target     prot opt source               destination
DROP       all  --  anywhere             anywhere             state INVALID
ACCEPT     all  --  anywhere             anywhere             state RELATED,ESTABLISHED
```

Notice the rules have been added under the `INPUT` and `OUTPUT` chains. The `FORWARD` chain remains empty.

Next, ensure that your firewall allows SSH traffic. You can do this in two ways: by broadly allowing SSH or by allowing SSH only from a subset of devices in your network. To allow SSH traffic originating from all devices in your network, use the following command:

```
$ sudo iptables -A INPUT -p tcp --dport 22 -m conntrack --ctstate NEW -j \
    ACCEPT
```

Creating broad rules can be helpful when connecting to or from multiple devices using SSH within your network. However, allowing the uninhibited use of programs and leaving protocols completely open is not the most secure solution. You should allow services like SSH only to and from specific IP addresses or ranges, as allowing remote access or file transfer between your endpoints and any other device is risky.

You can reduce your attack surface by specifying a source IP address or range (for example, 192.168.1.25) in your input chain with the `-s` ***`source`*** option, so if you're configuring iptables on a virtual machine, you might choose to allow connections from a single host for management purposes and deny access to all other endpoints in your network:

```
$ sudo iptables -A INPUT -p tcp -s 192.168.1.25 --dport 22 -m \
      conntrack --ctstate NEW -j ACCEPT
```

We append this rule to the `INPUT` policy chain using `-A`, destination port `22`, and protocol `TCP`. For `NEW` connections, iptables will `ACCEPT` traffic matching this rule. The port can be one of your choosing; just be sure that your SSH configuration matches your firewall rule. If the rule allows SSH on port 22 but your SSH configuration allows connections on port 2222, the firewall will block your SSH connections.

If you make a mistake, delete the rule by running the same command, substituting the `-D` option in place of `-A`:

```
$ sudo iptables -D INPUT -p tcp -s 192.168.1.25 --dport 22 -m conntrack \
    --ctstate NEW,ESTABLISHED -j ACCEPT
```

Alternatively, you can delete all the rules you've specified for any of your policy chains by using the **`-F`** *`chain`*, or **`--flush`** *`chain`*, parameter:

```
$ sudo iptables -F INPUT
```

With this basic set of rules, now you can tell iptables what to do with all other traffic (that you don't want entering or leaving your server or network). Once you've created rules to allow the specific traffic you want or need the firewall to allow, you can most likely block, deny, or drop everything else. You should do this after you've configured your firewall rules; otherwise, you might interrupt your connection and be unable to reconnect via SSH. Using the **`-P`** argument sets the default behavior of your policy chains and lets iptables know what to do with traffic that doesn't match your rules. To achieve this, set the policy chains' default behaviors to `DROP` this traffic:

```
$ sudo iptables -P INPUT DROP
$ sudo iptables -P FORWARD DROP
$ sudo iptables -P OUTPUT DROP
```

Using `-P` in this way is different from `-A` and `-I` used previously, because it doesn't affect the firewall rules themselves; instead, it deals with the overarching policies that govern traffic in your network. Where `-A` and `-I` append or insert rules for your firewall, respectively, `-P` configures the firewall behavior one level higher.

At this point, checking your iptables chains should return:

```
Chain INPUT (policy DROP)
target     prot opt source               destination
DROP       all  --  anywhere             anywhere             state INVALID
ACCEPT     all  --  anywhere             anywhere             state RELATED,ESTABLISHED
ACCEPT     all  --  anywhere             anywhere
ACCEPT     tcp  --  192.168.1.25         anywhere             tcp dpt:22 ctstate NEW
Chain FORWARD (policy DROP)
target     prot opt source               destination
Chain OUTPUT (policy DROP)
target     prot opt source               destination
DROP       all  --  anywhere             anywhere             state INVALID
ACCEPT     all  --  anywhere             anywhere             state RELATED,ESTABLISHED
```

Notice that the policy for all three chains has changed from `ACCEPT` to `DROP`, indicating the default behavior for each chain is to drop traffic that doesn't match any of the rules you've created. You should also be able to identify the rules you've added to the chains by comparing this output to the previous output listing the iptables rules. You may receive an error that DNS is failing, because the firewall is now blocking everything not explicitly allowed, including DNS (which runs on port 53). Resolve this issue by adding the following new rules:

```
$ sudo iptables -A OUTPUT -p udp --dport 53 -m conntrack --ctstate NEW -j ACCEPT
$ sudo iptables -A OUTPUT -p tcp --dport 53 -m conntrack --ctstate NEW -j ACCEPT
```

These commands append rules to the output chain, allowing this server to make outbound requests for domain name resolution on UDP and TCP port 53. With the addition of these rules, the server can resolve domain names.

Test your firewall by trying to ping the server from another device in your network; you should receive an error, as ICMP isn't allowed through the firewall. Likewise, if you try to ping anything from the server itself, you should receive a similar error:

```
$ ping google.com -c 5
PING google.com (<ip_address>): 56(84) bytes of data.
ping: sendmsg: Operation not permitted
ping: sendmsg: Operation not permitted
ping: sendmsg: Operation not permitted
ping: sendmsg: Operation not permitted
ping: sendmsg: Operation not permitted
--- google.com ping statistics ---
5 packets transmitted, 0 received, 100% packet loss, time 4000ms
```

ICMP can be such a useful troubleshooting tool that you might decide to allow ping through your iptables firewall. To do so, add the following rules:

```
$ sudo iptables -A INPUT -p icmp -j ACCEPT
$ sudo iptables -A OUTPUT -p icmp -j ACCEPT
```

You may discover that you need to open additional ports in the firewall. For example, if you have a proxy installed or if you build one after reading Chapter 6, you'll need to open the proxy port (3128) in your firewall:

```
$ sudo iptables -A OUTPUT -p tcp --dport 3128 -m conntrack --ctstate NEW -j ACCEPT
```

In most cases, you should block web browsing in general from servers—there are few, if any, legitimate reasons to use servers for this type of activity. Ideally, from both an administrative and a security standpoint, servers should be single-purpose. Allowing any additional service—especially browsing the internet—on a server results in a larger attack surface and creates potential vulnerabilities in your network.

If you decide to allow this traffic from your server(s) so the server can retrieve software updates, create output rules for ports 80 and 443, the default ports for HTTP and HTTPS traffic, respectively:

```
$ sudo iptables -A OUTPUT -p tcp --dport 80 -m conntrack --ctstate NEW,ESTABLISHED -j ACCEPT
$ sudo iptables -A OUTPUT -p tcp --dport 443 -m conntrack --ctstate NEW,ESTABLISHED -j ACCEPT
```

The only difference between the HTTP and HTTPS rules is the port number.

Every time you add a rule, you should test it. The easiest way to do so, in this case, will be to first test your ability to browse the internet by using a web browser on the server (if you have the GUI installed) or by using `curl` in the bash terminal. Start by installing `curl`:

```
$ sudo apt install curl
```

If you don't have rules allowing HTTP and HTTPS, the install command will fail, as updates are typically done over HTTP. However, if you do have those rules in place, `curl` should have installed successfully, so you can now ensure ports 80 and 443 are open:

```
$ curl http://icanhazip.com
ipaddress
```

The address *http://icanhazip.com/* is a public service provider that will return your current public IP address when queried with `curl`. If you're shown your current public IP address, your firewall is configured correctly.

If you receive an error, one of your rules may have a problem. Check for typos, and if all else fails, delete your rules and start again using the `-D` or `-F` parameters discussed earlier. Once the firewall is correctly configured, feel free to add further rules as you deem necessary.

One particular set of rules to add are those that block traffic to specific IP addresses. Since most public websites can have multiple IP addresses, however, blocking a site using iptables isn't the best option, as you'd have to create rules for each unique IP address. In most cases, you'd be better off using a proxy, which we'll cover in Chapter 6.

If you want to use iptables to block sites—say, for example, to block all traffic to and from *https://www.squirreldirectory.com/*, which currently resides at IP address 206.189.69.35—you would add the following rules to your `INPUT` and `OUTPUT` chains:

```
$ sudo iptables -A INPUT -s 206.189.69.35 -j DROP
$ sudo iptables -A OUTPUT -s 206.189.69.35 -j DROP
```

Typically, you'd add this type of rule to allow or deny traffic from a static, private IP address that isn't expected to change, and use a proxy for public IP addresses or URLs.

Logging iptables Behavior

You've now installed and configured the iptables firewall, but you haven't told it to log anything, so it produces no records of its behavior, which can make it difficult to troubleshoot issues or determine whether blocked traffic should have been blocked.

First, create a new, custom policy chain. Note that this configuration is an example of where rule order is critical. You can name the chain whatever you like, but here, we'll call it `LOGGING`:

```
$ sudo iptables -N LOGGING
```

The `-N` parameter is used to create new chains.

Next, add a rule at the end of each of the `INPUT` and `OUTPUT` chains that tells iptables to send any traffic that hasn't yet matched a rule to the new `LOGGING` chain:

```
$ sudo iptables -A INPUT -j LOGGING
$ sudo iptables -A OUTPUT -j LOGGING
```

Then, tell iptables to log only once per minute for each type of dropped packet:

```
$ sudo iptables -A LOGGING -m limit --limit 1/minute -j LOG \
    --log-prefix "FW-Dropped: " --log-level 4
```

This limit is optional, and you can set it to any period, such as `1/second`, `1/minute`, `1/hour`, or `1/day`. Limiting the number of log entries reduces both the noise within and the size of the logfiles. Add a prefix (`"FW-Dropped: "`) to the log information so the firewall log entries are easy to identify. Setting the logging level to `4` will log up to warning-level events, indicating an event that has a material effect on the server or the firewall. Increasing the number results in more events with lower severity being logged, which is useful when troubleshooting. Log levels 1 to 3 will log only events or errors with higher than warning-level severity.

Finally, the following command indicates to the firewall that, once logged, the packets should be dropped:

```
$ sudo iptables -A LOGGING -j DROP
```

Your firewall will now log all the dropped packets both inbound to and outbound from the server. By default, those logs will be kept in */var/log/messages*.

The last step is to save your firewall configuration. Remember that iptables configurations are temporary by default and won't survive a reboot, which is why we installed `iptables-persistent` in Project 12. To save your configuration, run the following command (`netfilter` is the command used by `iptables-persistent` for this purpose):

```
$ sudo netfilter-persistent save
run-parts: executing /usr/share/netfilter-persistent/plugins.d/15-ip4tables save
run-parts: executing /usr/share/netfilter-persistent/plugins.d/25-ip6tables save
```

With that, the firewall is ready to go.

You may consider adding temporary rules to your firewall, but remember the adage that "nothing is more permanent than a temporary firewall rule" (Austin Scott). In the case of adding a temporary rule to allow a user to download a file from the internet, for example, it would be better to find a different workaround, like using another host. If a rule like this is created and left in the firewall configuration, it creates a vulnerability and reduces the security offered by the firewall. Avoid temporary rules whenever possible.

pfSense

In addition to a firewall securing each endpoint in your network with iptables, you should implement a firewall like pfSense to secure your entire network at its border. Together, these firewalls add layers to your defense-in-depth strategy, making the job of any adversary more difficult with each level of complexity. You should place a perimeter firewall at the physical edge of your network—that is, as close to the internet as possible relative to the other endpoints in your network. For most, that position will be directly behind the modem/router or network boundary point that connects your network to your internet service provider. It is possible to achieve this logically, using virtual machines and the correct routing configuration. However, the best and most secure way to set up a perimeter firewall is to use a physical device.

Like iptables, the pfSense firewall is stateful. However, where iptables works as a feature installed on top of a base operating system like Ubuntu, pfSense is a fully fledged operating system. It's based on FreeBSD, an open source version of Unix (an operating system similar to Linux that uses its own kernel) that has user-friendly features like a web management interface and can be deployed as either a virtual machine or a physical appliance.

You have a few options when it comes to creating a physical firewall. The first is to build a device that suits this purpose from a computer with a small footprint, like the Intel Next Unit of Computing (NUC). However, for the same cost or far less, Netgate sells pfSense appliances that are easy to configure and basically ready to go out of the box.

For the sake of simplicity (and security), we'll discuss using a prebuilt device. This book will not cover building a device from scratch because the risk of misconfiguration is too high, especially when an inexpensive, secure solution is readily available. The Netgate 2100 Base pfSense+ costs around $400 at the time of writing. It's powerful enough to be capable of most anything you can throw at it, short of a full-blown enterprise network. The SG-3100 is a step up from the entry-level 1100 pfSense+ and is more fully featured. It also has higher bandwidth and is capable of greater throughput, so it's the ideal choice for smaller networks.

#13: Installing the pfSense Firewall

Upon receiving your pfSense device, remove it from the box and plug it into power. Connect an Ethernet cable from the WAN port on the device to any port on your cable, DSL modem, or network boundary point device. Connect another Ethernet cable from the LAN1 port to the Ethernet port on your computer.

To access the pfSense configuration page from your computer, browse to 192.168.1.1, the default IP address of the SG-3100. If that doesn't work, you may need to disconnect your computer from your regular network and manually set its IP address to 192.168.1.2 (or any other address in the 192.168.1.*x* range, except the pfSense IP of 192.168.1.1) using the following instructions. This is necessary only for the initial configuration of the device and should need to be done only once on the computer you use to set up the pfSense appliance.

macOS

1. Open **System Preferences**.
2. Click **Network**.
3. Select the Ethernet connection between your pfSense device and your computer, and then set the Configure IPv4 drop-down box to **Manually**.
4. Enter **192.168.1.2** into the IP Address field, set Subnet Mask to **255.255.255.0**, and enter **192.168.1.1** into the Router field.
5. Click **Apply**.
6. Open your web browser and browse to 192.168.1.1. You should be presented with the pfSense login page.

Windows

1. Open **Network and Internet Settings**.
2. Click **Change Adapter Options**.
3. Open the Ethernet connection between your pfSense device and your computer, and then click **Properties ▸ Internet Protocol Version ▸ (TCP/IP) ▸ Properties**.
4. Select the **Use the following IP address** radio button.
5. Enter **192.168.1.2** into the IP Address field, set Subnet Mask to **255.255.255.0**, and enter **192.168.1.1** into the Default Gateway field.
6. Click **OK** and close the remaining windows.
7. Open your web browser and browse to 192.168.1.1. You should be presented with the pfSense login page.

Linux

1. Open **Settings**.
2. Click **Network**.
3. On the Ethernet connection between your pfSense device and your computer, click the configure **Cog**.

4. Select the **IPv4** tab.
5. Select the **Manual** radio button.
6. Enter **192.168.1.2** into the IP Address field, set Netmask to **255.255.255.0**, and enter **192.168.1.1** into the Gateway field.
7. Click **Apply** and close the Settings windows.
8. Open your web browser and browse to 192.168.1.1. You should be presented with the pfSense login page.

NOTE *If you receive a warning message indicating the site is not private or is unsafe, click through to the login page. This warning appears because there's no SSL certificate configured, and you can ignore it for now. However, be wary of errors like this elsewhere; generally, an SSL certificate error (especially on the internet) is a serious warning that the page you're trying to access is insecure.*

On the pfSense login page, log in with the credentials provided when you received your device. Once you're logged in, accept the end-user license agreement (EULA) if one is presented. Take a moment to review the system information, and then click the **System** menu at the top of the page and start the **Setup Wizard**. Use the following steps to finish setting up pfSense:

1. At the welcome screen, click **Next**.
2. If the Support screen is displayed, click **Next**.
3. On the General Information screen, choose a hostname for the device, or leave it as the default, pfSense.
4. If you have a domain configured in your environment, enter it in the Domain field.
5. Ignore the DNS settings for now and click **Next**.
6. On the Time Server Information screen, accept the default Time server hostname, unless you have a time server in your environment, in which case enter its details here.
7. Be sure to select the correct time zone, and then click **Next**.

You should now see the Configure WAN Interface page. You can use this page to configure your pfSense appliance to connect to your internet service provider. We'll cover the most common configuration here, called *PPPoE*, that will most likely match the settings in your current modem/router. If not, contact your internet service provider for the correct configuration details for your connection.

8. In the SelectedType box, select **PPPoE**.
9. Skip the General configuration options to accept the default settings.
10. Static IP Configuration and DHCP client configuration should be grayed out, so move on to PPPoE configuration.
11. Enter the username and password provided to you by your internet service provider.

12. Accept all other settings as default and click **Next**.
13. Set the LAN IP address of the pfSense appliance. You can choose to keep the IP addressing scheme you identified in Chapter 1 by giving this device the first IP in the address range (192.168.1.1 in the case of an address scheme of 192.168.0.0/16), or you can change it by specifying a different LAN IP address on this page. If you'd like addresses in the 10.0.0.0/8 range, specify 10.0.0.1, and so on. Then click **Next**.
14. Change the administrator password. Be sure to select a strong passphrase at least 12 characters in length or longer, and save it in a password safe (we'll discuss this further in Chapter 11). Once done, click **Next ▸ Reload ▸ Finish**.

Your initial configuration is now complete. Assuming the device has been able to connect to your internet service provider with your credentials, you should be able to browse the internet. If not, you may have to do some troubleshooting. The best place for troubleshooting any issues is in the System Logs page within the Status menu at the top of the web interface. With any luck, any issues will become evident once you've looked over the logs. If you're sure you entered all of the configuration details correctly, reach out to your internet service provider to ensure your settings are correct.

Hardening pfSense

Your firewall is now configured and running, and it should already do a brilliant job of rejecting unsolicited traffic attempting to enter your network. However, you can take additional steps to ensure your device and network are even more secure.

While logged in to your pfSense device, click **System ▸ Advanced**.

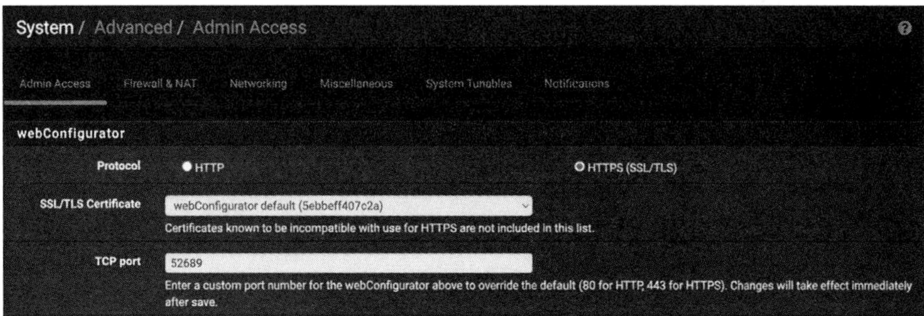

Figure 3-2: Advanced pfSense menu

In the Advanced menu tabs, you can change the protocols, ports, and proxy settings that pfSense uses, among other things. Click **Save** before leaving a tab if you change any settings.

In the Admin Access tab shown in Figure 3-2, set webConfigurator Protocol to **HTTPS** to ensure a secure, encrypted connection to the device. It's always preferable to use HTTPS instead of the unencrypted HTTP protocol because the added encryption ensures that, even if the network traffic is intercepted by an adversary, the adversary can't decrypt it.

In the next section of the Admin Access page (not shown in Figure 3-2), you can change the SSH options. I recommend not allowing SSH access to the device all the time—that would be similar to leaving your front door unlocked at night. If you allow SSH access only while you're actively using it, adversaries are able to attempt to access your network this way only while the service is available. Having the service turned off 99 percent of the time means attackers have only 1 percent of the time to attempt to breach the network. Disable this option unless you're actively connecting to the device via SSH. Once these settings have been updated, click **Save**.

On the Networking tab, you can enable or disable IPv6 traffic. If you're not actively using IPv6, disable it here to reduce your attack surface. Doing so should make the remaining settings on this page moot.

If you're using a proxy for your web traffic, enter your proxy details in the Miscellaneous tab. If you're planning to build your own proxy server using the steps detailed in Chapter 6, revisit this chapter and enter the proxy details at that stage.

pfSense Firewall Rules

The default pfSense firewall rules will block traffic from both RFC1918 private network connections and *bogon networks* from entering your network from the internet. RFC1918 addresses, discussed in Chapter 1, are IP address ranges reserved for private, internal network use only, meaning addresses in these ranges should not appear on the public internet. They include the following ranges: 192.168.0.0/16, 10.0.0.0/8, and 172.16.0.0/12. If any of these happen to appear on the internet, your firewall should find this suspicious and discard that traffic. Similarly, bogon networks or bogon addresses are those that are public but haven't been assigned to anyone by IANA. If an as-yet-unassigned address or address range is sending your network traffic, this is also suspicious, and the firewall should discard it.

While the default firewall rules are a good start, you should add a few rules manually to provide a higher level of security. For example, you shouldn't allow services such as *Server Message Block (SMB)*, the service that allows Windows computers to share files across a network, to send or receive outbound or inbound traffic from your network to the internet or receive inbound traffic from the internet.

NOTE *The WannaCry ransomware of May 2017 spread using an SMB vulnerability known as EternalBlue; blocking SMB at your perimeter firewall significantly reduces your risk of exposure to this vulnerability and the risk of other vulnerabilities like it being used to compromise your network.*

To add a rule that blocks SMB traffic, follow these steps:

1. In pfSense, at the top of the page, click **Firewall ▸ Rules**.
2. Click **LAN ▸ Add** to begin adding a rule.
3. Set the action to either **block** (drop the packets) or **reject** (drop the packets and notify the sender).

4. Set Address Family to **IPv4** and Protocol to **TCP**.
5. Set Source to **Any**, Destination to **Any**, and Destination Port Range (to and from) to **(other) 445**.
6. Ensure the **Log** box is ticked to log any dropped packets, and then click **Save**.

Once you're done, your firewall should no longer allow SMB traffic to pass your network boundary. Follow this same process for ports 137, 138, and 139, as these services (NetBIOS Name Resolution, NetBIOS Datagram Service, and NetBIOS Session Service) should never be allowed to cross the network boundary either, as all of these protocols are used for processes internal to a local network.

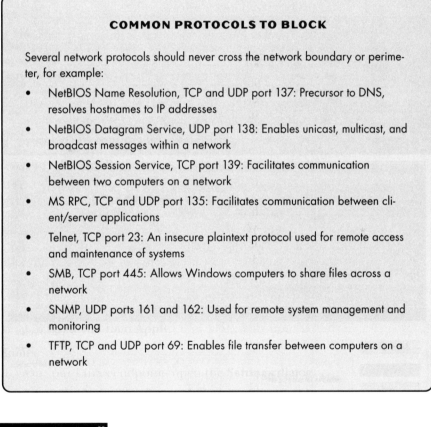

COMMON PROTOCOLS TO BLOCK

Several network protocols should never cross the network boundary or perimeter, for example:

- NetBIOS Name Resolution, TCP and UDP port 137: Precursor to DNS, resolves hostnames to IP addresses
- NetBIOS Datagram Service, UDP port 138: Enables unicast, multicast, and broadcast messages within a network
- NetBIOS Session Service, TCP port 139: Facilitates communication between two computers on a network
- MS RPC, TCP and UDP port 135: Facilitates communication between client/server applications
- Telnet, TCP port 23: An insecure plaintext protocol used for remote access and maintenance of systems
- SMB, TCP port 445: Allows Windows computers to share files across a network
- SNMP, UDP ports 161 and 162: Used for remote system management and monitoring
- TFTP, TCP and UDP port 69: Enables file transfer between computers on a network

#14: Testing Your Firewall

With one or more of these rules in place, test the firewall to ensure the blocked traffic is actually being blocked. The best tool for this purpose is *Nmap*, which is used for network scanning or network mapping. It's available in GUI form on Windows, Linux, and Mac (called *Zenmap*) and also as a command line tool. Installing the GUI version will make it available on the command line, so download and install the latest version from *https://www.nmap.org/*.

Otherwise, you can install it using the command line on Ubuntu:

```
$ sudo apt install nmap
```

Once you've installed Nmap, use the following command to scan port 445 from the command line, which we've told the firewall to block:

```
$ sudo nmap -p 445 -A scanme.nmap.org
--snip--
Nmap scan report for scanme.nmap.org (45.33.32.156)
Host is up (0.20s latency).
Other addresses for scanme.nmap.org (not scanned):
2600:3c01::f03c:91ff:fe18:bb2f
PORT     STATE    SERVICE      VERSION
445/tcp filtered microsoft-ds
Service detection performed. Please report any incorrect results at https://
nmap.org/submit/.
Nmap done: 1 IP address (1 host up) scanned in 2.54 seconds
```

You can use the same command in the Zenmap GUI—just exclude `sudo`. This command will perform a port scan from your device, which is behind your firewall, on the *http://scanme.nmap.org/* website, a public web page available for testing purposes from the creators of Nmap.

The command breaks down like this: `nmap` is the name of the program. The `-p 445` argument specifies the port or ports to be scanned, which can be either a comma-separated list (such as `-p 445,137,138,22`), a specific port as shown, or a port range like `-p1-1024`. The `-A` argument tells Nmap to try to identify the service and operating system on each scanned port, and `scanme.nmap.org` is the website or system to scan. If the results come back and the `STATE` shown for the port is `filtered`, the firewall has blocked the traffic, and the firewall rules are working. If the `STATE` shows `closed`, the firewall is allowing the traffic through, and the website itself, rather than the firewall, was returning a response saying the port is closed. If you receive this result, your firewall rule either isn't configured or isn't working.

Once your rules are working, go to the firewall logs to see the blocked packets. In pfSense, at the top of the page, click **Status ▸ System Logs ▸ Firewall** to see the last 500 entries in the firewall log, as shown in Figure 3-3.

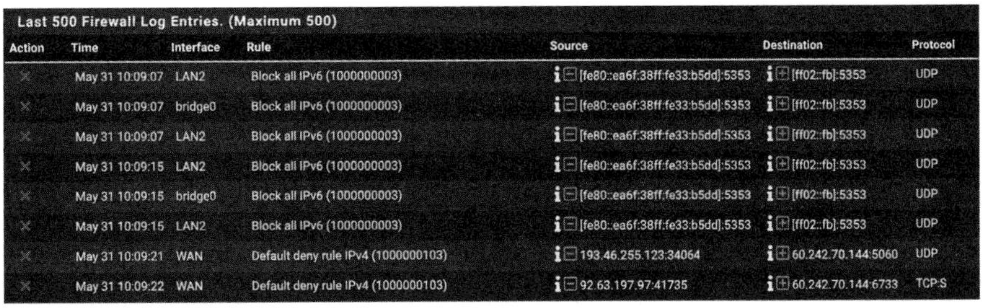

Last 500 Firewall Log Entries. (Maximum 500)

Action	Time	Interface	Rule	Source	Destination	Protocol
×	May 31 10:09:07	LAN2	Block all IPv6 (1000000003)	[fe80::ea6f:38ff:fe33:b5dd]:5353	[ff02::fb]:5353	UDP
×	May 31 10:09:07	bridge0	Block all IPv6 (1000000003)	[fe80::ea6f:38ff:fe33:b5dd]:5353	[ff02::fb]:5353	UDP
×	May 31 10:09:07	LAN2	Block all IPv6 (1000000003)	[fe80::ea6f:38ff:fe33:b5dd]:5353	[ff02::fb]:5353	UDP
×	May 31 10:09:15	LAN2	Block all IPv6 (1000000003)	[fe80::ea6f:38ff:fe33:b5dd]:5353	[ff02::fb]:5353	UDP
×	May 31 10:09:15	bridge0	Block all IPv6 (1000000003)	[fe80::ea6f:38ff:fe33:b5dd]:5353	[ff02::fb]:5353	UDP
×	May 31 10:09:15	LAN2	Block all IPv6 (1000000003)	[fe80::ea6f:38ff:fe33:b5dd]:5353	[ff02::fb]:5353	UDP
×	May 31 10:09:21	WAN	Default deny rule IPv4 (1000000103)	193.46.255.123:34064	60.242.70.144:5060	UDP
×	May 31 10:09:22	WAN	Default deny rule IPv4 (1000000103)	92.63.197.97:41735	60.242.70.144:6733	TCP:S

Figure 3-3: pfSense firewall log

In all likelihood, you'll see a lot of blocked traffic. At this stage, it's difficult to know what this blocked traffic could be. As an example, one of the entries at the top of my log shows a blocked connection from the IP address 80.82.77.245 on port 46732.

Upon further investigation, it appears as though this is a service that performs regular network scans of public IP addresses for "research purposes." That said, it could be anything; how do I know whether this "research" is legitimate or an adversary attempting to find holes in my firewall to penetrate my network? In most cases, it's impossible to know, but at least my firewall is actively blocking this activity, and I can find it in the firewall logs if I need to review it and act on it. We'll discuss what you can do with this information in greater detail in Chapter 10, which covers network security monitoring.

Summary

Your network and hosts are demonstrably more secure for having host- and network-based firewalls in place. In the projects for this chapter, you've created rules and rulesets to make it significantly more difficult for an adversary trying to infiltrate your network, and even more challenging to do so undetected.

While this chapter has armed you with the fundamentals and a greater understanding of firewalls, it's in your best interest to further research the ports and protocols you'd like to allow or deny within, as well as into and out of, your network. Every network will be different and have different requirements.

4

SECURING WIRELESS NETWORKS

Wireless networking has become ubiquitous and is synonymous with being online. Most places with an internet connection have a wireless modem or router serving a multitude of devices, from desktops to phones and internet of things (IoT) devices such as TVs, light bulbs, and refrigerators. Without wireless technology, modern life would be much less convenient, but convenience often forces us to give up some of our online security.

Wireless networking has caused our networks to extend beyond the cables that originally served as physical boundaries. They even bypass other physical barriers we take for granted: walls. As wireless technologies evolve, the effective distance of our wireless networks improves, so much so that we're now seeing larger networks that overflow from what used to be local area networks (LANs) inside our premises, all the way out to our neighbors. This is fantastic in terms of connectivity, but potentially disastrous regarding security.

This chapter will address some of the pitfalls associated with wider wireless networks. You'll learn about reducing your attack surface by disabling IPv6 and limiting the number of devices allowed on a wireless network. The chapter will also delve into MAC address filtering, which allows only known devices onto the internal network; disabling features when they're not in use; using secure authentication methods; and grouping devices or users based on their necessary privilege level within the network.

> **UPGRADING YOUR HARDWARE**
>
> If you received wireless networking equipment from your internet service provider, it's likely an entry-level device. Usually, this means it has fewer features or is less configurable than a higher-end product. If, while making your way through this chapter, you find that your device doesn't allow the level of management required, consider purchasing a model with higher specifications. Netgear's Nighthawk series routers, for example, are reasonably priced and fully featured, even at the mid-range.

#15: Disabling IPv6

IPv6, the newer version of the Internet Protocol, was designed to combat the fact that we'll eventually run out of publicly addressable IPv4 space. IPv6 expands the available address space by many orders of magnitude, but it's not as common as another mitigation: network address translation (NAT), which we described in Chapter 1. If you don't use IPv6 in your network but leave it enabled, you're providing adversaries one more potential *intrusion vector* (that is, another way to enter or otherwise compromise your network). As a general rule, you should disable or uninstall all protocols and applications that are not in active use to prevent attackers from using those tools (or the tools' vulnerabilities) against you. Disabling unused protocols reduces the attack surface of your environment, which should be as small as possible.

If you aren't actively using IPv6 in your network, disable it wherever you can, including in your Wi-Fi configuration. To disable IPv6, follow these steps:

Windows

1. Open **Network and Internet Settings**.
2. Click **Change adapter options**.
3. For each adapter in the resulting window, double-click the adapter and then click **Properties**.

a. Find the **Internet Protocol Version 6 (TCP/IPv6)** checkbox and uncheck it.
b. Click **OK** and close the remaining windows.

macOS

1. Open **System Preferences**.
2. Click **Network**.
3. For each adapter in the list, click **Advanced**.
   a. Open the **TCP/IP** tab.
   b. Ensure Configure IPv6 is set to **Off**.

Linux

1. Open **Settings**.
2. Select **Network** from the list on the left.
3. For each adapter, click the configuration **Cog**.
   a. In the **IPv6** tab, click the **Disable** radio button and then click **Apply**.

Your Modem or Router

Configuring your modem or router may be trickier, since every device has its own configuration menus and options. Some devices will have an IPv6 section; if this is the case, access that menu and disable IPv6 entirely. Or, you might find the IPv6 option in the DHCP settings. Others may be hidden within the Wireless or LAN options. In the pfSense device discussed in Chapter 3, the IPv6 settings are found under **Services ▸ DHCPv6 Server & RA**. Unless you configured a network interface in pfSense with a static IPv6 address, this will be disabled by default.

If you're unable to find the setting for IPv6 in your device, search the make and model on the internet. Once you've disabled IPv6, you're one step closer to being more secure.

#16: Limiting Network Devices

Most small, nonenterprise networks rarely specify or otherwise limit the devices present in their networks and suffer from being too open, allowing all devices to connect. While this setup provides convenience, particularly when you buy a new device or friends come over, it's an insecure practice that leaves a wide hole for potential adversaries, whether targeted or opportunistic.

You can avoid this security risk by identifying all the devices allowed to connect to the network and restricting access to just those devices. Creating an *asset list*—a table containing data about each device, such as its type (PC, laptop, mobile phone, and so on), location, hostname, MAC address (its hardware address), and IP address—will complement your network map and vice versa, helping you keep track of the various devices on your network.

Once you've collected this information for all the endpoints in your network, you can assign static IP addresses to known devices and reduce the assignable IP address range in your DHCP server. Make the range small enough to include enough addresses for the devices in your asset list and on your network map. By reducing the number of available addresses, you lower the risk of an adversary adding new devices to your network without detection. Even having taken this security measure, an adversary may be able to force one of your devices to disconnect and connect their own in its place. This is where MAC address filtering comes in.

MAC address filtering lets you allow or deny access to your network based on a device's MAC address. If you know the MAC addresses of all allowed devices, you can make unauthorized devices harder to add to the network and easier to detect.

Creating an Asset List

Unlike in large enterprises, making an asset list in smaller networks is fairly straightforward. First, create a chart like the one in Table 4-1 using pen and paper, Excel, or some other tool.

Table 4-1: An Asset List Template

Device	IP address	MAC address	Hostname (optional)	Location (optional)
My laptop				
Their laptop				
My phone				
Their phone				
TV				
Tablet				
Xbox				

You can choose to omit the hostnames and locations, but be sure to include the IP and MAC addresses of each device. If the devices are already connected to your network, you can retrieve this information from your router's DHCP section or your DHCP server if you have one. For devices without user interfaces, such as Wi-Fi-connected lights, this may be your best or only option. Alternatively, you can gather the details from each host.

Windows

1. Open **Network and Internet Settings**.
2. Click **Change adapter options**.
3. Identify the adapter that connects the device to your network. If connected to Wi-Fi, it will be the Wi-Fi adapter; otherwise, it's the Ethernet adapter. Double-click the adapter and then click **Details**.
4. Find the physical address and record this as the computer's MAC address in your asset list.

5. Locate the IP address and record this as well.
6. Click **Close** and close the remaining windows.

macOS

1. Open **System Preferences** and click **Network**.
2. Identify the adapter that connects the device to your network. If connected to Wi-Fi, it will be the Wi-Fi adapter; otherwise, it's the Ethernet adapter.
3. Click **Advanced** and then click the **TCP/IP** tab.
4. Record the IPv4 address.
5. Go to the **Hardware** tab and record the MAC address.
6. Click **OK** and close the Network window.

Linux

1. Open **Settings**.
2. Select **Network** from the list on the left.
3. Identify the adapter that connects the device to your network. If connected to Wi-Fi, it will be the Wi-Fi adapter; otherwise, it's the Ethernet adapter.
4. Click the configuration **Cog**.
5. In the **Details** tab, record the IP address and the hardware address (the MAC address).
6. Close the windows.

You should have successfully identified all known devices in the network. If any unknown devices are connected, you'll block them using the steps in the upcoming "MAC Address Filtering" section. Next, you'll assign each device a static IP address.

Static IP Addressing

IP addresses can be *static* or *dynamic*. By default, most routers use a Dynamic Host Configuration Protocol (DHCP) server to assign IP addresses to endpoints when they connect to the network. These assignments are called *DHCP leases* and are time-bound; a lease typically expires after 24 hours. Dynamic IP addresses may change each time the endpoint connects or the lease expires. However, you can alternatively assign each endpoint its own static IP address that it'll keep every time it connects to your network. This helps you know to which endpoint a given IP address corresponds and can prevent unknown devices from connecting by limiting available dynamic addresses.

You'll find the static IP address settings in the DHCP menu of most Wi-Fi routers. For this example, we'll be using the DHCP Leases menu of the Netgate SG-3100 covered in Chapter 3, but the process should be similar regardless of the device you're using. To reach the DHCP Leases menu in the SG-3100, click **Status ▸ DHCP Leases**. In similar devices, it might appear in the LAN or Advanced settings. You should see a table similar to Figure 4-1.

Leases

IP address	MAC address	Client Id	Hostname	Start	End	Online	Lease Type	Actions
192.168.1.42	aa:bb:cc:dd:ee:ff		Host_One	2021/06/09 02:05:30	2021/06/09 04:05:30	online	active	
192.168.1.41	ff:ee:dd:cc:bb:aa		Host_Two	2021/06/09 00:05:29	2021/06/09 02:05:29	online	active	

Figure 4-1: DHCP leases menu on the Netgate SG-3100 pfSense firewall

To create a static IP address (also called a *static lease*), click the **Add** button (in the SG-3100 it's the left, unfilled + button). The resulting page allows you to specify an IP address for the host you selected. Specify any address you'd like, as long as it's within your addressing scheme, and then click **Save**. For example, if your address scheme is *192.168.1.x*, you might choose *192.168.1.100*. The IP addresses you choose don't have to be consecutive; you can use *192.168.1.100* for this host and *192.168.1.54* for the next. After you've assigned the host's static address, it will probably need to reconnect to the network to acquire it; force it to do so by power-cycling the device (turn it off and on).

Once you've assigned static IP addresses to your authorized devices, update your asset list and network map. Then, to effectively ban additional devices from joining without authorization, reduce the range of addresses the DHCP server may assign.

By default, the DHCP server service makes the entire IP address range available for devices to connect to the network. If your IP addressing scheme is *192.168.0.0/16*, your network can have up to 65,534 hosts connected. No small network needs that many hosts, and leaving this wide open is a security risk.

To see the DHCP address range in the SG-3100, click **Services ▸ DHCP Server**. Your device should have an IP address range similar to Figure 4-2.

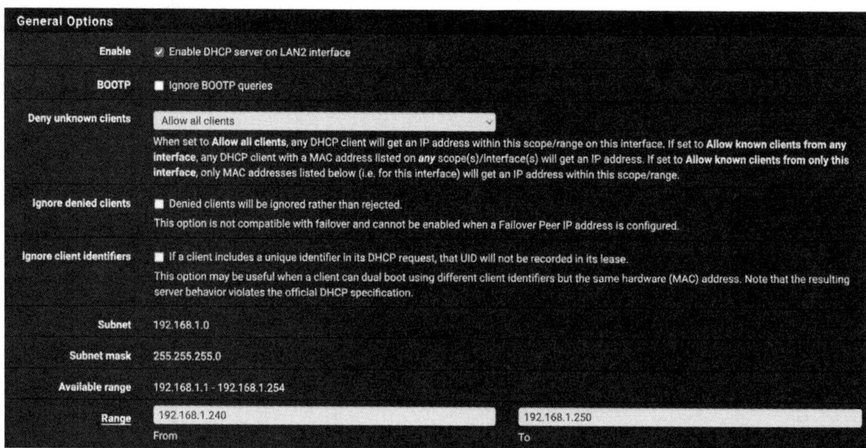

Figure 4-2: DHCP address range

The numbers may be different, but the general configuration should be close. To manually authorize every device that connects to your network, disable the DHCP server and add new static addresses for every endpoint. An alternative is to shorten the available DHCP address range. Instead of allowing the range to be open from *192.168.1.100* to *192.168.1.245*, you could specify of range of *192.168.1.100* to *192.168.1.105*, limiting the number of devices that can be assigned a DHCP address to six. When these IP addresses have been statically assigned to the devices within your network, no additional devices can receive an IP address from the DHCP server without one of those devices going offline or being removed from the network. Reducing the available address space reduces the ability for unauthorized devices to connect to your network, thereby minimizing your attack surface.

You might be wondering if these steps are necessary, when anyone wanting to connect to your wireless network will need to be nearby, and you probably don't let strangers into your home or office. Consider, though, that "close proximity" might be as far away as a car on the street outside your building, or the suite of offices next door.

MAC Address Filtering

MAC address filtering can be implemented as either a stand-alone defense or an additional layer of security. Most wireless routers allow you to specify the MAC addresses allowed to connect to your network, thereby blocking unspecified MAC addresses. MAC addresses are less likely to change than IP addresses, as they're tied to a device's hardware.

These days it's not that difficult to fake, or *spoof*, a hardware address. However, any additional obstacle you can place between an adversary and your network will make it more secure. As an example, to access the MAC address filtering page on an ASUS RT-AC5300 wireless router, you'd click **Wireless ▸ Wireless Mac Filter**, as shown in Figure 4-3.

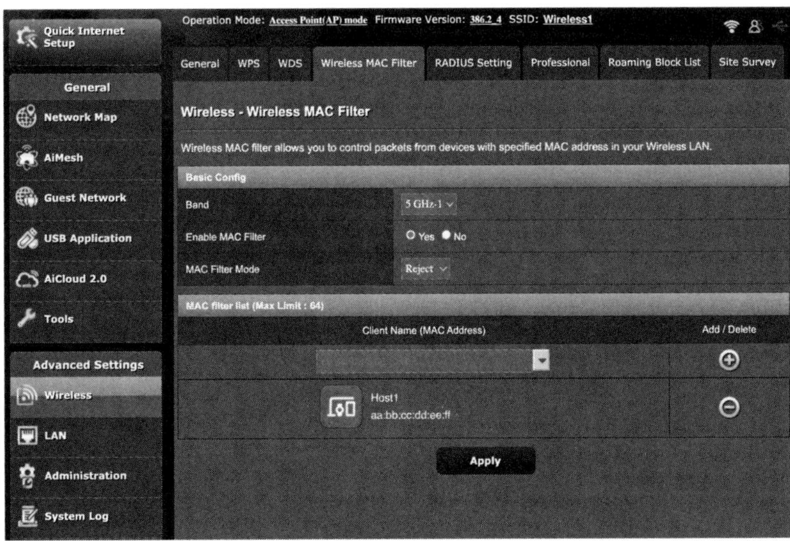

Figure 4-3: Wireless MAC address filtering on an ASUS AC-RT5300 router

The Basic Config options shown in Figure 4-3—the wireless band, whether the filter is enabled or disabled, and whether the filter mode is Accept or Reject—can be applied to either the 2.4 GHz or 5 GHz radio.

> **2.4 GHZ AND 5 GHZ WIRELESS BANDS**
>
> These two frequencies have several differences. One is the wavelength: the 2.4 GHz band will result in a wireless network that functions over greater distances, while the 5 GHz band will be less effective over longer distances, but it can provide faster speeds within its shorter range. There will likely be more interference on the 2.4 GHz band, as this is an older technology, so far more wireless networks and devices use this frequency (including microwaves, which can cause wireless interference). Finally, not all wireless devices are capable of handling both 2.4 GHz and 5 GHz wireless signals.

In Figure 4-3, the MAC filter for the 5 GHz band is Enabled, and the Mode option is set to Reject. This mode causes the filter to function as a *denylist*, meaning anything on the list will be blocked or denied access. An *allowlist*, on the other hand, is a list of endpoints that will be allowed access. Use a denylist when you know the MAC address of a device to which you want to deny access. In most cases, you'll use the Accept, or allowlist, mode instead. In Accept mode, the MAC filter list contains the MAC addresses that you've explicitly allowed access to the network.

Select **Enable Mac Filter** and **Accept** and then enter the MAC addresses from your asset list. Once you've added all the MAC addresses and saved your configuration, no devices except those specified can connect to the wireless network and acquire an IP address. You can test this by removing one of the less critical devices from the Accept list and trying to connect it to the network. If it refuses to connect, your MAC filtering is working correctly.

#17: Segmenting Your Network

Wireless networking grants you the ability to share an internet connection with guests by using a separate guest network without compromising your security. Most mid-range wireless routers offer this functionality. The ASUS RT-AC5300, for example, allows for multiple guest networks on both the 2.4 GHz and 5 GHz wireless frequencies, as shown in Figure 4-4.

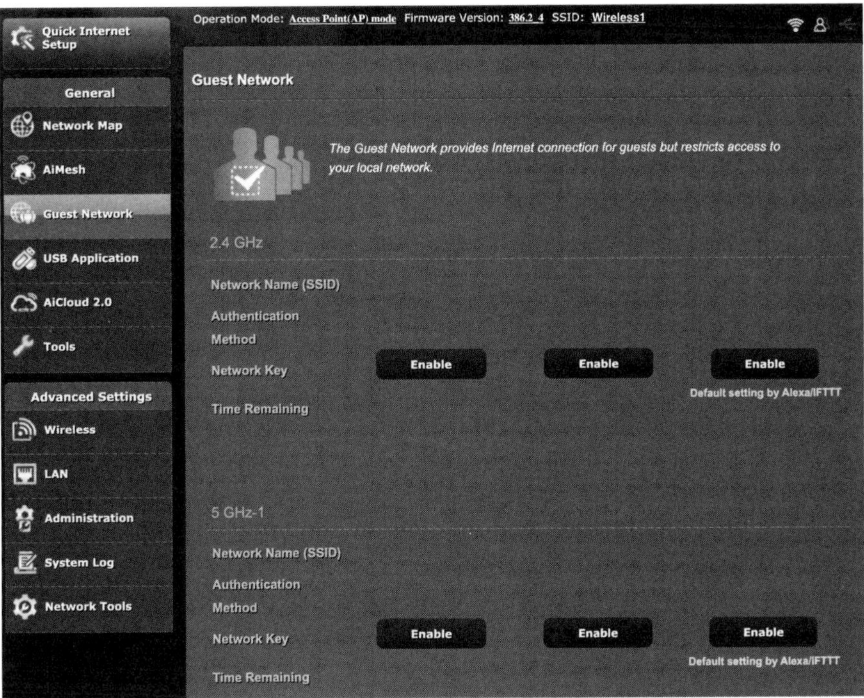

Figure 4-4: Multiple wireless network capability

A guest network is not only convenient for your visitors; it also allows you to group users and devices by their level of risk or trust. For example, on your private internal network, you might connect your primary devices: laptops, mobile devices, and so on. Then, on the guest network, you might connect your IoT devices: your Google Home, Amazon Alexa, LIFX or other smart lightbulbs, and other similar devices.

Certain categories of devices are inherently less secure. For instance, IoT devices are susceptible to botnet infections. A *botnet* is a group of internet-connected devices, usually linked via malware installed on each device. The malware causes the group to be controlled as a collective, usually for malicious activity, such as distributed denial-of-service attacks, data theft, or spamming. Allowing devices with lower standards of security onto the same network segment as your primary devices is risky. The best way to mitigate this risk is to separate them, either logically or physically.

As shown in Figure 4-4, you can allow guest devices on the network for an unlimited amount of time or a specific period of your choosing, which is useful for guests who may need access for only a few hours. By configuring your router to allow guests unlimited access, you trade security for convenience. Conversely, limiting the amount of time a guest can connect before needing to be re-authorized requires more work. Still, it's a far more secure manner of access control.

One last feature provided by some wireless routers and access points is the option to allow or deny access to your *intranet*, which is the internal network where your private devices are connected. Allowing guests access to this segment of your network lessens your security, as it provides them with access to your computers and mobile devices. If you let guests access your entire network, you might as well give them access to your primary wireless network instead of configuring a guest network. The ASUS wireless router I've been discussing has this capability; if you configure a guest network, you can choose to allow endpoints connected to that wireless network to access your intranet or allow them to access only the gateway to the internet. The router handles this access by allowing or disallowing devices connected to your guest network to see devices connected to your primary network. Banning access from the guest network to your intranet is the more secure option and one that you should implement. If your router has this capability, a fairly obvious checkbox should be present in the wireless network settings. If you can't find it, chances are your router doesn't have it (although you can make sure by reading the manual or doing a quick internet search).

#18: Configuring Wireless Authentication

You should protect your Wi-Fi network with encryption by creating a passphrase to access the network. An open wireless network—with no protection or encryption—provides a prime target for an adversary. Today, most networks use one of three security algorithms to secure their communications: WEP, WPA/WPA2, or WPA3.

WEP

Wired Equivalent Privacy (WEP) is the oldest of the three security protocols and by far the least secure. WEP uses either a 40- or 104-bit encryption key, both of which are small when compared to those of later protocols. WEP combines this encryption key with 24-bit initialization vectors (IVs) meant to provide enhanced security, but the shortness of these IVs means the algorithm will likely reuse keys, which in turn makes the encryption easier to crack. Understanding the details isn't necessary; just know that WEP is an insecure technology and shouldn't be used. In fact, vendors phased out WEP by 2001; it's no longer available on most hardware.

WPA/WPA2

Wi-Fi Protected Access (WPA), the successor to WEP, improved upon WEP's protection. Although it relied on the same RC4 encryption cipher, it also introduced the *Temporal Key Integrity Protocol (TKIP)*. TKIP strengthened wireless security by using a 256-bit key and implementing message integrity checking, larger 48-bit IVs, and mechanisms to minimize IV reuse.

In turn, WPA2 improved the original WPA protocol. Both WPA and WPA2 allow users to choose between personal and enterprise modes. Personal mode, called WPA-PSK, uses a preshared key (PSK) or passphrase to grant access, while enterprise mode requires an authentication server. WPA2 replaced both the RC4 encryption cipher and TKIP in favor of more secure algorithms and encryption protocols. Moreover, it implemented *Counter Mode CBC-MAC Protocol (CCMP)*, a more secure encryption mechanism. All of this made WPA2 far more secure than the earlier encryption protocols and facilitated roaming between access points, providing a smoother user experience. If possible, choose WPA2 or greater in your wireless network.

Having said that, an adversary could still capture your wireless traffic and brute-force your network password. Though WPA2 is good, there's no such thing as perfect security. As a result, ensure that you use strong passphrases to secure your wireless networks. Passphrases are discussed in detail in Chapter 11.

WPA3

Wi-Fi Protected Access version 3 (WPA3) is the latest wireless security technology. It's very recent and hasn't yet seen wide adoption. WPA3 improves security by keeping users who are connected to the same network from eavesdropping on each other's wireless communications—even if the wireless network is open and doesn't require a password to authenticate.

WPA3 achieves this by replacing the preshared key authentication used in WPA2 with a new protocol: *Simultaneous Authentication of Equals (SAE)*. This change also means adversaries can't capture the traffic needed to crack the network's password, making it even more difficult for them to gain unauthorized access to the network.

For now, WPA3 is in its infancy, so very few devices are compatible. Newer wireless routers and access points will come with WPA3 as standard. Even then, other devices will need to catch up before you can use it; there's little value in having a WPA3 router if your phones and computers can't connect to it. Once this changes, you should use WPA3 over any other wireless security standard.

To configure the ASUS router we've been discussing, in the wireless settings, under **Advanced Settings ▸ Wireless ▸ General**, you'd create your primary, internal network by specifying the network name (SSID) and a security key or passphrase, as shown in Figure 4-5. Then, in **General ▸ Guest Network ▸ Enable**, create one or more guest networks to which you'll connect all of your other devices by specifying a network name and security key or passphrase, just as you did for your primary wireless network.

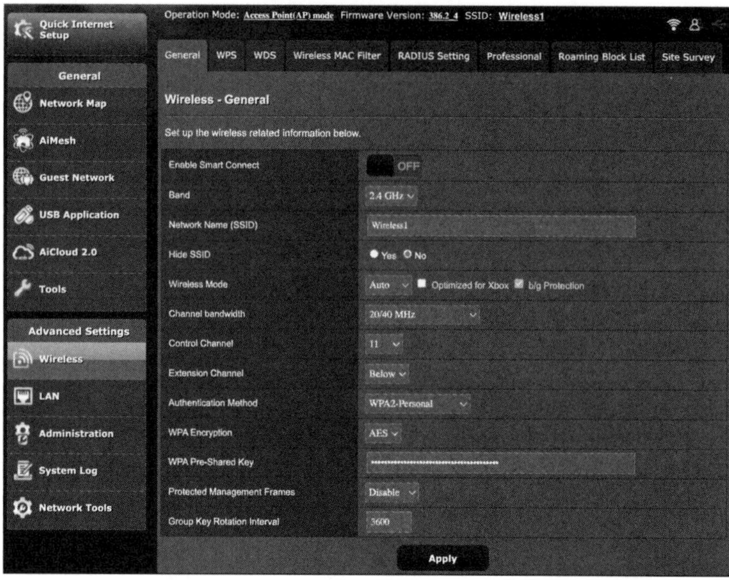

Figure 4-5: Primary wireless network settings

The ASUS router used in this example keeps your main wireless network and the guest networks divided. The same process could be followed on most modern mid- to high-end wireless routers. Any endpoints connected to the main wireless network will be unable to communicate with endpoints connected to the guest networks, and vice versa. However, if you create multiple guest networks, devices on any of those networks will be able to see and communicate with one another. Some wireless routers may provide the ability to keep each of your guest networks completely separate as well. Do your research before investing in a wireless router if you want this capability.

Be sure to follow secure practices and take advantage of any security options available, such as those discussed earlier. For example, the ASUS router has several features available for securing your wireless networks, as shown in Figure 4-6.

Guest Network index	2
Hide SSID	● Yes ○ No
Network Name (SSID)	GuestTest1
Authentication Method	WPA2-Personal
WPA Encryption	AES
WPA Pre-Shared Key	thisisatest
Access time	● 0 days hour(s) minute(s) ○ Unlimited access
Enable MAC Filter	Disable

Figure 4-6: Wireless network security settings

Where you have the ability to set a WPA passphrase or preshared key, do so. You should always take any opportunity to harden the network against opportunistic adversaries. In some cases, it's also beneficial to limit the access time allowed to endpoints connected to these networks. If you plan to use a secondary network for endpoints that are expected to be always on and connected, that option may not suit your needs. However, if you'll use these networks for guests, or endpoints that need only limited connectivity, limit the amount of time those endpoints are allowed to remain connected to a reasonable number of minutes or hours as you see fit. The last option shown in Figure 4-6, Enable MAC Filter, lets you allow or deny devices access to your networks based on their hardware addresses.

WIRELESS NETWORK TIPS

Most routers allow you to hide your wireless network by preventing the network name, or *SSID*, from being broadcast. Doing so will keep the network from appearing in the list of available networks on your device. Even if your network is hidden, you'll still be able to connect to it with the right access credentials. Hiding your network isn't recommended, however. Even though regular users won't be able to see it, an adversary with a network analyzer could still identify it. What's worse, a hidden wireless network actually creates more noise and is easier to discover than a nonhidden one. That's because devices connected to a hidden network have to constantly broadcast beacons to determine if the network is still available, generating traffic that an adversary can capture to attempt to breach the network. Hidden networks are great for protecting your network from your not-so-tech-savvy neighbors but will do the opposite for potential attackers.

Consider turning your Wi-Fi off when it isn't in use, such as when everyone in the house is asleep or when your office has closed down for the night. If the wireless is turned off, adversaries won't be able to detect it, much less breach it. The same goes for your guest network; if it isn't being used, turn it off to reduce your attack surface.

Summary

In this chapter, we've discussed common wireless network security risks and methods to mitigate them within your network by implementing measures such as IP and MAC address filtering and reducing the available address space in your DHCP server. Creating and maintaining an asset list and network map can help to ensure no unauthorized devices are connecting to your network. Eavesdropping is the easiest risk to mitigate. Add encryption to your network in the form of WPA security (ideally WPA3, as it becomes more common) and implement a passphrase rather than a password for network access.

5

CREATING A VIRTUAL PRIVATE NETWORK

A *virtual private network (VPN)* is a means of providing privacy and security for communications over the public internet. If you don't want a malicious third party to intercept your Google search traffic as it traverses the internet from your local laptop to Google's servers, you should use a VPN to encrypt the traffic between the two endpoints. If you frequently transfer sensitive files or data, such as personally identifiable information or banking information, it's wise to protect this information using encryption.

The other primary function of a VPN is to extend a private network, such as those in homes and offices, from one geographic location to another. A VPN creates a tunnel over the internet from one network to a second network. This means that if a user usually based in Australia is traveling in Europe, they could connect to their home network from Europe as if they were physically located in Australia. Conversely, if a user located in Australia wants to *appear* as if they're physically located in Europe, they can place the VPN endpoint in Europe, usually via some third-party service.

This chapter outlines a method for creating a private VPN whose *exit node* (that is, the place where the VPN tunnel ends) is located somewhere outside of your local network, in a different geographic location somewhere in the world, to make your actual physical location private. We'll discuss how to achieve this with OpenVPN or Wireguard.

Drawbacks of Third-Party VPNs and Remote Access Services

Although you could subscribe to a VPN service like NordVPN or ExpressVPN, operating your own VPN is beneficial because you control everything about it, including connection and traffic logging levels, as well as the cost of the service. Also, whereas third-party services provide some benefits, such as the possibility of using multiple exit nodes in different locations, they usually don't offer the ability to connect into your own network remotely. One last challenge of using third-party VPN services is that they usually set a limit to the number of devices you can connect at a time. A privately managed VPN has no such limitation.

Recently, there's been a boom in the number of applications designed to allow remote access to endpoints from the wider internet. This includes software and vendors such as Teamviewer and AnyDesk. Although these solutions are convenient and have a low barrier to entry, they increase the attack surface of your private network by opening up remote access from your computer to the internet, something you should rarely do, if ever. There have also been several well-known compromises of these solutions, indicating that they are vulnerable to attack. A VPN provides a much more secure solution.

OpenVPN

OpenVPN is one of the most common VPN solutions available. Because of its age and ubiquity, you can be confident in its security when compared to newer solutions, which have been less rigorously tested for bugs and vulnerabilities. OpenVPN comes built-in to a variety of networking hardware, which is beneficial because in a lot of cases your router can act as your VPN endpoint inside of your network (that is, the VPN server). This means your router can also act as a VPN client, connecting to a VPN server in the cloud, and then everything connected to the router on your internal network can send and receive traffic via your VPN tunnel. Encrypting your internet traffic in this way provides much greater privacy than using the internet without a VPN. Ideally, though, you'll want more control over the VPN exit node than this allows; most routers use either a cut-down version of Linux or a proprietary operating system, so you'll learn how to create a VPN server using Ubuntu for greater flexibility.

EasyRSA

EasyRSA is a command-line utility for creating and managing certificate authorities. To encrypt and protect traffic, OpenVPN requires a *certificate authority (CA)* to issue certificates. *Digital certificates* are used to enable trust between different parties, usually networks and computers. *Public key infrastructure (PKI)* is responsible for the distribution, authentication, and revocation of public key certificates, which are used to verify ownership of digital certificates. These certificates contain the public key that an entity uses as part of a public/private key pair to encrypt data, which can then be decrypted only by the public key owner with the matching private key. This method secures most communication on the internet today.

The CA you create will generate, sign, verify, and revoke (if necessary) all the certificates required to encrypt and secure communications between the VPN server and VPN clients. Technically, you can install both OpenVPN and the CA on the same server, but doing so is less secure than installing them on separate servers. Any adversary who gains access to the server would have access to the certificates and private keys used by the server, as well as the ability to generate new certificates. Therefore, you'll need two Ubuntu servers: one to act as the OpenVPN server and one to serve as the certificate server. You'll use the certificate server to sign requests generated on the OpenVPN server for both the VPN server and any client devices connecting to the VPN, whether they're laptops, workstations, mobile devices, or any other type of device.

Wireguard

Wireguard, a relatively new alternative to OpenVPN, is simple and incredibly fast by comparison. The drawback of being newer is that although Wireguard is open source, it's had less time to be tested for bugs and vulnerabilities. However, it has gathered a sizable following in the security community and a good reputation for being reliable and secure.

NOTE *If you plan to connect to your private network remotely, keep in mind that you'll need a static IP address on your home or office internet connection, as well as some port forwarding on your border router. Most internet service providers supply static IP addresses upon request, usually for a nominal fee.*

#19: Creating a VPN with OpenVPN

In this first project, you'll start by creating an OpenVPN server and a certificate authority to secure communication via the VPN. Next, you'll generate the relevant certificates, create the OpenVPN configuration files, configure the host firewall, and start the VPN. Finally, you'll configure each of the VPN clients that will use this VPN to send and receive traffic, and you'll connect to and test the VPN connection.

The entire process of spinning up an OpenVPN server in the cloud and connecting a client to it should take no longer than a couple of hours. Adding subsequent clients should take up to 30 minutes per endpoint. You'll need to enable and configure a firewall on your server as part of creating your VPN. Ubuntu's built-in firewall, the *Uncomplicated Firewall (UFW)*, is designed to reduce the complexity of firewall configuration. It's much simpler than solutions like iptables (covered in Chapter 3). We'll introduce you to UFW and its use in this project as an alternative host firewall solution. Alternatively, you can apply what you learned in Chapter 3 and implement the same rules described for UFW in an iptables deployment. Even if you have a perimeter firewall in place like pfSense, be sure to enable either the host-based firewall offered by Ubuntu or iptables, as laid out in Chapter 3, to provide an additional layer of protection at the host level. Implementing a host-based firewall also allows more granular configuration of the servers' network connections.

Once you enable the firewall, you'll have to adjust the settings of the Ubuntu installation so that OpenVPN traffic is capable of traversing that firewall. (I'll cover how to do this later in the project.)

Securing internet traffic originating inside your network will require a VPN exit node elsewhere, as well as a certificate server, so follow Project 3 in Chapter 1 to create two base Ubuntu servers in the cloud, using the cloud service provider of your choice.

Once your Ubuntu servers are up and running, log in to the server you plan to use as your OpenVPN server (as opposed to the certificate authority) via SSH as a standard, non-root user:

```
$ ssh user@your_server_IP
```

Once logged in to the OpenVPN server, at the bash terminal, use `apt` to install OpenVPN:

```
$ sudo apt install openvpn -y
```

You also need to install EasyRSA on both the OpenVPN server and the certificate server. Install the latest version using `apt` as well:

```
$ sudo apt install easy-rsa -y
```

Make sure to install this on both Ubuntu servers. EasyRSA will be installed to the */usr/share/easy-rsa/* directory by default.

Set Up the Certificate Authority

Next, you must configure and build the certificate server to act as a CA. The easiest way to do this is to make a copy of the template that EasyRSA provides and then modify its configuration to suit your needs. You can then initialize the PKI, build the CA, and generate its public certificate and private key.

Navigate to the *easy-rsa* folder on the certificate server and then create a copy of the *vars.example* file. Call it *vars*:

```
$ cd /usr/share/easy-rsa/
$ sudo cp vars.example vars
```

Keep in mind that most of the time when a command in bash runs successfully, there will be no output to the screen, and you'll be returned to the prompt.

Open the resulting *vars* file in a text editor:

```
$ sudo nano vars
```

In the file, find the *organizational fields* that contain information about the organization for which the certificates will be generated by this server; for example:

```
--snip--
#set_var EASYRSA_REQ_COUNTRY    "US"
#set_var EASYRSA_REQ_PROVINCE   "California"
#set_var EASYRSA_REQ_CITY       "San Francisco"
#set_var EASYRSA_REQ_ORG        "Copyleft Certificate Co"
#set_var EASYRSA_REQ_EMAIL      "me@example.net"
#set_var EASYRSA_REQ_OU         "My Organizational Unit"
--snip--
```

Each of these lines in the file is a comment by default, so they won't be read or interpreted when the file is run; they'll be ignored or suppressed. Remove the hash (#) at the beginning of each line to ensure they're read when this file is invoked. Alter the values in quotations on the right to match your organization or personal network. The values can be anything you choose, but they can't be blank. Here's an example:

```
--snip--
set_var EASYRSA_REQ_COUNTRY    "AU"
set_var EASYRSA_REQ_PROVINCE   "Queensland"
set_var EASYRSA_REQ_CITY       "Brisbane"
set_var EASYRSA_REQ_ORG        "Smithco"
set_var EASYRSA_REQ_EMAIL      "john@smithco.net"
set_var EASYRSA_REQ_OU         "Cyber Unit"
--snip--
```

Save and close the file. Execute the easyrsa script within the *easy-rsa* folder (which should still be your current working directory) to initialize the PKI and then build the CA with the same easyrsa script, which will generate both the CA public certificate (*ca.crt*) and the private key (*ca.key*):

```
$ sudo ./easyrsa init-pki
--snip--
Your newly created PKI dir is: /usr/share/easy-rsa/pki
$ sudo ./easyrsa build-ca nopass
--snip--
CA creation complete and you may now import and sign cert requests.
Your new CA certificate file for publishing is at:
/usr/share/easy-rsa/pki/ca.crt
```

When prompted for the server's Common Name, you can enter any string of characters you'd like, but it's often easier to use the hostname of the server or press ENTER to accept the default Common Name. The output will contain the path to your PKI directory and *ca.crt* file; the *ca.key* file will be inside the *private* folder in the same location. The nopass option keeps you from being prompted for a password every time the CA is queried during this process.

That concludes the configuration of the CA server for now. The next set of configuration steps takes place on the OpenVPN server.

Create the OpenVPN Server Certificate and Key

Each client you plan to connect to the VPN needs its own public certificate and private key. These files allow the certificate server, the VPN server, and any other clients on the VPN to authenticate the client and enable communication between all devices within the VPN. The VPN server also needs its own certificate and key for the same reasons. This part of the project describes how to sign a certificate and generate a key for the OpenVPN server. You'll follow a similar process for connecting clients to the OpenVPN server.

On the OpenVPN server, navigate to the *easy-rsa* folder, and initialize the PKI for this server in the same way as before:

```
$ cd /usr/share/easy-rsa
$ sudo ./easyrsa init-pki
```

Just as every client connected to the VPN requires a certificate and key, the OpenVPN server itself needs a certificate signed by the CA. To this end, generate a certificate request from the OpenVPN server:

```
$ sudo ./easyrsa gen-req server nopass
Using SSL: openssl OpenSSL 1.1.1f 31 Mar 2020
Generating a RSA private key
................................+++++
.......................................+++++
writing new private key to '/usr/share/easy-rsa/pki/private/server.
key.2ljAQtgUYY'
-----
You are about to be asked to enter information that will be incorporated
```

```
into your certificate request.
What you are about to enter is what is called a Distinguished Name or a DN.
There are quite a few fields but you can leave some blank
For some fields there will be a default value,
If you enter '.', the field will be left blank.
-----
Common Name (eg: your user, host, or server name) [server]:

Keypair and certificate request completed. Your files are:
req: /usr/share/easy-rsa/pki/reqs/server.req
key: /usr/share/easy-rsa/pki/private/server.key
```

When prompted, press ENTER to accept the default Common Name for the VPN server, server, or give it a custom name. The output indicates that an RSA private key is generated and shows where the script stored the resulting server key and certificate request.

Copy the generated *server.key* file to the OpenVPN configuration directory on the VPN server:

```
$ sudo cp /usr/share/easy-rsa/pki/private/server.key /etc/openvpn/
```

Copy the *server.req* file to your certificate server using rsync, replacing the user and CA-ip placeholders with the relevant username and IP address for your certificate server:

```
$ sudo rsync -ruhP /usr/share/easy-rsa/pki/reqs/server.req user@CA_ip:/tmp/
```

Next, enter the following commands to log in to your certificate server and then import and sign the VPN certificate request generated earlier, enabling the VPN communications to be encrypted and secured:

```
$ ssh user@CA_ip
$ cd /usr/share/easy-rsa/
$ sudo ./easyrsa import-req /tmp/server.req ❶ server
$ sudo ./easyrsa sign-req ❷ server
```

The first easyrsa import-req command imports the request. The second argument is the Common Name you created for your VPN server earlier ❶. To sign the request, pass easyrsa sign-req the argument server ❷ to specify the request type and then the Common Name again. (Later, when signing client requests, you'll use the same command with client as the argument.)

When asked to confirm whether the details are correct, double-check to ensure the Common Name is set as expected and then type yes and press ENTER to complete the import and signing process. You'll need to copy the resulting *server.crt* certificate file belonging to the OpenVPN server (along with the CA certificate) back to the OpenVPN server from the CA server so that each can authenticate the other:

```
$ sudo rsync -ruhP /usr/share/easy-rsa/pki/issued/server.crt user@vpn_ip:/tmp/
$ sudo rsync -ruhP /usr/share/easy-rsa/pki/ca.crt user@vpn_ip:/tmp/
```

On the OpenVPN server, move the relevant files to the */etc/openvpn/* directory:

```
$ sudo mv /tmp/server.crt /etc/openvpn/
$ sudo mv /tmp/ca.crt /etc/openvpn/
```

Next, you'll need a Diffie-Hellman key to exchange keys between devices. A *Diffie-Hellman key exchange* is a way to communicate public and private key information between two parties over a public communication channel securely. Without this capability, it wouldn't be possible to create secure encrypted channels over a public network like the internet.

You'll also need an *HMAC signature* to make the process more secure. An HMAC signature, used in HMAC authentication and with a secret key, is a method of verifying the integrity of a message or payload. Using an HMAC signature in this process will maintain the key exchange's integrity and allow you to verify the keys' authenticity.

On your VPN server, navigate to your *easy-rsa* directory and generate a shared secret key using the easyrsa script created earlier:

```
$ cd /usr/share/easy-rsa/
$ sudo ./easyrsa ❶ gen-dh
$ sudo ❷ openvpn --genkey secret ta.key
$ sudo cp /usr/share/easy-rsa/ta.key /etc/openvpn/
$ sudo cp /usr/share/easy-rsa/pki/dh.pem /etc/openvpn/
```

The gen-dh argument ❶ creates the Diffie-Hellman key, which may take a long time and generate a lot of output. The openvpn --gen-key secret ❷ command quickly generates the HMAC signature, and you'll see no output if it's successful. These processes create the */usr/share/easy-rsa/ta.key* and */usr/share/easy-rsa/pki/dh.pem* files. Copy each of them to the OpenVPN configuration directory, */etc/openvpn/*, on your OpenVPN server:

```
$ sudo cp /usr/share/easy-rsa/ta.key /etc/openvpn/
$ sudo cp /usr/share/easy-rsa/pki/dh.pem /etc/openvpn/
```

At this point, you've created all the required certificates and keys for the servers.

Create a Client Certificate

Next, you'll need to create client certificates and keys to allow clients to connect to the VPN, which are the same as the server certificates but relate to each individual client device. The most efficient way to do this is to create the necessary files on the server, rather than on the client, which prevents you from having to transfer files between devices unnecessarily. On the OpenVPN server, create a safe location for the files:

```
$ sudo mkdir -p /etc/openvpn/client-configs/keys/
```

Navigate to the *easy-rsa* directory, generate a new certificate request for the client, copy the key to the directory you just created, and securely copy the request file to your CA server as shown here:

```
$ cd /usr/share/easy-rsa/
$ sudo ./easyrsa gen-req ❶ myclient nopass
$ sudo cp /usr/share/easy-rsa/pki/private/myclient.key \
   /etc/openvpn/client-configs/keys/
$ sudo rsync -ruhP /usr/share/easy-rsa/pki/reqs/myclient.req user@CA_ip:/tmp/
```

You'll be asked for a passphrase for the request; enter one and be sure to save it for later reference. You'll also be asked for a Common Name for your VPN client. This name will need to be different for each client that you provide access to the VPN, so consider using the client hostname (`myclient` in this example; change *`myclient`* ❶ to the client name of your choice).

On your certificate server, navigate to the *easy-rsa* directory:

```
$ cd /usr/share/easy-rsa/
```

Import the request using the client's Common Name (`myclient` in this example) and then sign it using the `client` directive, rather than the `server` directive you used earlier:

```
$ sudo ./easyrsa import-req /tmp/myclient.req myclient
$ sudo ./easyrsa sign-req client myclient
```

Confirm that the Common Name is correct and then type **yes** and press ENTER to complete the command.

Finally, securely copy the newly generated certificate back to your OpenVPN server:

```
$ sudo rsync -ruhP /usr/share/easy-rsa/pki/issued/myclient.crt user@vpn_ip:/tmp/
```

For the VPN to function correctly, the *ta.key* and *ca.crt* files you created earlier, as well as the *myclient.crt* file, need to be in the client configuration directory on the OpenVPN server. On your VPN server, copy those files to the */etc/openvpn/client-configs/keys/* directory:

```
$ sudo cp /usr/share/easy-rsa/ta.key /etc/openvpn/client-configs/keys/
$ sudo mv /tmp/myclient.crt /etc/openvpn/client-configs/keys/
$ sudo cp /etc/openvpn/ca.crt /etc/openvpn/client-configs/keys/
```

And with that, you've created the necessary files to connect a client to the OpenVPN server. You can repeat this process as many times as necessary. Just be sure to change the client name from `myclient` to something else each time you generate files for a new client.

Configure OpenVPN

Now that the certificate server is set up, you can configure the OpenVPN server. To do so, you'll copy a template OpenVPN configuration and modify it to suit your needs.

On your OpenVPN server, copy the configuration template to the OpenVPN configuration directory:

```
$ sudo cp /usr/share/doc/openvpn/examples/sample-config-files/server.conf /etc/openvpn/
```

Open the resulting *server.conf* file in a text editor (this example uses nano):

```
$ sudo nano /etc/openvpn/server.conf
```

As with any configuration file, open it and familiarize yourself with its contents. You might notice that these configuration files use both # and ; to mark lines as comments.

Once you feel comfortable with the options available, you might decide to alter the port or protocol your VPN uses. Find the lines that start with `port` or `proto`, and notice a semicolon is used to comment out the inactive lines:

```
--snip--
port 1194
--snip--
;proto tcp
proto udp
--snip--
```

OpenVPN can run over either UDP or TCP, but it uses UDP by default, and the default port is 1194. However, you can tell it to run over any port you like, but if you make changes, you'll need to make those same changes in any commands or files that follow. Also, make sure that the certificates and keys mentioned in this file match your configurations from earlier sections of the chapter:

```
--snip--
ca ca.crt
cert server.crt
key server.key
--snip--
```

When you reach the Diffie-Hellman section, ensure that the file matches the one you created earlier; the configuration file lists *dh2048.pem* by default, which will need to be changed to *dh.pem*:

```
--snip--
#dh dh2048.pem
dh dh.pem
--snip--
```

In addition, the redirect-gateway and dhcp-option DNS directives should not be commented out, so remove the semicolons at the beginning of those lines:

```
--snip--
push "redirect-gateway def1 bypass-dhcp"
--snip--
push "dhcp-option DNS 208.67.222.222"
push "dhcp-option DNS 208.67.220.220"
--snip--
```

These directives ensure that all traffic will traverse the VPN and not the unsecured internet. You can leave DNS with the default settings, or you can set it to any DNS servers you desire, such as Quad9 (*9.9.9.9*), Google (*8.8.8.8*), or your Pi-Hole DNS server if you have one configured as described in Chapter 7.

Next, check that the tls-auth directive is set to 0 and not commented out with a semicolon and that the cipher is set to AES-256-CBC. Then, immediately after the cipher directive, add an auth directive:

```
--snip--
tls-auth ta.key 0
--snip--
cipher AES-256-CBC
auth SHA256
--snip--
```

The tls-auth directive ensures that the HMAC signature you configured earlier will indeed be used to secure the VPN. Several settings are available for the cipher, and AES-256 is a reasonable choice as the encryption offered is good and well supported. The SHA256 indicates the algorithm used for the HMAC message digest, meaning the hash calculated will be an SHA256 hash, which is considered secure and less prone to hash collisions than some other hashing algorithms.

To make the VPN more secure, remove the semicolons from the user and group directives, which makes the VPN service run with fewer privileges and ideally mitigates the risk of privilege escalation attacks:

```
--snip--
user nobody
group nogroup
--snip--
```

After making these changes, save and close the configuration file.

The OpenVPN configuration is complete, but you'll need to make some changes to the server's network settings. First, you must configure IP forwarding or the VPN won't do anything with the traffic received:

```
$ sudo sysctl -w net.ipv4.ip_forward=1
```

Reload sysctl to make the change take effect, as follows.

```
$ sudo sysctl -p
net.ipv4.ip_forward = 1
```

The command may output the lines modified in the *sysctl.conf* file.

Configure the Firewall

The first step in this process is to find your VPN server's public network interface; your server may have multiple network interfaces, and selecting the wrong interface for the following commands would result in a VPN that is unable to route traffic to the internet correctly:

```
$ ip route | grep -i default
default via 202.182.98.1 dev ens3 proto dhcp src 202.182.98.40 metric 100
```

In this output, the network interface is called `ens3`, but yours might be different. The *default route* shown by `ip route` will be the public network interface of your host. You'll need this to configure your firewall correctly.

In most firewalls, the order in which you set your rules is the most important consideration. In UFW, rules are evaluated from rule files in the following order: first *before.rules*, then *user.rules*, and finally *after.rules*. The firewall must correctly identify and push through the VPN traffic, so rules are needed at the top of the firewall configuration. To do this in UFW, open the *before.rules* file in a text editor:

```
$ sudo nano /etc/ufw/before.rules
```

Then add these lines at the top of the file to allow OpenVPN client traffic via the public network interface you identified in the previous commands:

```
*nat
:POSTROUTING ACCEPT [0:0]
-A POSTROUTING -s 10.8.0.0/24-o ens3 -j MASQUERADE
COMMIT
```

The network *10.8.0.0/24* indicates the addresses that clients connecting to your VPN will be assigned. These addresses should be different from the addresses used in your network. If you use *192.168.1.x* addresses in your network, do not use *192.168.1.x* addresses for your VPN network addressing. As long as your network uses addresses other than *10.8.0.x,* the previous configuration is safe to use.

Save and close the file. UFW also needs to accept, rather than drop, forwarded packets. You can allow this by changing the UFW configuration file:

```
$ sudo ufw default allow FORWARD
```

Finally, the firewall needs to allow the port and protocol used for the VPN to send and receive traffic, as well as SSH for server administration. Enter the following command to allow the correct port and protocol based on the configurations you set in *etc/openvpn/server.conf*:

```
$ sudo ufw allow 1194/udp
```

Next, allow OpenSSH:

```
$ sudo ufw allow OpenSSH
```

Restart the firewall for the changes to take effect permanently:

```
$ sudo ufw disable
$ sudo ufw enable
```

Your SSH connection might be interrupted as the firewall restarts, and you may need to log in again.

Start the VPN

At this point, you're ready to start the VPN. Do so using `systemctl`, the utility used to control services in Ubuntu, passing it your server's Common Name:

```
$ sudo systemctl start openvpn@server
```

Check the VPN's status:

```
$ sudo systemctl status openvpn@server
```

If it's working properly, the output should say `active (running)`.

Press Q to return to the terminal and then make the VPN start whenever the server boots:

```
$ sudo systemctl enable openvpn@server
```

Your VPN should now be up and running and ready for client connections.

Configure a VPN Client

Clients must have *.ovpn* files configured to connect to the VPN server and send and receive traffic across the secure tunnel. Creating these configurations can be tedious if you have several clients to connect, so we'll use an easily repeatable procedure to do it for us. We'll generate configuration files on the OpenVPN server and then transfer those configuration files to the relevant clients.

On your OpenVPN server, create a safe location for the client configuration files (such as */etc/openvpn/client-configs/files/*), copy another template provided by OpenVPN, and open the resulting *base.conf* file in a text editor:

```
$ sudo mkdir -p /etc/openvpn/client-configs/files/
$ sudo cp /usr/share/doc/openvpn/examples/sample-config-files/client.conf \
    /etc/openvpn/client-configs/base.conf
$ nano /etc/openvpn/client-configs/base.conf
```

Familiarize yourself with the file's contents. If you made changes to the port or protocol in previous steps, make the same changes in this file.

```
--snip--
;proto tcp
proto udp
--snip--
remote vpn_ip 1194
;remote vpn_ip 1194
--snip--
```

Also, uncomment the `user` and `group` directives:

```
--snip--
user nobody
group nogroup
--snip--
```

Comment out the SSL/TLS parameters:

```
--snip--
#ca ca.crt
#cert client.crt
#key client.key
--snip--
```

Comment out the `tls-auth` directive:

```
--snip--
#tls-auth ta.key 1
--snip--
```

Set the `cipher` and `auth` directives to the values found in the other configuration files:

```
--snip--
cipher AES-256-CBC
auth SHA256
--snip--
```

Finally, add the following line to the end of the file:

```
--snip--
key-direction 1
```

The `key-direction` directive indicates to the client which device in the client-server pair will provide the key and therefore the encryption for the VPN tunnel. This can be set to either `0` or `1`, but this configuration should be set to `1`, as this should provide better overall security by forcing different keys to be used for client-server and server-client communication. Save and close the file.

You can easily create client configurations by writing and executing a script to pull all of these elements together. Create an *.sh* file in which to put your script, make it executable, and then open it with a text editor (nano in this example):

```
$ sudo touch /etc/openvpn/client-configs/client_config.sh
$ sudo chmod +x /etc/openvpn/client-configs/client_config.sh
$ sudo nano /etc/openvpn/client-configs/client_config.sh
```

Copy the script in Listing 5-1 into the file.

```
#!/bin/bash
KEY_DIR=/etc/openvpn/client-configs/keys
OUTPUT_DIR=/etc/openvpn/client-configs/files
BASE_CONFIG=/etc/openvpn/client-configs/base.conf

cat ${BASE_CONFIG} \
    <(echo -e '<ca>') ${KEY_DIR}/ca.crt \
    <(echo -e '</ca>\n<cert>') ${KEY_DIR}/${1}.crt \
    <(echo -e '</cert>\n<key>') ${KEY_DIR}/${1}.key \
    <(echo -e '</key>\n<tls-auth>') ${KEY_DIR}/ta.key \
    <(echo -e '</tls-auth>') > $ {OUTPUT_DIR}/${1}.ovpn
```

Listing 5-1: A script for generating client configuration (.ovpn) file

Save and close the file. The first line tells bash that what follows in this file is a script. The next three lines are variables, which you can modify if your key directory, output directory, or base config files and folders are different from the examples in this chapter.

Execute the script from within the *client-configs* directory as shown in Listing 5-2, with a client name as the only parameter. The client name should match one in the certificate and key files you created in earlier steps. To generate configuration files for further clients, be sure to generate their certificates and keys, and then use those files to create the relevant *.ovpn* file for that client with the script in Listing 5-1. Don't forget this entails creating a certificate request, transferring it to your certificate server for signing, and then transferring it back to your VPN server, in the *client-configs* directory.

Listing 5-2 shows a run of the script for the `myclient` client, and a command to list the resulting file.

```
$ cd /etc/openvpn/client-configs/
$ sudo ./client_config.sh myclient
$ ls -lah /etc/openvpn/client-configs/files/
total 20
drwxrwxr-x 2 test test 4096 Apr 28 23:22 ./
drwxrwxr-x 4 test test 4096 Apr 28 23:21 ../
-rw-rw-r-- 1 test test 11842 Apr 28 23:22 myclient.ovpn
```

Listing 5-2: Executing the script from Listing 5-1

Once the *.ovpn* file is created for this client, download the file to your local machine via rsync and then import it into the OpenVPN client for that device.

```
$ rsync -ruhP user@vpn_ip:/etc/openvpn/client-configs/files/myclient.ovpn ./
```

OpenVPN has client applications for most operating systems, including Windows, Linux, macOS, iOS, and Android. You can find these on the OpenVPN website: *https://openvpn.net/community-downloads/*.

With that done, you can now import the *.ovpn* configuration file, connect to your VPN, and use the internet in a much more private and secure manner. If you plan to connect to your VPN using a Linux client, you can install OpenVPN using the following command:

```
$ sudo apt install openvpn -y
```

Then, connect to your VPN using your configuration file and this command:

```
$ sudo openvpn myclient.ovpn
```

See "Test Your VPN" on page 89 for additional testing you can do to ensure your VPN is secure.

#20: Creating a VPN with Wireguard

Modern versions of Ubuntu (those from March 2020 onward) have Wireguard built into the kernel, so it's simple to install and get up and running. Wireguard isn't built into a lot of networking hardware at this stage, so you'll have to configure each of your endpoints to connect to it manually, rather than simply configuring your router and passing all network traffic through the VPN tunnel. In this project, you'll create a Wireguard server using the instructions to create a virtual machine in the cloud, and then you'll install and configure Wireguard. We'll create the relevant public and private key pairs for the server and any clients, configure the server firewall as required, configure and connect a client, and test the VPN to ensure that it's working correctly. Your internet traffic will then be safe and secure, as long as you're connected to your Wireguard VPN.

Installing Wireguard

Create a new Ubuntu server using the instructions provided in Project 3 in Chapter 1. Log in to the server via SSH as a standard, non-root user:

```
$ ssh user@your_server_IP
```

Then, use `apt` to install Wireguard, specifying -y to skip the confirmation prompt:

```
$ sudo apt install wireguard -y
```

Next, you'll create the necessary public and private keys required to connect to and encrypt your VPN.

Set Up the Key Pairs

Due to the sensitive nature of the files or folders you're about to create, it's wise to enforce more restrictive permissions than usual. You can run the following command to ensure that only the owner of a file can read and write to that file:

```
$ umask 077
```

This `umask` command won't last after you exit the terminal session, but only the owner is allowed to read and write to the folders and files you create during this session.

Now, using the `wg genkey` command, create the private Wireguard key:

```
$ wg genkey | sudo tee /etc/wireguard/private.key
```

The output shown in the terminal is your private key, which will be stored in the *private.key* file specified in the command. Do not share this key. Treat it like a password—it's how your VPN will be secured.

With the private key created, you'll need a corresponding public key to provide to your clients so they can authenticate to the server:

```
$ sudo cat /etc/wireguard/private.key | wg pubkey | sudo tee /etc/wireguard/public.key
```

This command first reads the contents of the *private.key* file using `cat`. Then, the `wg pubkey` command uses the private key to generate the public key. The public key is then output to the terminal and saved to the *public .key* file.

Now that you have your public/private key pair, you can configure your VPN server and clients.

Configure Wireguard

Wireguard requires a configuration file to function. This file is not created when Wireguard is installed, so you need to create one from scratch. Create and open the */etc/wireguard/wg0.conf* file using a text editor:

```
$ sudo nano /etc/wireguard/wg0.conf
```

Add the following contents to the file:

```
[Interface]
PrivateKey = your_private_key
Address = 10.8.0.1/24
ListenPort = 26535
SaveConfig = true
```

Replace *your_private_key* with the private key you created earlier. Your key will be the contents of your */etc/wireguard/private.key* file. The address will be the address of your server within the subnet you want your VPN clients to be assigned when they connect to your server; ensure that this subnet is different from your private network. For example, if you use *192.168.1.x* addresses in your network, avoid using *192.168.1.x* addresses for your VPN. The listening port should be any port between 1025 and 65535, chosen at random. This port is the one your server and clients will use to communicate. Once complete, save and exit the configuration file.

At this point, the server's network settings require some modification. Configure IP forwarding so the VPN will forward the traffic it receives using the following command and then restart `sysctl` so that the changes take effect:

```
$ sudo sysctl -w net.ipv4.ip_forward=1
$ sudo sysctl -p
```

Next, you need to configure the firewall to allow VPN traffic to ingress and egress the server.

Configure the Firewall

In this section we'll discuss the use of the *Uncomplicated Firewall (UFW)*, Ubuntu's built-in firewall that is designed to reduce the complexity of firewall configuration. To configure the firewall, first identify the correct network interface for the VPN. Specifying the wrong interface will result in a nonfunctional VPN. Enter the following command to locate your server's default network interface:

```
$ ip route | grep -i default
default via 172.16.90.1 dev ens33 proto dhcp metric 100
```

In this output, the network interface is called `ens33` (yours might be different). The *default route* shown by `ip route` will be your host's public network interface. You'll need this to configure your firewall correctly.

Next, add the following rules to the bottom of your Wireguard configuration file by opening */etc/wireguard/wg0.conf* with a text editor again and replacing `ens33` with your network interface name:

```
$ sudo nano /etc/wireguard/wg0.conf
--snip--
SaveConfig = true
PostUp = ufw route allow in on wg0 out on ens33
PostUp = iptables -t nat -I POSTROUTING -o ens33 -j MASQUERADE
PreDown = ufw route delete allow in on wg0 out on ens33
PreDown = iptables -t nat -D POSTROUTING -o ens33 -j MASQUERADE
```

Save and close the file. This allows Wireguard to modify the firewall configuration after Wireguard starts and before it stops to enable the VPN to function correctly.

Additionally, you need to allow traffic via the listening port you configured earlier in the chapter (port 26535 in the example):

```
$ sudo ufw allow 26535/udp
```

Next, allow OpenSSH:

```
$ sudo ufw allow ssh
```

Finally, with this rule updated, you need to disable and enable UFW to reload the rules (your SSH session might be interrupted, and you may need to log in again):

```
$ sudo ufw disable
$ sudo ufw enable
```

And with that, your firewall configuration is complete.

Identify the DNS Server

To secure your internet traffic, your VPN needs to have correctly configured DNS to prevent DNS leaks, which can compromise your security. To solve this problem, you'll force your Wireguard VPN to use the DNS that's used by the Wireguard server itself. Identify that DNS server(s) with the following command:

```
$ resolvectl dns ens33
```

The resulting output is the DNS address you will provide to the client in its configuration later in this project—take note of it.

Start the VPN

Ideally, the VPN should start and be ready to accept client connections whenever the server starts up. You can achieve this by creating and starting a Wireguard system service using `systemctl`:

```
$ sudo systemctl enable wg-quick@wg0.service
$ sudo systemctl start wg-quick@wg0.service
```

Once done, check the status to ensure Wireguard is running:

```
$ sudo systemctl status wg-quick@wg0.service
```

If it's working properly, the output should say `active`. If the service is not active or has a failed status, double-check your configuration file and firewall status to ensure there are no typos or other errors in your configuration.

Configure a VPN Client

There are official client applications available for Wireguard for Windows, macOS, Android, and iOS—the setup of which is reasonably similar across the board. The Linux client setup is a little more involved, but if you've been able to configure the Wireguard server successfully, configuring a Linux client will seem very familiar.

Windows, macOS, Android, or iOS Client Configuration

To configure a client on any of these operating systems, follow these steps:

1. Download and install the relevant client program from *https://www.wireguard.com/install/*.
2. In the client interface, click + or **Add Tunnel ▸ Add Empty Tunnel** to create a new VPN profile from scratch.
3. Note that the public and private keys for the client are displayed.
4. Supply a friendly name in the Name field.
5. Ignore any On Demand settings or check boxes.
6. Add the following details to the configuration, below the PrivateKey automatically generated for the client:

```
--snip--
Address = 10.8.0.2
DNS = 108.61.10.10

[Peer]
PublicKey = server_public_key
AllowedIPs = 0.0.0.0/0
Endpoint = server_public_ip:listening_port
```

   `Address` is the IP address you want your client to have within the VPN subnet and should be different for every VPN client. `DNS` should be the IP address of the DNS server you identified in "Identify the DNS Server" on page 85. `PublicKey` is the public key you created for your Wireguard server earlier in the process. `AllowedIPs` is a setting used for *split tunneling*; traffic to and from the networks or addresses listed with this directive will be sent through the VPN tunnel, and all other traffic will go straight out and circumvent the VPN. Setting this to `0.0.0.0/0` sends all traffic from your client through the VPN. `Endpoint` is the public IP address of your VPN server, followed by the listening port you specified earlier (26535 in the example).

7. Save the configuration.
8. On the Wireguard server, stop the Wireguard service, noting that there will be downtime for any users currently connected, using the following:

```
$ sudo systemctl stop wg-quick@wg0.service
```

9. Open the */etc/wireguard/wg0.conf* configuration file with a text editor:

```
$ sudo nano /etc/wireguard/wg0.conf
```

10. Add the client details to the bottom of the configuration file, keeping in mind that each peer you add will need its own [Peer] section added to this file:

```
--snip--
[Peer]
PublicKey = client_public_key
AllowedIPs = 10.8.0.2
```

This instance of PublicKey is the public key created for your Wireguard client by the client application. Within the [Peer] section of the file, AllowedIPs refers to the IP addresses allowed to send traffic through the VPN tunnel. Set this to the specific host IP you want your client to have on the VPN network, which must match the IP you configured for this peer in the client configuration.

11. Save and close the file.
12. Start the Wireguard service and double-check that the status says active:

```
$ sudo systemctl start wg-quick@wg0.service
$ sudo systemctl status wg-quick@wg0.service
```

Back on your client, activate the VPN connection. Once successfully connected, ping your Wireguard server's VPN address (such as 10.8.0.1):

```
$ ping 10.8.0.1
PING 10.8.0.1 (10.8.0.1): 56 data bytes
64 bytes from 10.8.0.1: icmp_seq=0 ttl=57 time=43.969 ms
64 bytes from 10.8.0.1: icmp_seq=0 ttl=57 time=43.969 ms
64 bytes from 10.8.0.1: icmp_seq=0 ttl=57 time=43.969 ms
64 bytes from 10.8.0.1: icmp_seq=0 ttl=57 time=43.969 ms
--- 10.8.0.1 ping statistics ---
4 packets transmitted, 4 packets received, 0.0% packet loss
round-trip min/avg/max/stddev = 43.969/43.969/43.969/0 ms
```

A successful result indicates your VPN connection is working between your client and server. Repeat this process for any additional clients.

Linux Client

To configure a Linux client, follow these steps:

1. Install Wireguard and resolvconf (used for DNS configuration):

```
$ sudo apt install wireguard resolvconf -y
```

2. Generate the client public/private key pair for the client:

```
$ wg genkey | sudo tee /etc/wireguard/private.key
$ sudo cat /etc/wireguard/private.key | wg pubkey | sudo tee \
    /etc/wireguard/public.key
```

3. Create the Wireguard client configuration file:

```
$ sudo nano /etc/wireguard/wg0.conf
[Interface]
PrivateKey = client_private_key
Address = 10.8.0.3
DNS = 108.61.10.10

[Peer]
PublicKey = server_public_key
AllowedIPs = 0.0.0.0/0
Endpoint = server_public_ip:listening_port
```

4. Save and close the file.
5. On the Wireguard server, stop the Wireguard service:

```
$ sudo systemctl stop wg-quick@wg0.service
```

6. Open the */etc/wireguard/wg0.conf* configuration file with a text editor:

```
$ sudo nano /etc/wireguard/wg0.conf
```

7. Add the client details to the bottom of the configuration file:

```
--snip--
[Peer]
PublicKey = client_public_key
AllowedIPs = 10.8.0.3
```

   This instance of `PublicKey` is the public key created for your Wireguard client by the client application. Within the `[Peer]` section of the file, `AllowedIPs` refers to the IP addresses allowed to send traffic through the VPN tunnel. Set this to the specific host IP you want your client to have on the VPN network.

8. Save and close the file.
9. Start the Wireguard service and double-check that the status says active:

```
$ sudo systemctl start wg-quick@wg0.service
$ sudo systemctl status wg-quick@wg0.service
```

   Back on your client, activate the VPN connection using the following command:

```
$ wg-quick up wg0
```

Once successfully connected, ping your Wireguard server's VPN address (such as 10.8.0.1). A successful result indicates your VPN connection is working between your client and server. To disconnect a Linux client from your VPN server, use the following command:

```
$ wg-quick down wg0
```

Repeat this process for any additional clients you want to add.

Test Your VPN

Regardless of which VPN you chose, find your public IP address from a website such as *https://www.whatismyip.com/* while not connected to the VPN. Once done, connect to your VPN and refresh the page. Your public IP address should now be the IP address of your VPN server. Another way to test your VPN is to use a service such as DNS leak at *https://dnsleaktest.com/*. Performing a standard test should show you clearly whether there are any issues with your VPN configuration. If your actual public IP is masked and the DNS leak test shows only the DNS servers you've configured the VPN to use, then you've been successful in setting up your own private VPN server.

Summary

Connecting multiple clients to either your OpenVPN or Wireguard servers will allow traffic to pass between them as if they were on the same network. This means you can easily manage multiple devices remotely simply by having them all connected to your VPN at the same time. This chapter covered setting up your own private VPN, which provides you with complete control, using either OpenVPN or the much lighter and faster Wireguard. Your private internet traffic will now be truly private and secure while you are connected to your VPN.

6

IMPROVING BROWSING AND PRIVACY WITH THE SQUID PROXY

A proxy server acts as an intermediary between you and the internet. When you request a web page, the proxy receives the request and then forwards it on to the web server (if necessary). A proxy allows you to protect your privacy by obfuscating the metadata that is usually available to the services we interact with daily on the internet. Proxies also allow the administrator to block access to certain content, like social media or online gambling.

This chapter will show you how to install, configure, and use the *Squid proxy*, a solution that runs on most operating systems. With Squid, you'll be able to speed up access to websites, enhance your security, and allow or prevent access to specific domains or websites. Chapter 7 covers another proxy solution, Pi-Hole, which offers the same benefits as Squid, but additionally blocks ads and prevents other tracking and privacy issues as well. Choosing the best proxy for your needs will depend on which you find easier to use and which provides you the best user experience.

Why Use a Proxy?

Every time you visit a website, your computer makes a request to a web server that responds by sending you the information necessary to view the website. The communication between your browser and the server may expose your personal information (the browser you're using, your public IP address, and so on) through *metadata*. The metadata allows the web server to make guesses about you and your device, such as your location, what time of day it is where you are, and your browsing habits. For lots of reasons, you might want to keep this information private. Additionally, loading web pages and their content consumes bandwidth, so as more people use an internet connection, the connection can begin to slow down, negatively affecting everyone using it.

One great thing about proxies is that they *cache* any traffic that passes through them. This means that every time a web page is retrieved, the proxy will keep a local copy of that page. The next time someone tries to browse to that site, the proxy first checks its cache for a copy, and if it holds a copy, it presents that copy to the user rather than sending a request to the web server for a fresh copy of the web page. By default, Squid will keep a cached copy of a website for a set period before it no longer considers the cache "fresh" and will then retrieve the latest version of the page, whether or not the content has changed. This reduces the load on the network, the time it takes to load frequently visited sites, and the overall amount of bandwidth used, leading to a better experience for everyone involved.

Proxies also reduce the amount of *personally identifiable information (PII)* leaked to web servers. PII is any data or information that can be used to identify any specific individual (such as you). For example, a proxy can identify itself to a web server as any web browser. You might be using Google Chrome, but the proxy could present Firefox to the server instead. The proxy can also have a different public IP address to hide the one you're using if it's located somewhere other than where you are (like in the cloud), obscuring your physical location and internet service provider.

Even though it isn't directly relevant to small network administrators, you might be interested to know that commercial organizations often rely on proxies (including Squid) for the benefits we've already discussed, as well as for content delivery, such as streaming audio and video. Content providers, such as Netflix and YouTube, strategically place proxy servers globally to keep local copies of content. This practice allows users of those services to access the content from a source closer to home, rather than all users accessing the content from a single location, which would be far less efficient and would result in poor performance in a lot of cases.

#21: Setting Up Squid

The Squid web proxy provides all the benefits you just learned about: it reduces bandwidth, making surfing the web faster for users. It's also capable of anonymizing your personal information if configured correctly; information about your identity, such as where your web requests are coming from or the web browser you're using, can be stripped or changed before traffic is sent to the internet. Many enterprise-grade devices use Squid. While you could use many other proxy solutions, such as NGINX, Apache Traffic Server, or Forcepoint, Squid is free and open source, so it provides greater access to underlying configurations and data than a commercial solution might.

A wealth of information is available online about using Squid to protect and enhance your network. You can find more information on Squid proxy configuration in the Squid wiki at *https://wiki.squid-cache.org/SquidFaq/*.

This project will cover the initial installation and configuration of Squid, configuring clients in your network to use the proxy, testing the proxy once configured, and performing some additional steps to allow or deny access to certain internet resources using the proxy.

Configuring Squid

Create a base Ubuntu server following the steps in Chapter 1. If you want to hide your location or prefer not to give away your internet service provider (in addition to preventing your metadata being recorded), create the proxy server in the cloud in a country different from your own. Otherwise, locate the proxy server inside your network. Don't forget to add your new server to your network map and asset list you created in previous chapters. Once you've done so, log in to the server via SSH as a standard, non-root user. To install the proxy, use the following command:

```
$ sudo apt install squid
```

The installation should complete in less than a minute. By default, you'll find the configuration file located at */etc/squid/squid.conf*, the logfiles at */var/log/squid/*, and the cache data (that is, cached website information) at */var/spool/squid/*.

Open the *squid.conf* configuration file with a text editor to familiarize yourself with the settings:

```
$ sudo nano /etc/squid/squid.conf
```

Squid has many possible configurations, so it's easy to become overwhelmed. Notice, though, that many settings aren't active as they're commented out by default. Let's start by focusing on the active settings. You can explore other changes when your proxy server is functioning as you want it to.

Search by pressing CTRL-W; then type your search term and press ENTER to find the section marked `Recommended minimum configuration:`

```
--snip--
# Recommended minimum configuration:
#

# Example rule allowing access from your local networks.
# Adapt to list your (internal) IP networks from where browsing
# should be allowed
acl localnet src 0.0.0.1-0.255.255.255  # RFC 1122 "this" network (LAN)
acl localnet src 10.0.0.0/8             # RFC 1918 local private network (LAN)
--snip--
```

This section details the *access controls lists (ACLs)* that tell Squid which endpoints should have permission to access internet resources via the proxy server. An ACL is a list of ports, addresses, or resources that you've specifically allowed or banned from communication within the network.

An ACL consists of several elements. First is a unique name, such as `localnet`, that identifies a specific ACL. Each named ACL then contains an ACL type (such as `src`) followed by a value or list of values, such as IP addresses or port numbers. These values can be entered over multiple lines, and Squid will combine them into a single list.

Keywords like `src` indicate to Squid the direction in which the traffic is flowing; `src 10.0.0.0/8`, for example, indicates any traffic coming from an address in the *10.0.0.0/8* IP address range to any IP address in any range.

Comment out any lines that don't apply to your network. For example, if your internal IP addresses follow the *10.x.x.x* format, leave the relevant directive as is and comment out all other lines beginning with `acl localnet src` by adding a `#` at the start of each line:

```
--snip--
#acl localnet src 0.0.0.1-0.255.255.255  # RFC 1122 "this" network (LAN)
acl localnet src 10.0.0.0/8              # RFC 1918 local private network (LAN)
#acl localnet src 100.64.0.0/10          # RFC 6598 shared address space (CGN)
#acl localnet src 169.254.0.0/16         # RFC 3927 link-local machines
#acl localnet src 172.16.0.0/12          # RFC 1918 local private network (LAN)
#acl localnet src 192.168.0.0/16         # RFC 1918 local private network (LAN)
#acl localnet src fc00::/7               # RFC 4193 local private network range
#acl localnet src fe80::/10              # RFC 4291 link-local machines
--snip--
```

The second portion of the recommended minimum configuration section tells Squid which ports can send and receive traffic:

```
--snip--
acl SSL_ports port 443
acl Safe_ports port 80          # http
acl Safe_ports port 21          # ftp
acl Safe_ports port 443         # https
#acl Safe_ports port 70         # gopher
```

```
#acl Safe_ports port 210         # wais
acl Safe_ports port 1025-65535  # unregistered ports
#acl Safe_ports port 280         # http-mgmt
--snip--
```

Here, SSL_ports and Safe_ports are ACL names, and the port type tells Squid to interpret the number that follows as a port number used for communication by a specific service (see Chapter 1). The acl SSL_ports port 443 line sets the port your proxy should use for secured, filtered tunnels, such as those used for HTTPS traffic. Directives containing the label Safe_ports determine the ports on which Squid should allow connections. If you don't need a certain protocol or port, comment it out to reduce your attack surface. To be prudent, you might keep only ports 80 and 443 and comment out the acl Safe_ports port 1025-65535 line, thereby blocking ports from 1025 through 65535. However, doing so may cause some applications or services to malfunction if they require other ports. You can use Google and the website or manual for a given application to determine what other ports it might need to function correctly.

A little further in the configuration file, you'll find directives that enable these ACLs:

```
--snip--
# Recommended minimum Access Permission configuration:
#
# Deny requests to certain unsafe ports
http_access deny !Safe_ports

# Deny CONNECT to other than secure SSL ports
http_access deny CONNECT !SSL_ports
--snip--
```

The http_access deny !Safe_ports directive tells Squid to prohibit communication between all ports except those listed in the Safe_ports list. Likewise, the http_access deny CONNECT !SSL_ports line tells Squid to prohibit filtered tunnels on any port other than the one specified in SSL_ports.

The next section of the configuration file relates to your local network as opposed to the internet:

```
--snip--
# Example rule allowing access from your local networks.
# Adapt localnet in the ACL section to list your (internal) IP networks
# from where browsing should be allowed
#http_access allow localnet
http_access allow localhost

# And finally deny all other access to this proxy
http_access deny all
--snip--
```

Remove the # from the http_access allow localnet directive to enable the localnet settings you specified earlier, which allow endpoints on your local network to access the internet through your proxy. Finally, http_access deny all ensures the proxy denies all other traffic to keep it from affecting your internal network. By denying all traffic that isn't specifically allowed, you'll protect your network from unwanted traffic, which can include malware.

If you want to change the port on which Squid listens for requests, modify the following line in your configuration file:

```
--snip--
# Squid normally listens to port 3128
http_port 3128
--snip--
```

Your devices will use this port to connect to the proxy server so they can send requests, receive traffic, and generally browse the internet.

Once you've finished your edits, save and close the configuration file. Reload the updated Squid configuration using the following command so the changes take effect (be aware, though, that reloading the configuration can interrupt any open connections):

```
$ sudo systemctl reload squid
```

You can now make sure that Squid was able to start successfully and is running with the following command:

```
$ sudo systemctl status squid
  squid.service - Squid Web Proxy Server
     Loaded: loaded (/lib/systemd/system/squid.service; enabled; vendor preset: enabled)
     Active: active (running); 2min 5s ago
--snip--
```

A green dot before `squid.service` and a status of `active (running)` indicates Squid is running as expected. If Squid didn't start properly due to an error, you'll see a failed message with a red dot before `squid.service`:

```
$ sudo systemctl status squid
  squid.service - Squid Web Proxy Server
     Loaded: loaded (/lib/systemd/system/squid.service; enabled; vendor preset: enabled)
     Active: failed (Result: exit-code); 2min 5s ago
--snip--
```

Go back and check your configuration again or validate your configuration file using this command:

```
$ squid -k parse
2024/05/06 00:44:06| Processing: acl denylist dstdomain .twitter.com
2024/05/06 00:44:06| Processing: http_deny denylist
2024/05/06 00:44:06| /etc/squid/squid.conf:1406 unrecognized: 'http_deny'
2024/05/06 00:44:06| Processing: anonymize_headers deny From Referer Server
2024/05/06 00:44:06| /etc/squid/squid.conf:1408 unrecognized: 'anonymize_headers'
2024/05/06 00:44:06| Processing: anonymize_headers deny User-Agent WWW-Authenticate
2024/05/06 00:44:06| /etc/squid/squid.conf:1409 unrecognized: 'anonymize_headers'
2024/05/06 00:44:06| Processing: http_access allow localnet
--snip--
```

This output shows what you'd see if you used the unrecognized directives `http_deny` and `anonymize_headers`. When you've resolved any errors with the configuration, start Squid with the `start` command:

```
$ sudo systemctl start squid
```

You've now finished the basic Squid proxy configuration.

Configuring Devices to Use Squid

Next, you'll need to configure the proxy settings on each device that will use the proxy. We'll explain how to configure Windows, macOS, and Linux devices.

Windows

1. On your Windows host, open the **Windows Settings** dialog.
2. In the Find a Setting box, search for *Proxy Settings*.
3. Turn on the **Use a Proxy Server** toggle in the Proxy window.
4. Enter your proxy server's IP address and port—for example, *192.168.1.50:3128*.
5. Be sure to tick the **Don't Use the Proxy Server for Local (Intranet) Addresses** checkbox.

macOS

1. Open **System Preferences**.
2. Choose **Network** and select your wireless or Ethernet adapter.
3. Click **Advanced ▸ Proxies**.
4. Check the box for **Web Proxy (HTTP)**. Enter your proxy server's IP address and port number—for example, *192.168.1.50:3128*. Do this for each of the protocols listed, which you configured earlier in your */etc/squid/squid.conf* file.
5. Enter your local network into the Bypass Proxy Settings for these Hosts & Domains box.
6. Click **OK** and then **Apply**.

Linux

1. On your Linux endpoint, open the **Settings** dialog.
2. Go to the **Network ▸ Network Proxy** settings.
3. Set the proxy to **Manual** and enter the HTTP Proxy IP address and port number—for example, *192.168.1.50:3128*.
4. Make sure to enter your local network in the Ignore Hosts box, and then close any open settings windows.

Testing Squid

With both the Squid server and at least one of your devices configured, make sure the device is actually using the proxy and that the proxy functions as expected. On the Squid server, use the following command to view the Squid proxy logfile as it's populated:

```
$ sudo tail -f /var/log/squid/access.log
--snip--
1619747519.519      54 172.16.90.1 TCP_TUNNEL/200 39 CONNECT play.google.
    com:443 - HIER_DIRECT/172.217.25.174 -
1619747519.755      54 172.16.90.1 TCP_TUNNEL/200 39 CONNECT mail.google.
    com:443 - HIER_DIRECT/216.58.200.101 -
1619747519.776      55 172.16.90.1 TCP_TUNNEL/200 39 CONNECT mail.google.
    com:443 - HIER_DIRECT/216.58.200.101 -
1619747520.190     161 172.16.90.1 TCP_MISS/200 985 GET
--snip--
```

Your output will differ depending on the applications you're using in your network.

If you don't see any output (and your host is unable to browse the internet), update your iptables or other firewall rules using the steps in Chapter 3 to allow traffic to and from the Squid proxy on port 3128 (or whichever port you configured Squid to listen on).

If you browse to Facebook from a host configured to use your proxy server while the tail command is running, you should see this request appear in the log as multiple requests to Facebook services:

```
--snip--
1584414232.470     3 192.168.1.51 NONE/503 0 CONNECT pixel.facebook.com:443 - HIER_NONE/- -
1584414237.647     0 192.168.1.51 NONE/503 0 CONNECT pixel.facebook.com:443 - HIER_NONE/- -
1584414242.652     0 192.168.1.51 NONE/503 0 CONNECT pixel.facebook.com:443 - HIER_NONE/- -
1584414247.864 69023 192.168.1.51 TCP_TUNNEL/200 6426 CONNECT static.xx.fbcdn.net:443 - HIER_
    DIRECT/157.240.8.23 -
1584414248.566     0 192.168.1.51 NONE/503 0 CONNECT pixel.facebook.com:443 - HIER_NONE/- -
1584414254.535     0 192.168.1.51 NONE/503 0 CONNECT pixel.facebook.com:443 - HIER_NONE/- -
--snip--
```

If not, try restarting the proxy server, your host, or both.

Blocking and Allowing Domains

Now that your proxy works, you'll probably want to block (denylist) or allow (allowlist) some domains. For example, if you have children, you may want to prevent them from visiting distracting or inappropriate websites. To do this, open the *squid.conf* file in a text editor:

```
$ sudo nano /etc/squid/squid.conf
```

Now, find the comment that reads `INSERT YOUR OWN RULE(S) HERE`. In that section, you can define rules (that is, ACLs) of your own. As mentioned, an ACL is made up of an ACL name, an ACL type such as `allow` or `deny`, and a list of elements, such as IP addresses or domains. Your configuration will consist of one or more of these rules, identifying what is and is not allowed through the proxy. (Previously, you enabled rules like `http_access allow localnet` and `http_access deny !Safe_ports` to use the ACLs from the recommended minimum configuration section.)

For example, to denylist Facebook, enter the following lines after the `include` directive:

```
--snip--
include /etc/squid/conf.d/*

acl denylist dstdomain .facebook.com
http_access deny CONNECT denylist
--snip--
```

The `acl` directive at the beginning of the line tells Squid to treat what follows as a list of items to either allow or deny. Next, `denylist` is the unique name of the list; choose any name you'd like, so long as it consists of alphanumeric characters. The `dstdomain` directive indicates that what follows is a list of destination domains. The period at the start of a domain indicates to Squid that it should denylist the entire domain, including subdomains. For example, *www.facebook.com* is a top-level domain name that might have a subdomain of *campus.facebook.com* or *hertz.facebook.com.* If you omit the leading period, Squid will block only the parent domain (*facebook.com*). Finally, the `http_access` directive with `deny` and `CONNECT` parameters tells the proxy to forbid connections to the domains or URLs specified in the ACL.

Save the configuration file and reload Squid to make the change take effect:

```
$ sudo systemctl reload squid
```

Now, try browsing to *www.facebook.com* from a host configured to use the proxy server. You should see an error page as in Figure 6-1.

Figure 6-1: Web browser error caused by Squid

To allow access to Facebook again, either delete or comment out the lines you added, save the configuration file, and reload Squid.

You can repeat the process for additional domains by adding them to the same denylist ACL:

```
acl denylist dstdomain .facebook.com .twitter.com .linkedin.com
```

Alternatively, you could create separate ACLs for each website or for groups or categories of websites as you desire.

Allowlisting works in pretty much the same way; any domains that are added to the allowlist will be allowed, but only for users who are authenticated to the proxy:

```
--snip--
include /etc/squid/conf.d/*

acl allowlist dstdomain .facebook.com .twitter.com .linkedin.com
http_access allow CONNECT allowlist
--snip--
```

If you add new ACL rules, be aware of where they are located in relation to each other in the configuration file. Squid will interpret the ACL rules in the order they appear, much like a firewall. If there's a `deny all` rule at the beginning of the list of ACL rules, Squid will interpret this rule first and then ignore any further rules in the file. That means you should put any custom rules before the following lines:

```
--snip--
# And finally deny all other access to this proxy
http_access deny all
--snip--
```

Protecting Personal Information with Squid

Squid is highly configurable and allows you as the administrator to set how much information about your users and their devices you want exposed to the internet. By default, there is no anonymization of the traffic that passes from a client device through the proxy to the internet.

To prevent anyone outside your network knowing where your traffic is coming from (that is, the server information or from which website or resource you may have been referred, like Amazon or a blog), use the `request_header_access` directive to deny this information:

```
--snip--
include /etc/squid/conf.d/*

request_header_access From deny all
request_header_access Referer deny all
request_header_access Server deny all
--snip--
```

To further anonymize your traffic, it may be wise to also deny the `User-Agent`, `WWW-Authenticate`, and `Link` header values, which may leak additional information about your browser or browsing activity:

```
--snip--
include /etc/squid/conf.d/*

request_header_access From deny all
request_header_access Referer deny all
request_header_access Server deny all
request_header_access User-Agent deny all
request_header_access WWW-Authenticate deny all
request_header_access Link deny all
--snip--
```

Anonymizing your traffic with these options will limit the amount of PII you're sending over the internet, making you more difficult to track and protecting, to some extent, your browsing history and habits.

NOTE *Some websites and services use user agents to determine how to display content to users, so be mindful that by removing the header information, you may experience content differently.*

Disabling Caching for Specific Sites

There may be some websites that you don't want Squid to cache, as you always want to retrieve the latest version from the web server rather than the cached version from your proxy. This is achieved by denying caching of that site or sites:

```
--snip--
include /etc/squid/conf.d/*

acl deny_cache dstdomain .facebook.com
no_cache deny deny_cache
--snip--
```

Remember to add an ACL entry for each website you want to prevent Squid from creating and keeping a cached copy.

Squid Proxy Reports

You may have noticed that the Squid logs can be difficult to read and take some getting used to. Third-party solutions are available that make activity reporting and reviewing logs easier. One of the simpler solutions is *Squid Analysis Report Generator (SARG)*. SARG is a web-based report generator and viewer that allows you to view your Squid logs in a browser window, rather than from the terminal.

On your Squid server, install SARG:

```
$ sudo apt install sarg
```

The SARG report files will be accessed via a web browser, so you also need to install a web server. Install Apache:

```
$ sudo apt install apache2
```

Next, open the SARG configuration file that should be located at */etc/sarg/sarg.conf*:

```
$ sudo nano /etc/sarg/sarg.conf
```

Find the line that starts with `access_log`, which specifies the Squid access log location:

```
--snip--
access_log /var/log/squid/access.log
--snip--
```

Then, close the file and use the `find` command to make sure it matches the actual location of the logfile:

```
$ sudo find / -name access.log
/var/log/squid/access.log
```

Open the file in a text editor and find the output directory tag (the line that starts with `output_dir`), comment out the line containing `/var/lib/sarg`, and replace it with a line that sets the directory to the Apache web location */var/www/html/squid-reports/*:

```
--snip--
#output_dir /var/lib/sarg
output_dir /var/www/html/squid-reports/
--snip--
```

Save and close the file. Feel free to peruse the other settings if you would like.

To generate a SARG report, run the following command on your Squid server:

```
$ sudo sarg -x
```

In your web browser, navigate to the reports location on your proxy server: *http://<proxy_ip_address>/squid-reports*. You should see a basic website, as shown in Figure 6-2.

Figure 6-2: SARG reports summary

Click the relevant report on the page displayed, and you should see information about each user connection through the proxy, how much data was transferred for each connection, how long the connection lasted, and a timestamp indicating when the connection was established, as shown in Figure 6-3.

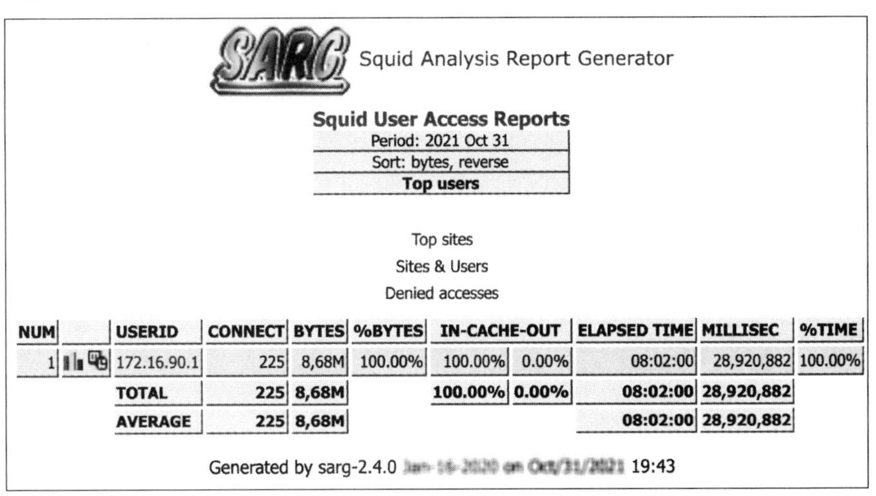

Figure 6-3: SARG report output

The report shows the users, or hosts, that have used the proxy; the level of traffic they have sent and received (represented as bytes); and various other useful things about the use of the proxy. There are also links included for subreports, such as the top sites accessed via the proxy; the sites and users report, which lists the sites accessed and a list of the users or hosts that accessed each; and any cache or website access that was denied by the proxy based on the rules and configuration you provided.

Try using your new proxy server for a few weeks to see if it helps your bandwidth usage and browsing speed. Once you're comfortable, you could investigate and begin experimenting with the proxy's more advanced features, such as preventing users from downloading large files (this might be advisable if your internet service provider has data caps and charges for bandwidth).

Summary

Using a proxy server such as Squid offers you a great deal of control over what's allowed in and out of your network. You'll be able to control the PII exposed from your endpoints, such as the web browser you're using, to improve your network's online privacy. A proxy server also provides a better overall browsing experience.

7

BLOCKING INTERNET ADVERTISEMENTS

Companies monetize the internet through advertising, which has caused the number of online ads to proliferate (or more accurately, explode). These ads have become more insidious over time, as websites track your activity to display the promotions most likely to lead to purchases. Even worse, advertising has caused slower internet connections through websites becoming so bloated with autoplaying advertisements.

You can block ads from your network in several ways. This chapter will first discuss various browser ad-blocking solutions. Then, we'll build an ad-blocking DNS proxy server using Pi-Hole to provide users with a much better browsing experience while also improving data and privacy protection.

Browser-Level Ad Blocking

Most modern browsers have some form of ad-blocking technology built-in to the application itself. By default, some browsers prevent various trackers and scripts from operating as designed. These include social media trackers, cookies, fingerprinters, and cryptominers. Blocking *social media trackers* disallows sites such as Facebook, Twitter, and LinkedIn from tracking you as you browse websites that implement social media buttons or instant sharing links. *Cookies* are files used by sites to track information and user preferences between visits; this can leak your private information from one site to another. *Fingerprinters* are similar in that they identify a specific user by a number of metrics collected from their browsing habits, which allows advertisers to track your activity during a browsing session. Finally, *cryptominers* are applications (some might say malware) that use your computer hardware to mine cryptocurrency, such as Bitcoin. This is a highly resource-intensive process that can cause system instability. All of these can negatively impact your browsing experience and should be blocked.

Besides the built-in functionality provided by some web browsers, some of the most popular browser ad blockers are browser *extensions*, also known as *add-ons*—software that you can add to your browser to improve its functionality or add capabilities. For example, *Adblock Plus*—installable in most browsers—works by intercepting advertisements before they're displayed to the user, though the ads are still downloaded to your computer.

Many websites can identify when browser extensions are in use and will either modify their content or completely block users from viewing web pages until the extension has been disabled or the site is allowlisted to play ads. Browser extensions are discussed further in Chapter 11. The following projects cover how to set up browser ad blocking for Google Chrome, Mozilla Firefox, and Brave browsers.

#22: Blocking Ads in Google Chrome

Chrome's ad blocker (*https://www.google.com/chrome/*) is designed to hide ads on websites that have too many ads or whose ads detract from the user experience, such as by flashing or making noise. Chrome also blocks ads on sites that put content behind a *paywall*, which obscures the website entirely until the user either allows the ads to display or pays a fee to view the content. This behavior applies to the Android version of Chrome in addition to the desktop version. It's possible to activate or deactivate the built-in ad blocker, as well as to allowlist specific sites:

1. At the top right of the Chrome browser, click the **More** icon (three horizontal lines).
2. Click **Settings ▸ Advanced ▸ Site Settings ▸ Ads**.
3. If the text "Blocked on sites that tend to show intrusive ads (recommended)" is displayed, Chrome is currently blocking ads for you.

4. If you'd like to turn ad blocking off, hit the toggle to switch the setting to **Allowed**.

Another way to protect your privacy online is to use a private browsing window. Chrome's *incognito mode* either won't save your personal information or immediately deletes it (including tracking information such as cookies) when you close the browser. Your browsing history and internet searches won't be saved. To open an incognito window, follow these steps:

5. At the top right of the Chrome browser, click the **More** icon (three horizontal lines).
6. Click **New Private Window**.

A new browser window will open that has a different appearance when compared to a normal Chrome window—text such as "You've gone Incognito" is typically displayed. This is how you know you're browsing privately.

#23: Blocking Ads in Mozilla Firefox

Firefox's *Private* browsing (*https://www.mozilla.org/*) windows block not only ads but also tracking content, including videos and other media displayed on a web page. To open a new Private window, follow these steps:

1. At the top right of the Firefox browser, click the **More** icon (three horizontal lines).
2. Click **New Private Window**.

You can change Firefox's default behavior to disable tracking content in all Firefox windows, rather than just Private windows. To modify these settings, follow these steps:

1. Click **More** in the top right of the Firefox window.
2. Click **Preferences ▸ Privacy & Security**.
3. Set your Enhanced Tracking Protection settings to Standard (the default), Strict (provides greater privacy but may break some websites), or Custom.
4. Configure your Cookie settings to delete cookies on browser exit by ticking the **Delete Cookies and Site Data When Firefox is Closed** checkbox.
5. Make Firefox forget your browsing history by setting the History dropdown menu to **Never Remember History**.
6. Set permissions for things like your webcam and microphone so that Firefox isn't able to watch or listen without authorization.

You can find more information on disabling trackers and other security and privacy settings in the Mozilla knowledge base at *https://support.mozilla.org/en-US/kb/enhanced-tracking-protection-firefox-desktop/.*

#24: Controlling Brave's Privacy Settings

Brave (*https://brave.com/*) is a relatively new web browser based on Google's Chromium (so it shares a lot of the same features as Chrome); all the extensions that are compatible with Chrome are also compatible with Brave. The great thing about Brave, when compared to other browsers, is that its goal is to provide a private, tracker- and ad-free experience for users. By having an aggressive approach to blocking ads in the browser, Brave claims not only to save you time and bandwidth while using the internet but also to reduce the amount of battery your browser uses.

Brave provides much more granular control over your security and privacy settings, and it makes these settings much easier to get to than other browsers:

1. At the top right of the Brave browser, click the **More** icon (three horizontal lines).
2. Click **Settings ▸ Shields**.
3. Set Trackers & Ads Blocking to Standard or Aggressive.
4. Turn on **Upgrade Connections to HTTPS**.
5. Set Cookie Blocking to Only Cross-site or All (your browser won't remember your session information once closed).
6. Set Fingerprinting blocking to Standard or Strict (might break some websites).

Experiment with these settings, as well as the social media blocking settings, until you find a combination that works for you.

#25: Blocking Ads with Pi-Hole

Blocking ads with a browser extension or built-in tools is a great start to enhancing your internet browsing experience. However, those options apply to only one device at a time, and managing settings for multiple devices can quickly become onerous. Not only that, but some websites can block browser extensions. Blocking ads at the DNS level mitigates all of these issues.

The *Domain Name System (DNS)* enables your computer (or browser) to communicate with websites on the internet. All websites have an IP address (or more than one) assigned to them. Compared to IP addresses, the URLs that you use to access websites (for example, *www.facebook.com*) are human-readable and easy to remember. Your computer translates that URL into an IP address to find the web server on the internet that serves Facebook to you—enter DNS. DNS acts like the postal service, in that IP addresses are equivalent to physical addresses, and URLs are like street names. DNS allows you to send and receive internet traffic to a specific address (or server) without having to remember the exact address (the IP address) of that server.

Given that advertising domains also use DNS to serve you ads, let's build a *Pi-Hole* server to send all of those requests to a blackhole and provide your users with a better browsing experience. Pi-Hole is similar to the Squid proxy discussed in Chapter 6; it sits between you and the websites you want to browse, observing all internet traffic, identifying advertising at the DNS level via a curated list of known advertising domains and addresses, and allowing only legitimate, non-ad traffic to pass through to your browser. Pi-Hole is capable of blocking a larger percentage of ads than browser solutions, and it's much harder for websites to detect and circumvent.

Set up an Ubuntu server in your local network, as discussed in Chapter 1, and add it to your network map and asset list. It's possible to use a server located in the cloud, but exposing a DNS server to the open internet creates some technical challenges we won't cover in this chapter. The right mitigating controls can solve these challenges, so if you choose to use a cloud server, proceed cautiously and do some research into how to mitigate the risks. If you've installed a perimeter firewall as discussed in Chapter 3 and you create your Pi-Hole server using a virtual machine, the server should be located behind the firewall (that is, on the network side of the firewall, rather than the internet side).

It's possible to use Pi-Hole in conjunction with Squid (discussed in Chapter 6) by using Pi-Hole to handle DNS requests and Squid to handle HTTP traffic. However, by default Squid uses an internal DNS client—this can't be changed without rebuilding Squid, which is outside the scope of this book. If you choose to use both Squid and Pi-Hole, you can follow the instructions supplied for configuring each solution separately on your endpoints and achieve the same outcome.

Configure Pi-Hole

Begin by creating a base Ubuntu server, as described in Chapter 1. Then, install the Pi-Hole server using the following steps:

1. Log in to your Ubuntu server via SSH as a standard, non-root user. Then, download the Pi-Hole installation script from *https://install.pi-hole.net/*, make it executable, and execute the script using `sudo`:

```
$ ssh user@your_server_ip
$ wget -O basic-install.sh https://install.pi-hole.net
$ chmod +x basic-install.sh
$ sudo ./basic-install.sh
```

2. At this point, the automated installer will take over your terminal window. Read the various informational screens that come up, pressing ENTER to move to the next one.

3. When prompted to select an upstream DNS server, as shown in Figure 7-1, choose whichever upstream (authoritative) DNS provider you're comfortable with. Google or Quad9 is a good choice.

NOTE *Use the arrow keys or TAB to navigate through the options, spacebar to select options, and ENTER to accept settings.*

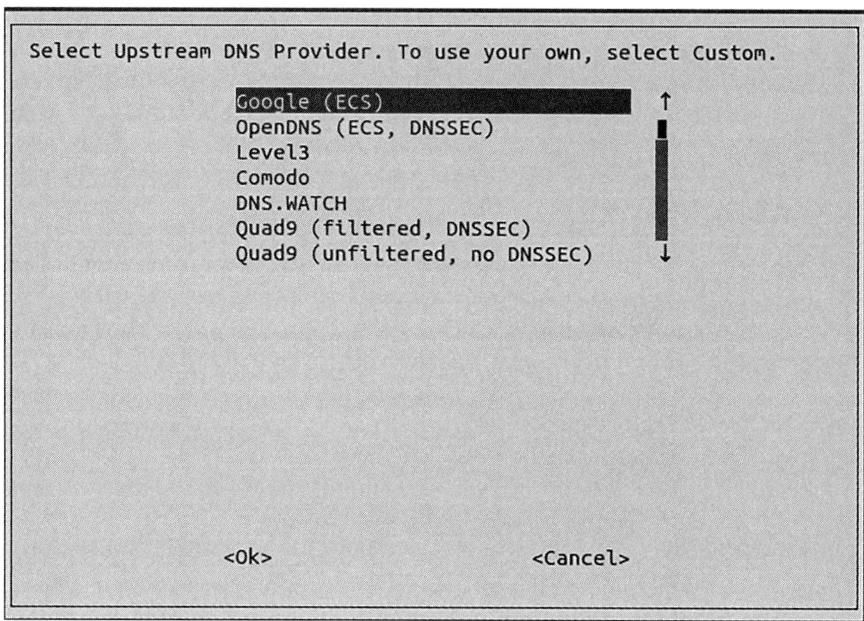

Figure 7-1: Upstream DNS provider

To perform DNS lookups, your Pi-Hole server will need an authoritative DNS server to query when it attempts to resolve domains that aren't already cached by the proxy server. An *authoritative* DNS server is a nameserver that holds the actual DNS records for a particular domain or address, such as *www.google.com*. By contrast, your server is *recursive*, an intermediary between you and your host and one or more authoritative DNS servers. When you make a request for a website, your device will pass this request to the Pi-Hole server, which will then farm this request out to an authoritative server to find the address of the website you want to view.

4. Select all the available blocklists when prompted.

   Pi-Hole uses *blocklists* (curated lists of advertising domains maintained by third parties) to identify and intercept advertisements on the internet. The chosen lists can be changed later.

5. Select IPv6 in addition to IPv4 at the protocol screen if you use IPv6 in your network.

In most cases, IPv6 isn't necessary. IPv6 provides internet-addressable IP space to endpoints, which you don't need to do in this situation. It's best to disable IPv6 to reduce your attack surface, unless you have a legitimate use for it.

6. The following screen indicates the static IP address and gateway of your server. If the address details listed on this page are correct, press ENTER to accept them. Otherwise, select **No** and press ENTER; then set your desired static IP details manually.

   The gateway for your Pi-Hole could be your firewall or router. Once you've configured or accepted the IP settings for your server, the automated installer will warn about configuring your router or DHCP server to reserve the IP address for this server. If you don't do this, your network may encounter address conflicts, but most routers will be able to avoid this conflict without your input. (See "Static IP Addressing" in Chapter 4 for configuring static IP addresses on a router.) Press ENTER to acknowledge the warning.

7. Select **On** to install the web interface, which makes the server configuration easier to manage (even for advanced administrators), and then press ENTER.
8. Select **On** to install the web server offered by the automated installer, unless you plan to install your own (this is beyond the scope of this book).
9. Select **On** to log the DNS queries that pass through your Pi-Hole server. Since Pi-Hole is a proxy, it will record and cache all web requests that pass through it. This means that any endpoint configured to use your Pi-Hole server for DNS will have its browsing history recorded. If this poses concerns for your users, either get their permission or turn logging off. You don't need logging to use Pi-Hole's ad-blocking features, but enabling it can help troubleshoot any issues.

10. Select a privacy level that is acceptable within your network.

    Pi-Hole uses *Faster Than Light (FTL)* DNS, which provides statistics about Pi-Hole activity and displays it graphically. You'll be able to see information such as how many ads were blocked, and for which endpoints, over a given period. FTL gets this data by parsing the Pi-Hole text logs. Like logging, this isn't necessary for Pi-Hole to function and can cause privacy concerns for your users. Be sure to get their permission ahead of time, or set the privacy levels to Hide Domains and Clients, as shown in Figure 7-2. Doing so will prompt FTL to collect anonymized data, allowing the statistics and graphical displays to function while preserving the privacy of your users. You could also decide to disable statistics entirely by turning logging off in the previous step.

```
Select a privacy mode for FTL.
https://docs.pi-hole.net/ftldns/privacylevels/

( ) 0  Show everything
( ) 1  Hide domains
(*) 2  Hide domains and clients
( ) 3  Anonymous mode

          <Ok>                         <Cancel>
```

Figure 7-2: FTL DNS settings

11. When the installation finishes, you'll be presented with a screen showing your configuration, as well as the URL and administrator password for the web interface, as shown in Figure 7-3. Be sure to record these values, ideally in a password vault (discussed in Chapter 11) for security and safety purposes; then press ENTER to return to the terminal.

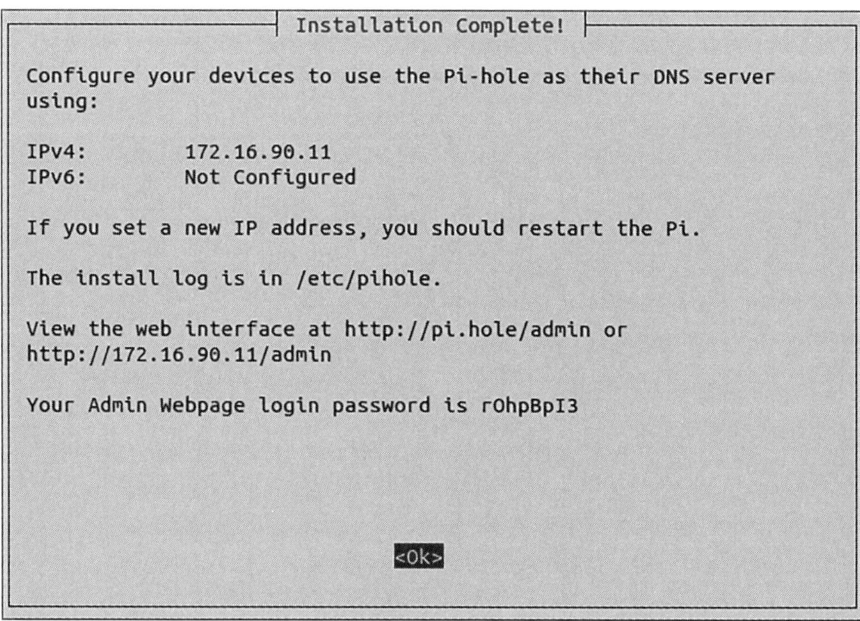

Installation Complete!
Configure your devices to use the Pi-hole as their DNS server using:
IPv4: 172.16.90.11
IPv6: Not Configured
If you set a new IP address, you should restart the Pi.
The install log is in /etc/pihole.
View the web interface at http://pi.hole/admin or http://172.16.90.11/admin
Your Admin Webpage login password is rOhpBpI3
<Ok>

Figure 7-3: Pi-Hole installation complete

You can change the administrator password with the following command:

```
$ sudo pihole -a -p
```

To keep Pi-Hole up-to-date, periodically run the following command:

```
$ sudo pihole -up
```

Ensuring that Pi-Hole and its components are up-to-date is crucial in keeping your Pi-Hole server, and your network, secure.

Using Pi-Hole

Browse to the administrator URL displayed in the last configuration step (*http://<your_server_ip>/admin/*) where you should see the user dashboard. When a new update is available, you'll be notified at the bottom of this screen, as in Figure 7-4. At this time, it's not possible to update Pi-Hole from the web interface; it must be updated using the commands in the previous section.

Donate if you found this useful.

Pi-hole v5.2.4 · Update available! **Web Interface** v5.4 · Update available!
FTL v5.7 · Update available!

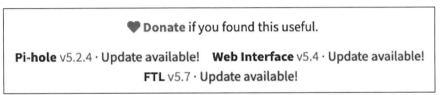

Figure 7-4: Pi-Hole update required

Click **Login** on the left side of the screen and authenticate with your administrator username and password. The dashboard will then display more detailed information. You'll find additional options in the administrator menu once logged in, as shown in Figure 7-5.

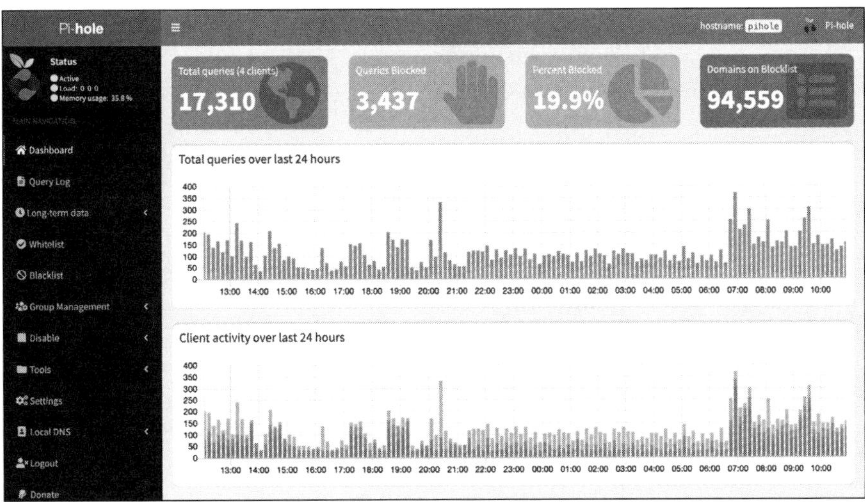

Figure 7-5: Pi-Hole administrator dashboard

Brief descriptions of the important options in the navigation dashboard are as follows:

Query Log A chronological, searchable history of all browser requests for websites that pass through the Pi-Hole proxy server.

Long-term Data A more extensive history of requests to the proxy server that you can filter based on ranges of dates.

Whitelist Websites that Pi-Hole blocks by default but to which you'd like to allow access.

Blacklist Domains that the proxy may not block by default but that you'd like to block explicitly.

NOTE *While we've been using allowlist/denylist, Pi-Hole uses whitelist/blacklist for its menu options and configuration. When discussing Pi-Hole, we'll adhere to this terminology.*

Disable Disable the proxy for a set period.

Tools Used to debug or update the blocklists, and review backend proxy logs. The backend logs provide debug information about Pi-Hole itself, rather than web traffic.

Tools ▸ Network Displays all clients connected to the Pi-Hole server to help identify which endpoints are using the proxy and which may be bypassing it (your network map and asset list will come in handy).

Settings ▸ System Contains the Pi-Hole proxy settings (including settings configured during installation); displays critical information; allows you to disable, restart, and power off the server; and lets you flush (delete) DNS proxy logs.

Settings ▸ DNS Change the authoritative DNS servers used for domain name translation and modify the network interface on which requests are received and passed through the proxy filter (though the default settings are usually the safest).

Settings ▸ DHCP Allows the Pi-Hole server to act as a DHCP server if desired.

Settings ▸ Privacy Increase or decrease the level of privacy used when reporting about queries by choosing to link endpoints with their browsing activity or anonymize the data captured by the proxy.

Settings ▸ Teleporter Imports or exports Pi-Hole settings to or from another server.

Logout Logs you out of the administration dashboard.

Explore the various menus and options to familiarize yourself with Pi-Hole's settings and configurations. Consider reading the manual as well to get a better understanding of how Pi-Hole works and how powerful it really is.

Configure DNS on Your Endpoints

At this point, there's only one thing left to do: make your clients use the Pi-Hole server as their DNS server. You need to configure your DHCP server or router to push the DNS settings to devices that access the internet. Alternatively, you can configure each endpoint individually using its internal network settings. You might want to do this if you'd like only specific devices on the network to connect through the proxy while letting others connect to the internet directly. That said, making all devices go through the Pi-Hole server will provide the best experience to users and allow you to have better control of network traffic and identify issues earlier. The server will also cache more websites as users browse to them, which will make browsing to frequently visited sites faster for everyone.

NOTE *Your router is capable of specifying the DNS server your endpoints use to access the internet. In the ASUS router we've been using as an example, it's under Advanced Settings ▸ LAN ▸ DNS Server. Enter your Pi-Hole server's IP address in the DNS Server1 box and click* ***Apply*** *to set the DNS server connected clients will use.*

If you want only some of your endpoints to use the Pi-Hole server, either you can configure those clients using their local DNS settings or you can use the DNS settings in your pfSense firewall (if you implemented pfSense, as discussed in Chapter 3).

Windows DNS Settings

To configure the DNS settings on a Windows client, follow these steps:

1. Open **Settings ▸ Network & Internet4Change Adapter Options**.
2. Right-click **Ethernet Adapter**.
3. Click **Properties**.
4. Click **Internet Protocol Version 4 (TCP/IPv4) ▸ Properties**.
5. Select the **Use the Following DNS Server Addresses** radio button.
6. Enter the IP address of your Pi-Hole server in the Preferred DNS Server box.
7. Click **OK** and close all remaining windows.

macOS DNS Settings

To configure your Mac to use your Pi-Hole server for DNS, follow these steps:

1. Open **System Preferences ▸ Network**.
2. Select your network adapter (**Ethernet** or **Wi-Fi**) in the connection list on the left.
3. Click **Advanced ▸ DNS**.
4. Add your Pi-Hole server's IP address to the DNS servers list on the left.
5. Click **OK ▸ Apply**.

Linux DNS Settings

To route DNS requests through your Pi-Hole server on Linux endpoints, follow these steps:

1. Open **Settings ▸ Network**.
2. Click the configuration **Cog** to the right of your Wired or Wireless connection.
3. Select the **IPv4** tab.
4. Enter your Pi-Hole server's IP address in the DNS box.
5. Click **Apply**.

pfSense DNS Settings

Using pfSense, you're able to configure DNS settings either per client within the static IP addressing settings you will have used earlier or en masse by pointing your pfSense appliance at your Pi-Hole server for DNS. To send all DNS requests through your Pi-Hole server, enter your Pi-Hole IP address in the DNS servers box on the **Services ▸ DHCP Server** page. If you want to specify which endpoints will use the Pi-Hole server for DNS, follow these steps:

1. Browse to the **Services ▸ DHCP Server** page of your pfSense appliance.
2. Find the Static Mapping option for the relevant endpoint in the DHCP Static Mappings table at the bottom of the page.
3. Click the **Edit** pencil icon for that endpoint.
4. Enter your Pi-Hole server's IP address in the DNS box.
5. Click **Save ▸ Apply Changes**.

Once you've configured your endpoints using any of the previous options, you can test your ad-blocking capability using a website like *https://canyoublockit.com/*. Such websites provide several options for testing your ad blockers, whether they're browser-based or something more substantial like Pi-Hole, from simple to advanced testing methods. If you run these tests and see no ads, your ad blocker is working. If you still see ads, review the earlier sections of this chapter and ensure your settings are correct. Log in to your Pi-Hole server and check the dashboard to see if your DNS queries are being seen by, and are therefore passing through, the server.

Summary

Regardless of how you choose to use Pi-Hole, you now have a means of monitoring and controlling internet usage in your network, and everyone should have a better internet browsing experience. You can choose to use Pi-Hole in addition to the Squid proxy you might have implemented in Chapter 6, or you can use either Squid or Pi-Hole without the other. Whichever solution you choose, you'll experience the benefits associated with that technology. Alternatively, you can forego DNS-level ad blocking if you prefer to use browser-based blocking utilizing browser add-ons; the choice is yours.

8

DETECTING, REMOVING, AND PREVENTING MALWARE

Malware such as viruses, trojans, and ransomware are significant threats to internet users and likely will be for the foreseeable future. As a result, it's important to arm yourself and your users with an antivirus solution that detects and removes malware. Additionally, keeping your endpoints up-to-date can prevent malware from infecting your network and in some cases provide more protection than an antivirus (AV) solution.

Antivirus solutions can be tricky to manage because they typically are not cross-platform (that is, they work on only one operating system). If you have multiple operating systems in your network, you'll need to find an effective AV product for each of them. Although this chapter discusses installing, configuring, and scanning with specific products, most options and settings will be the same across most antivirus solutions. The names of the settings and configuration options may differ slightly, but the same logic and processes should work for most products.

After exploring some antivirus solutions for various operating systems, we'll consider the differences between malware signatures and heuristic scans, the pros and cons of each approach, and the concept of creating an antivirus farm to catch as much malware as possible across different endpoints. Finally, we'll cover patch management for various operating systems and how best to keep your endpoints up-to-date.

Microsoft Defender for Windows

The latest iteration of the built-in Microsoft antivirus solution is *Microsoft Defender*. Defender automatically updates its virus definitions and scans for threats on a regular schedule, so Windows computers have decent protection out of the box.

Defender's automatic scans are *quick scans* that check only the folders where threats are commonly found. While a quick scan offers fast results and uses few system resources, it's unlikely to discover and remove malware residing outside of these folders. A *full scan* scans all your files and running programs, performing a thorough search for malware. It's recommended to run full scans somewhere between once a week and once a month. The longer the period between full scans, the more time an adversary has to wreak havoc on your systems.

You also have the option to choose custom and offline scans. A *custom scan* lets you select which folders and files to scan. An *offline scan* is similar to the Boot to Safe Mode method of malware removal available in earlier versions of Windows. Windows is now capable of automatically rebooting to a state that allows Microsoft Defender to remove persistent malware via this offline scan. This option is a last resort, rather than a scan you would run regularly. If you believe your computer is infected but are unable to find the infection using a full scan, run the offline scan to be certain. Failing this, your only recourse is to wipe your hard drive and re-install Windows from scratch.

To run scans, open **Settings ▸ Update & Security ▸ Windows Security ▸ Virus & Threat Protection**. Click **Scan Options**, select the type of scan you want, and then click **Scan now**.

In the Virus & Threat Protection4Manage Settings menu, ensure Real-time Protection is turned on to enable Defender to protect your computer constantly. You can also add file and folder exclusions from this menu. You might add exclusions when you have files or programs that are legitimate and not a risk to your system, but Defender classifies them as malware and tries to quarantine them anyway.

One setting in particular could be considered a risk to your privacy, Automatic Sample Submission, which allows Microsoft Defender to upload your files to Microsoft's servers in the cloud automatically to be analyzed and scanned for malware. This practice poses a risk: private or confidential data could be leaked to a third party without your knowledge, as Defender won't ask or advise you of files being uploaded to Microsoft. To turn off this setting, toggle Automatic Sample Submissions.

Related to this setting is the Cloud-Delivered Protection setting. This one isn't as risky, as it relays only file metadata to Microsoft rather than entire file contents. Cloud-Delivered Protection will still work with Automatic Sample Submission turned off, although it might not perform as well.

Windows will keep Microsoft Defender up-to-date, but it never hurts to update manually occasionally. To update, click **Check for Updates** on the main Virus & Threat Protection page.

XPROTECT FOR MACOS

macOS has a built-in antivirus solution called XProtect. When you download an application from the internet, XProtect will check its definitions file of known-bad files, which is updated when you receive software and operating system updates for your computer. This is less beneficial than an antivirus program that performs a heuristics-based scan (see the upcoming "Signatures and Heuristics" section for more information on heuristics) that evaluates files based on their content or behavior, rather than a specific file signature.

Choosing Malware Detection and Antivirus Tools

When deciding on the antivirus and malware detection tools you'd like to use, consider whether it's worth paying for a commercial tool (or the premium version of a free tool) and whether the tool will use signatures or heuristics to detect malware.

In general, if all you want is a simple malware scanning tool, there's rarely a good reason to pay for a commercial product. Typically, you'll pay for advanced features, such as an email or web browser scanner built-in to the malware file scanner.

Oftentimes, paid solutions allow for some form of centralized management. Whether that's a web portal or a management server or agent, you gain visibility and the ability to manage all of your devices from one place. If you have a larger network, there's value in having this capability; if your network consists of less than 30 devices, you probably don't need it.

Antivirus Farm

There's also a benefit in foregoing a single solution in favor of using multiple antivirus products in smaller networks. *Antivirus farms* use several products aiming to catch more malware than a single solution might. It also makes the attacker's job more difficult; instead of evading a single antivirus product, they need to evade multiple to move laterally through a network.

Antivirus farms are helpful because every antivirus vendor curates their own databases of *malware signatures*—sequences of bytes in the executable that can be used to identify that specific malware sample. These databases have to be optimized every so often; otherwise, the virus definitions that you download with the software would become too large and unwieldy to be useful. Therefore, older virus definitions may be removed from these databases over time, which means having products from multiple vendors will likely lead to greater coverage of known threats.

Signatures and Heuristics

You should also aim to use antivirus products that perform both signature-based detection and heuristics. *Signatures* identify known-malicious software by the contents of an executable or other file, though it's trivial for an attacker to change the signature of their malware by changing the contents slightly. This is a major weakness when it comes to malware detection software. *Heuristics*, on the other hand, analyze the way a file behaves and the commands a file might run to determine whether it's malicious. This is a much more reliable way of detecting known and unknown threats. How do you tell whether a particular antivirus program performs signature-based detection or heuristic scanning? The best way, if it's not listed on their website, is to contact the vendor and ask. There will always be a contact method listed on their website.

#26: Installing Avast on macOS

Apple devices, commonly believed to be less prone to malware, are becoming infected more often, which means you should install antivirus software on any Macs on your network. There are many options, both free and commercial, when installing a third-party heuristics-based antivirus solution on your Apple computer. Among these, Avast has topped many lists for several years. To install and configure Avast, use the following steps:

1. Download Avast from *http://www.avast.com/* and install the software. When the installation has completed, you should be presented with the Avast Security window (see Figure 8-1).

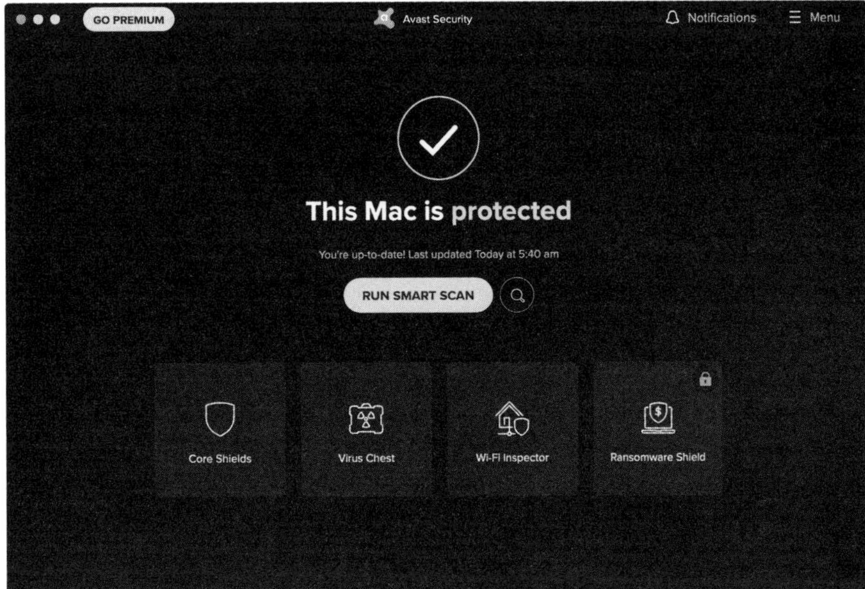

Figure 8-1: Avast Security window

2. Click **Menu ▸ Preferences** to reach Avast's settings page.
3. In the General tab, ensure that the **Turn on Automatic Updates** checkbox is ticked.
4. In the Privacy tab, *untick* the two checkboxes allowing your data to be shared with Avast. Similar to Windows Defender, it's best to protect your privacy.
5. In the Core Shields tab, enable each of the security checks Avast will run, such as file scanning and web and email protection.
6. Click the **Add Exceptions** button under each of the shields to specify any necessary exceptions. Add exceptions if you have files or programs that you know to be legitimate or low risk but that your antivirus classifies as potentially malicious.
7. In the Scans tab, ensure the checkboxes **Scan Whole Files**, **Scan External Drives**, **Scan Mounted Network Volumes**, **Scan All Time Machine Backups**, and **Scan Archives** are ticked. By doing so, you can be certain your antivirus is doing as much as possible to identify threats and protect you from them.

A *Smart Scan* is designed to scan the most vulnerable areas of your computer quickly. While this is less resource intensive and less time consuming, it's not likely to catch all threats on your computer because it doesn't scan all areas of your hard drives. A *Deep Scan* is more comprehensive and includes all areas of storage on your device, optionally including external storage, network locations, Time Machine backups, memory, and rootkit detection. A *Targeted Scan* scans only specified areas.

All of these scans are run from the Scan Central screen in Avast on your Mac. Click the **Search** button to select the type of scan you want to run and then click **Scan Now**. Selecting Targeted, USB/DVD, or Custom Scans will prompt you for the locations to scan. Avast will scan your computer for threats, and if any are detected, it will ask what you'd like to do with the relevant files. Select all the files and click **Resolve Selected** to move them all to the Virus Chest; then click **Done**. Your computer should now be clean of all potentially malicious files and applications.

#27: Installing ClamAV on Linux

Linux is susceptible to viruses as well. However, Linux operating systems rarely come with a built-in antivirus application, and there are fewer available than for other operating systems. Most of the available solutions are commercial and therefore have a cost attached, such as Avast Core Security for Linux, though there is an open source solution: ClamAV.

ClamAV is a free application that can be used on Windows, macOS, and Linux. To install it on Ubuntu, log in to your server via SSH as a standard, non-root user. Run the following command to install the version of ClamAV that allows you to automate your virus scanning activity, as well as the GUI, clamtk, which may be useful later:

```
$ sudo apt install clamav clamav-daemon clamtk
```

With the installation complete, your antivirus definitions (the database that tells ClamAV what is malware) should be up-to-date, but you can run the following commands to update the virus definitions—either now or in the future—to stop, update, and then restart ClamAV:

```
$ sudo systemctl stop clamav-freshclam
$ sudo freshclam
$ sudo systemctl start clamav-freshclam
```

To run a malware scan, use the `clamscan` *`folder_to_scan`* command. To scan everything on the system, use / to indicate to ClamAV to scan everything in the root of the filesystem, supply the `-r` parameter to make the scan recurse all directories, and use `sudo` so that ClamAV has the necessary permission to read all files in the filesystem:

```
$ sudo clamscan -r /
--snip--
----------- SCAN SUMMARY -----------
Known viruses: 8927215
Engine version: 0.102.3
Scanned directories: 89954
Scanned files: 362758
Infected files: 0
Total errors: 82216
Data scanned: 8767.58 MB
```

```
Data read: 14195.27 MB (ratio 0.62:1)
Time: 1171.021 sec (19 m 31 s)
```

When the scan completes, clamscan will output a scan summary.

In addition to known malware, ClamAV can detect *potentially unwanted applications (PUAs)*, including software such as adware, peer-to-peer (p2p) programs, remote administration tools, bitcoin miners, and bundleware (software included with but not related to the application being installed), which are not inherently malicious but may pose a risk to or negatively impact your endpoints' security and performance. To scan for PUAs, include the `--detect-pua=yes` argument when running ClamAV.

If your scans are taking too long, you can use other advanced parameters to reduce their duration. You can limit the size of the files ClamAV will scan with `--max-filesize=n`, where *n* is the maximum file size in kilobytes. Any files larger than the size you specify will be skipped and assumed to be clean, reducing the time it takes your scan to complete. Similarly, `--max-scansize=n` scans only archive files (*.rar* files, *.zip* files, and so on) up to the specified size—all other archives will be skipped. To limit the depth of the recursion (that is, how many directories will be scanned below the directory where you start the scan), use the `--max-dir-recursion=n` parameter. For more parameters, use the `-h` argument, as in `sudo clamscan -h`, to print the help menu.

To run a scan on a regular schedule, use Crontab, a Linux utility designed to execute programs at preset times or intervals. In your terminal, use the `crontab -e` command to edit the scheduled tasks file:

```
$ sudo crontab -e
[sudo] password for user:

# Edit this file to introduce tasks to be run by cron.
#
# Each task to run has to be defined through a single line
# indicating with different fields when the task will be run
# and what command to run for the task
#
# To define the time you can provide concrete values for
# minute (m), hour (h), day of month (dom), month (mon),
# and day of week (dow) or use '*' in these fields (for 'any').
#
# Notice that tasks will be started based on the cron's system
# daemon's notion of time and timezones.
#
# Output of the crontab jobs (including errors) is sent through
# email to the user the crontab file belongs to (unless redirected).
#
# For example, you can run a backup of all your user accounts
# at 5 a.m every week with:
# 0 5 * * 1 tar -zcf /var/backups/home.tgz /home/
#
# For more information see the manual pages of crontab(5) and cron(8)
#
# m h  dom mon dow   command
```

The large comment at the start of the file explains how to specify tasks with an example. The last line of the comment provides the syntax for scheduling execution of scripts and applications. The order is minute, hour, day of month, month, day of week, and command to execute. Minutes and hours must be numbers, 0 to 59 and 0 to 23, respectively, and you can specify a list of minutes or hours by separating the values with commas (that is, you can run a command at 1, 2, and 3 AM by specifying `1,2,3`). You can specify days numerically (1 to 7, where 1 is Sunday), or as Sun, Mon, Tue, and so on. Months are 1 to 12 (where 1 is January). An asterisk (*) stands for all possible values for a field; if you want your command to run every month, put an asterisk in the month (`mon`) position.

Say you want to run `clamscan` over the entire filesystem at 1 AM every Sunday, including scanning for potentially unwanted applications. At the bottom of the Crontab file, add a new line and enter the following:

```
0 1 * * sun clamscan -r / --detect-pua=yes -l /path_to_logfile/clamav.log
```

By default, you won't be able to see the results of your scans unless you specify the logfile with the `-l` parameter. If you want to scan a specific folder, like the user home folders (*/home/*), every day, in addition to the full system scan, add another entry to the Crontab, following the previous example as a guideline.

Add another line to the Crontab to ensure ClamAV is kept up to date:

```
0 0 * * mon systemctl stop clamav-freshclam && freshclam && systemctl start clamav-freshclam
```

You can link multiple commands together and separate them with a pair of ampersands to run them in series. Find more information on Crontab (or any other terminal command) with the `man` function. Enter **`man crontab`** to open the manual for the application on the command line.

#28: Using VirusTotal

VirusTotal (VT) tests files to determine whether they're likely to be malicious (*https://www.virustotal.com/*) by taking the concept of an antivirus farm and implementing it on a large scale. It's a publicly available service where you can upload any file to scan for malware, and VT will scan it with more than 60 antivirus programs. It will then produce a report to let you know whether it contains malware or behaves in a way that may negatively impact your endpoints, security, or privacy. This capability is especially useful if you believe a file is malicious but is undetected by your antivirus.

Be aware that anything uploaded to VT becomes public, so anyone can search for and download the files you upload. To use VT without making your private information public, search VT for the hash of the file you want to check. *Hashing* is a process for calculating a fixed-length string based on the contents of a file. Hashing is expected to be a one-way process, meaning you can't take the hash of a file and reverse it to get the original file contents. By creating the hash of a file, you should get a unique string of characters that identify said file. Some hashing algorithms can result in *collisions*, where two files yield the same hash, though the chances of this happening in most modern hashing functions are slim to none. You can get the hash of a file by using built-in tools in any operating system.

Windows PowerShell In Windows, open a PowerShell window and enter the following command to get the MD5 hash of any file:

```
$ Get-FileHash path_to_file -Algorithm MD5
```

You can then search for the hash directly in the VirusTotal web portal.

Linux and macOS Terminal You can get the MD5 hash of a file in both Linux and macOS using the following command:

```
$ md5sum path_to_file
```

Then, search for the resulting hash in the VT web portal.

If a file with the same hash has been uploaded to VT at any point in the past, you'll be presented with the public report for that file, detailing the malware scan results from all the providers in VT. If it hasn't been uploaded previously, there's a good chance the file isn't malicious.

#29: Managing Patches and Updates

Along with using antivirus tools, patch management is an important defense because malware exploits are written to attack a specific vulnerability in a network, application, protocol, or operating system. Adversaries pay close attention to Windows updates and patches for other operating systems, as the patch notes call out the vulnerability it's designed to remediate. Attackers use that vulnerability information to write malware specifically for that security flaw, and anyone who hasn't downloaded the update can fall victim. This is why operating systems constantly ask you to install updates and patches.

In most cases, end users don't install updates right away, and adversaries have a window of opportunity to target unpatched systems. It's in your best interest to install software updates as soon as they become available. Luckily, the process of updating is exceedingly simple and easy to automate. This project describes how to configure system updates on individual systems, and the following section discusses a solution for patch management across multiple endpoints.

Windows Update

For Windows updates, open **Windows Settings ▸ Update & Security**. Windows checks for updates automatically at least once per day (assuming the device is left on at all times). To check for, download, and install updates manually, click the **Check for Updates** button.

If you'd prefer not to worry about updates for a while, click **Pause Updates for 7 Days**. Updates are critical for keeping your system secure, so pausing the updates is not recommended.

You can restrict Windows from updating your computer during certain times by setting active hours. If you use your computer primarily between 9 AM and 5 PM, you can tell Windows not to update during this window, which is a better option than pausing updates for an extended period of time.

In Advanced Options, you can allow Windows to update other Microsoft products via Windows Update—I recommend turning this on. You can also make Windows force devices to restart after updates are installed, which is useful if you, as the administrator, want to force your end users to restart their machines. You'll be unpopular, but your network will be more secure.

In the Advanced Options ▸Delivery Optimization menu, you can enable the option to download updates from other PCs in your network. This reduces the bandwidth required to download the same updates to multiple computers from the internet. You should turn on this setting, with the caveat that downloads be allowed only from PCs on your local network and not from PCs on the internet.

Back in the Advanced Options pane, the last settings of particular interest are the Privacy settings. You can increase your privacy within this menu by disallowing Windows and Microsoft from sending you targeted ads and content based on your location, browsing habits, and application usage statistics.

macOS Software Update

Apple devices are much simpler than Windows or Linux because their update process can be almost entirely automated and requires very little user input. To ensure your Apple computers are kept up-to-date, open **System Preferences ▸ Software Update**. To allow automatic updates, check **Automatically Keep My Mac Up-to-date**.

With this check box ticked, click the **Advanced** button to select what actions should be taken automatically. From this menu (Figure 8-2), choose whether your computer can check for updates, download updates, or complete the installation process without user input, and then click **OK** to save the settings. In most cases, allowing your computer to keep itself up-to-date with no input from the user is desirable; the computer will still confirm with the user before restarting after any updates that require a reboot (which doesn't happen often).

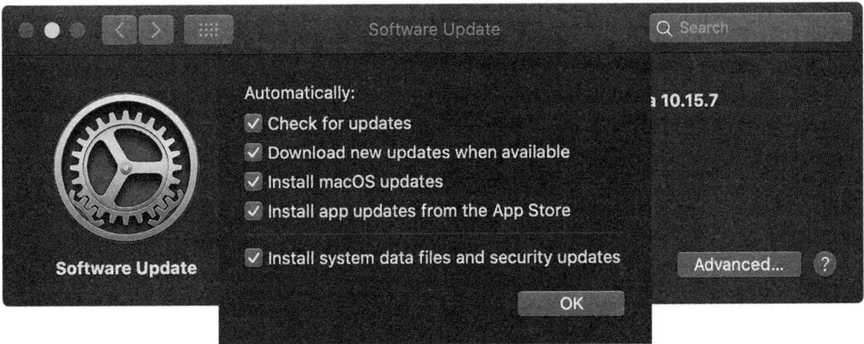

Figure 8-2: macOS advanced software update configuration

Keeping your devices up-to-date in this way ensures they are as secure as possible and protects your and your users' privacy.

Linux Updates with apt

As discussed in Chapter 1, the Linux operating system comes in multiple implementations, called *distributions*. Each of those distributions uses a package manager to maintain and update the software that the system or user installs. Throughout this book, we use Ubuntu Linux, which uses the Advanced Package Tool (APT) package manager. Package managers simplify the process of keeping your Linux endpoints up-to-date and secure.

To update an Ubuntu system, log in via SSH as a standard, non-root user. When you log in, you should be presented with a welcome message, including information about required and recommended updates:

```
--snip--
 * Documentation:  https://help.ubuntu.com
 * Management:     https://landscape.canonical.com
 * Support:        https://ubuntu.com/advantage

105 updates can be installed immediately.
68 of these updates are security updates.
To see these additional updates run: apt list --upgradable
--snip--
```

To make sure the list of updates is complete, run the **`apt update`** command:

```
$ sudo apt update
```

Once the list is up-to-date, run the **`upgrade`** command to update all of the software packages:

```
$ sudo apt upgrade
```

The command output will show the number of packages to update, the disk space they'll use, and various status messages. When prompted, type **Y** and press ENTER to continue.

As with Windows and macOS, some updates require you to reboot the system. If that's the case, you'll see something like:

```
A reboot is required to replace the running dbus-daemon.
Please reboot the system when convenient.
```

To make Ubuntu update the system and installed packages automatically, use the following command:

```
$ sudo dpkg-reconfigure -plow unattended-upgrades
```

The command will produce the prompt shown in Figure 8-3.

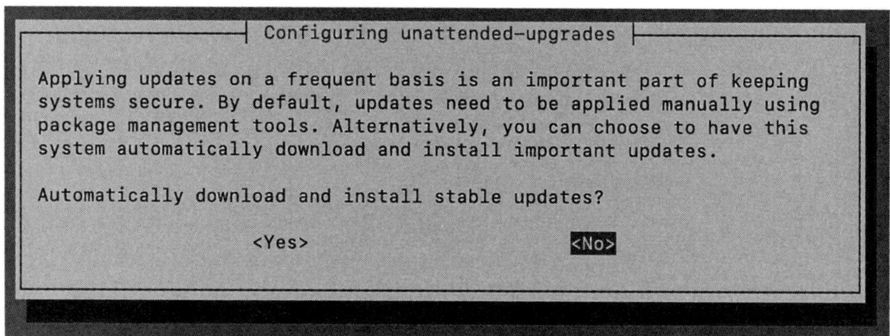

Figure 8-3: Ubuntu unattended updates

By selecting **Yes** and pressing ENTER, you'll ensure your servers are kept up-to-date, thereby making them inherently more secure. However, you should still check for updates manually and reboot your server once a month.

#30: Installing Automox

Depending on the size of your network, keeping all your endpoints up to date manually or even semi-manually might feel tedious or overwhelming. A centralized patch management solution like Automox allows you to easily manage all of these things in one place. Automox operates on a per-endpoint subscription model: you can start managing one or more Windows, macOS, or Linux systems (workstations or servers) for a nominal monthly fee, which allows you to patch all of your endpoints, with both system and third-party software patches, from one dashboard. Automox also maintains an asset and software inventory, which is the first step anyone should take to keep their network secure.

Installing Automox

Head to the Automox website (*https://www.automox.com/*) to sign up for an account (or free trial). Then log in to your account dashboard at *https://console.automox.com/*. The dashboard is where you'll see a summary of your managed endpoints and the updates they require. Of course, until you add some endpoints to your account, this dashboard will be sparse. In the following sections you'll require a user key to connect your endpoints to Automox. Your key can be found by going to your profile settings page in the Automox web UI, under the Keys tab.

Windows

To install the Automox agent on Windows endpoints, access the **Devices** tab from your Automox console, and then click the **Add Devices** link at the top of the page. You'll be presented with an OS selection pop-up. Select Windows, and then download the agent.

Once the agent is downloaded, run the installer (an *.msi* file) as an administrator. Follow the installation wizard, entering your Automox user key from the console when prompted. When the installation has completed, refresh your Automox dashboard to see the newly added endpoint (Figure 8-4).

Figure 8-4: Automox asset list

macOS and Linux

In a Terminal window on a Mac or Linux computer, run the following command, substituting your user key for *yourkey*:

```
$ curl -sS "https://console.automox.com/downloadInstaller?accesskey=yourkey" | sudo bash
```

Refresh your console again to see the newly added endpoint(s).

Using Automox

Now that you've installed Automox on your endpoints, you'll be able to manage operating system and third-party software patches from a central console. From the Devices tab, you can view all of your managed endpoints and add them to groups—if you'd like to manage them that way. You can also scan your endpoints to identify hardware changes and check for new updates they require, reboot your endpoints remotely, or remove endpoints from your account. By clicking an endpoint, you can see its hardware configuration, IP and MAC addresses, device type, operating system, CPU and RAM details, and other critical information, as shown in Figure 8-5. You can also force updates to be applied to the endpoint immediately, rather than wait for the endpoint to be updated according to the update policies specified in the System Management tab.

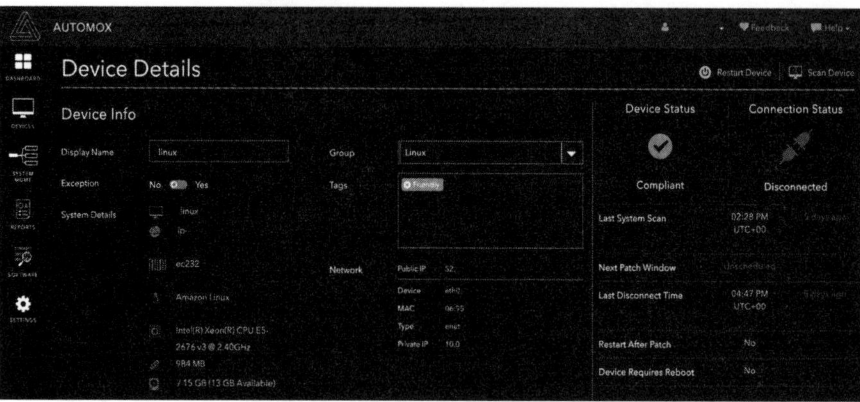

Figure 8-5: Automox device details

The System Management tab allows you to create and assign patching policies, which is useful if you want to schedule patch installation. For example, you may decide to automatically install any critical patches daily at 5 PM. Alternatively, you might want to force the installation of all required patches at 12 AM every Saturday, when people are less likely to be using their computers. You will need to define your own requirements and decide what patching schedule works best for you and your network.

In the Reports tab, you can generate reports of actions taken by Automox to keep your endpoints up-to-date, report on the state of any or all endpoints in your console, or identify noncompliant endpoints. Depending on the size of your network, it may be easier to view this information in your dashboard than to run these reports.

Automox will provide you with an inventory of all the software installed on your managed endpoints and their patch level in the Software tab. This allows you to easily identify software that requires updating and to update it if possible. You can also use this list to identify software that you don't want in your environment, whether it's potentially unwanted applications or specific software, like games or other software that violates an organizational policy.

Finally, the Settings tab allows you to create new users to allow other administrators to access your Automox console to manage your endpoints. You can also find and add your agent access keys in this tab. One thing you should absolutely take advantage of is the two-factor authentication setting. By enabling two-factor authentication, you make your account more secure and therefore make unauthorized access to your devices and patch management information much more difficult (discussed further in Chapter 11).

Summary

Keeping your systems up-to-date is critical in keeping your network secure. Whether you choose to use the built-in antivirus and patching options for your operating system or a managed patching solution like Automox, updates should be regularly scheduled and virus scans regularly run; otherwise, you leave your network vulnerable to all sorts of adversaries and unnecessary risk.

9

BACKING UP YOUR DATA

Having a reliable, well-defined, and well-implemented backup strategy is one of the best defenses any network can have against malicious or accidental data loss. Whether you mistakenly delete a folder of critical documents, an adversary executes ransomware inside your network, or a natural disaster destroys your devices, backups can save you from catastrophe.

This chapter introduces various backup considerations, including different backup types, creating backup schedules, the value of onsite and offsite backups, what to back up, and backup storage options. Finally, we'll show how to implement different solutions within your network.

Backup Types

You should consider three types of backups when implementing your backup schedule: *full*, *incremental*, and *differential*.

Full Backup

A full backup contains a complete copy of everything you want to back up from a specific host or location (called a *backup set*). For example, you might decide you want to regularly create backup copies of everything in your user profile on your computer. Alternatively, you may want a copy of the entire disk or volume, including operating system files. Either of these options is viable and could be considered a different backup set.

Full backups provide quick, easy restoration of all files from a backup set. Because all data is contained in a single backup, the process to restore will be faster than other backup options. However, full backups require more storage, especially if you're keeping more than one, and they take the longest amount of time to create.

Differential Backup

Differential backups contain only copies of the data that's changed since the last full backup, thus lending themselves to more frequent use than full backups. If you decide to take a full backup once a month, it's a good idea to schedule a differential backup once a week. It's recommended to create a full backup regularly to keep the size of your differential backups under control (rather than taking one full backup of your backup set and then creating differential backups only from that point forward).

Differential backups take up a lot of storage space, as the first backup contains copies of all the files modified since the last full backup, and then the next differential backup contains all of that data, *plus* all of the additional modified files between the first and second differential backups. Without a full backup at some point in the chain, differential backups will become exponentially larger as time goes on. Also, if one or more of the differential backups is incomplete, you won't be able to achieve a full recovery from the partial differential backup and the full backup of the data.

Incremental Backup

Incremental backups create copies of any data that has changed since the last backup *of any kind*, whether it's a prior full, differential, or incremental. This type of backup takes the least amount of space and requires the least amount of time to create. If you create a full backup once a month and a differential backup once a week, you'd do well to create your incremental backups daily to ensure that any changes made to your data will be captured.

Incremental backups are difficult in that it can be challenging to restore all your files across multiple backups, as each will have to be opened individually and specific files restored from the desired backup point. That means using all the available restore points to complete a full restoration, whereas a differential backup requires only the most recent differential and the most recent full backup to complete a full restoration.

Devising a Backup Schedule

Backups are of little value if not taken regularly. Your most critical data probably changes daily, so having a two-month-old backup of a document isn't helpful if it becomes corrupted or otherwise permanently unavailable. Therefore, it's essential to decide how often backups should be created. Your backup strategy will be highly individual and unique to your particular set of circumstances and requirements, though there are some best practices you can follow.

It's usually best to create full backups less frequently than differential or incremental backups, because of how much space and time they take up. Taking differential or incremental backups allows modified data to be backed up more frequently, and these backup types are less prone to failure due to time constraints than a full backup would be. As a general rule, taking a full backup of your primary systems or critical data once a month is a good place to start, and you can adjust your backup strategy as needed.

Depending on the backup software you choose, you may have access to some, all, or none of these specific scheduling options. Some software, for example, technically has all of this functionality and will allow you to restore data from your backups from different points in time, but the differential/incremental/full backup and restore options will not be displayed to you directly. Most operating systems come with an integrated backup solution (discussed later). Depending on your requirements, the built-in options might be sufficient. Otherwise, you can consider various paid solutions.

Onsite and Offsite Backups

Depending on the criticality of the data you choose to back up, keeping *offsite backups* in addition to *onsite backups* might be a good idea. Onsite backups are held in the same physical location as your original data, such as your home or office. Offsite backups are stored away from your primary location. Storing your backups in multiple locations provides data redundancy; if your onsite backups and original data are destroyed, an offsite backup may be your only option for recovery. Typically, an offsite backup will be stored offline, not connected to your network, and ideally in something like a fireproof safe. Alternatively, you might choose to use a cloud solution, but that comes with its own security risks.

Having an offsite backup may create additional administrative overhead. In most cases, you'll create your backup onsite, either by using a backup application or by copying the onsite backup in its entirety, and then remove that backup physically from the premises. This should be done on a regular schedule in the same way as onsite backups, as it affords you more options in the event of an emergency.

What to Back Up and What Storage to Use

Choosing exactly what you want to back up can be a challenge at first. Do you need to be able to recover an entire device from a previous checkpoint, or do you need only specific files? If you don't need to recover the whole operating system, it's best to determine which files and folders are critical or would be useful to recover. Consider how long you can be without the data before it really starts to impact you, your users, or your business. The time it takes to restore data from backup depends entirely on how much data you have to restore.

The other consideration when determining what to include in your backup strategy is what kind of storage, and how much, you have available to store your backups. You could choose to create backups of files on the device itself, but doing so isn't very useful if the device is lost, stolen, destroyed, or otherwise unavailable. A better option is to use an external hard drive, which can be obtained from any local computer store in any capacity that suits your needs. It's a cheap, easy option that allows you to create onsite backups and secondary backups that can be easily stored offsite. Finally, you could purchase dedicated storage for your backups in the form of a *network-attached storage (NAS)* device. An NAS connects to your network, has high storage capacity, and usually includes additional features like drive redundancy and automation. It offers greater performance and reliability than a stand-alone external hard drive but is often more expensive and requires some administration.

Whichever storage solution you choose, it should match your needs in terms of what you plan to back up. Full-disk backups of your devices will take up a lot of space, as internal storage for computers is typically up to or greater than 1TB. If you're planning to back up only critical personal files, you won't need as much storage for your backups. Chances are you'll start with an external hard drive and then upgrade your storage as your needs increase over time. The solution you choose will depend largely on your operating system, whether your endpoint is physical or virtual, and how much data you want to keep in your backup set.

If you want to maintain your own backups, most operating systems have built-in backup solutions, some of which are more fully featured than others.

#31: Using Windows Backup

To access the built-in backup solution for Windows, open **Windows Settings ▸ Update & Security ▸ Backup**. You'll need to connect a drive to the computer that will store your backup data. Once connected, click **Add a Drive** and select it, as shown in Figure 9-1. Note that in Windows 11,

Windows Backup is found under **Windows Settings ▸ Accounts ▸ Windows backup**, and the settings are per user. You can use Windows Backup in Windows 11 to sync your files, applications, and preferences to OneDrive, but the option to back up a local drive to an external or network drive is no longer available.

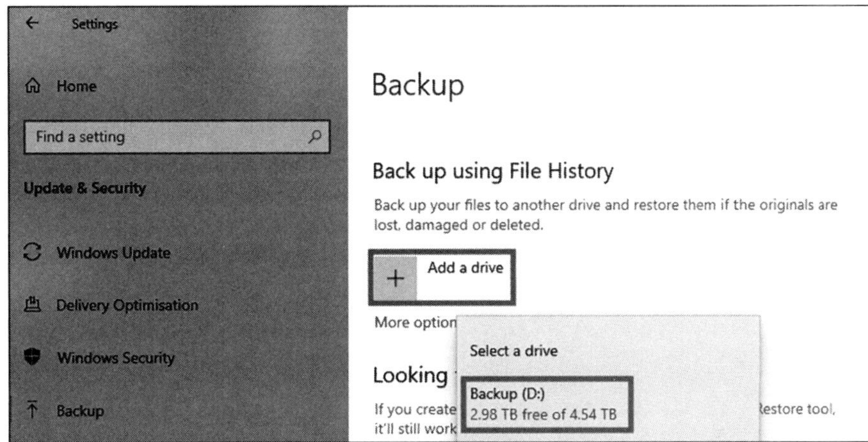

Figure 9-1: Windows backup to an external drive

When you've selected the drive, the Automatically Back Up My Files option will be turned on. This will keep various copies of the more critical data in your user profile folder (*C:\Users\<username>*) such as your *Documents*, *Desktop*, and *Downloads* folders, as well as application settings from the *AppData* folder. You can choose which folders to include in your backup by clicking More Options.

Windows Backup is essentially a full backup plus differential backup strategy. It'll take a complete backup of your chosen files to start with and will then keep every new version or modification to any of those files on an hourly basis by default, forever (or until your backup drive space is exhausted). This allows you to view and restore your files from any point in the backup timeline. There are a few limitations to this, including being unable to save your backup to a network location and not being able to take full system images.

#32: Using Windows Backup and Restore

Windows Backup, discussed in the previous project, is great for backing up specific files and folders, but not for taking full system backups. Luckily, all versions of Windows since Windows 7 include *Back up and Restore*, which is useful for creating full system backups including system images that can completely restore a system (if it were to become corrupted by ransomware, for example). It's also capable of creating backups to an external or network drive, though it doesn't keep older versions of your files or file history.

In Windows 10, you can get to Back up and Restore by going to **Windows Settings ▸ Update & Security ▸ Back up ▸ Go to Back up and**

Restore (Windows 7). In Windows 11, Back up and Restore is found in **Control Panel ▸ System Security ▸ Back up and Restore (Windows 7)**. You'll be presented with the screen shown in Figure 9-2.

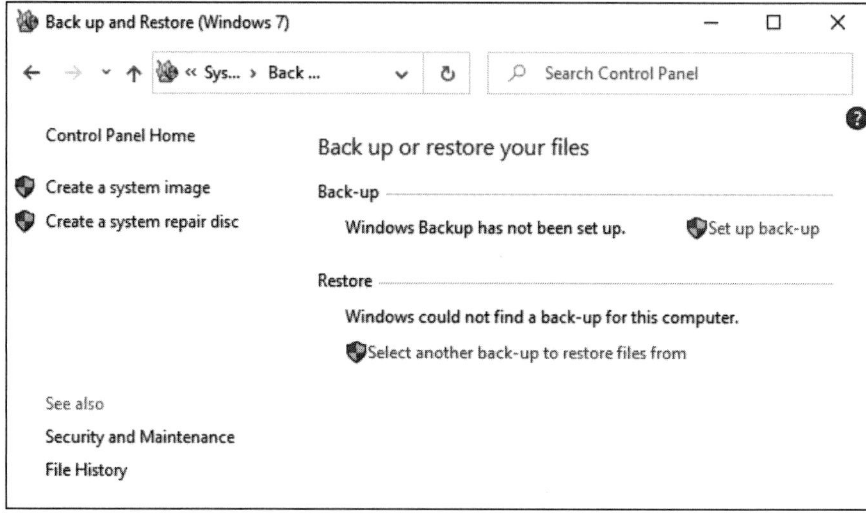

Figure 9-2: Windows Back up and Restore window

On the left, you have options to create a *system image* or a *system repair disc*. In case your computer becomes inaccessible due to issues with the hardware or the operating system, you'll be able use either of these to restore the computer to its current, known-good configuration, with all of your files intact in their present state.

1. Click the **Set Up Back-up** button on the right to create a regular backup schedule of your personal and system files.
2. Attach an external drive and click **Refresh** to select it as a backup location, or specify a network drive or location by clicking **Save On a Network** and specifying the necessary username and password (if any); then click **Next**.

At this point, Windows will ask you what you want to include in your backup. By default, you can let Windows choose what to include, which will be your personal files and folders from *C:\Users\<username>*.

3. Select the **Let Me Choose** radio button and then click **Next**.
4. Choose what to back up.
   a. Enable or disable backup of new users' files (assuming new user accounts will be created on this computer).
   b. Include and exclude any personal libraries such as *Documents* or *Pictures* and locations like your *Desktop* and *Downloads* folders.
   c. Select any folders from the drives on your computer.

    d. If you'd like to regularly back up your entire system, ensure that the checkbox to include a system image of your device is checked. When you're happy with the settings, click **Next**.

5. At this point, you can choose the schedule on which you want this backup to run, which can be daily, weekly, or monthly.
6. Click **Save Settings and Run Backup** to take the first full backup of your data.

You now have a regular backup of your folders to either an external or network drive on your Windows system.

#33: Using macOS Time Machine

Apple devices come with their own built-in solution for backing up your data called *Time Machine*, accessed via **System Settings ▸ Time Machine** (Figure 9-3).

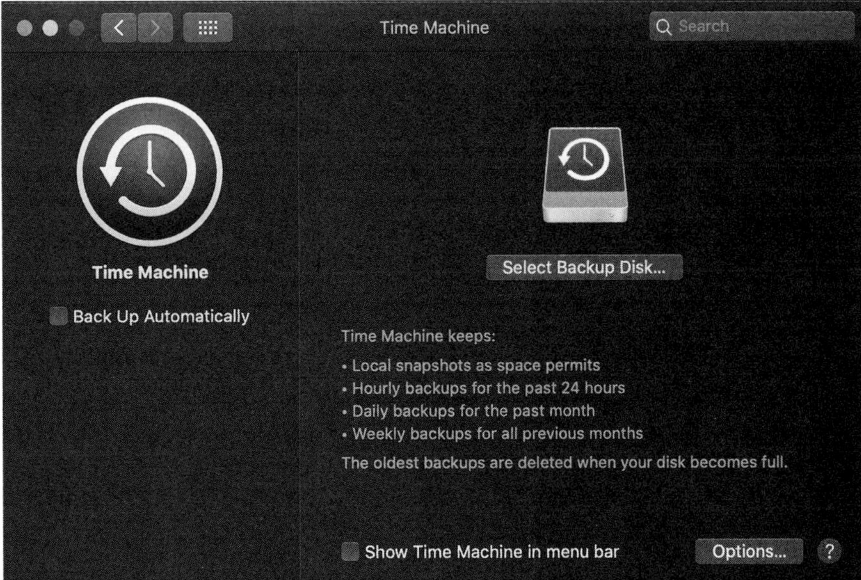

Figure 9-3: macOS Time Machine

Time Machine can back up your data either to an external drive directly connected to your computer or to network-attached storage. This network storage can be in the form of an Apple Airport Time Capsule (designed explicitly for Time Machine backups), a drive connected to an Apple Airport Extreme base station, another Mac that has been shared as a Time Machine backup destination, or a dedicated NAS device that supports Time Machine over SMB. If you have any of these in your network already, I recommend using that solution. If you don't have one of these available, the simplest and cheapest solution to back up your Mac is to use an external drive rather than a network location. Typically, when you plug in a high-capacity drive to your Apple device, you'll be presented with a prompt asking if you'd like to use that drive for Time Machine backups. Alternatively, you can select a specific backup disk using the Select Backup Disk option shown in Figure 9-3.

Time Machine doesn't provide the option to schedule backups; it'll back up your data at predefined times. Time Machine keeps 24-hourly snapshots of your data, rolling daily backups for one month, and rolling weekly backups for as long as there's space remaining on your backup drive. Once the space is exhausted, Time Machine will delete its oldest backup set to accommodate the more recent versions of your data. Check **Back Up Automatically** to allow Time Machine to do so.

The options for selecting the data you want to back up are somewhat limited. By default, Time Machine will back up your entire device, including system files, applications, accounts, preferences, emails, music, photos, movies, and documents. Click **Options** to exclude any of these using the dialog shown in Figure 9-4.

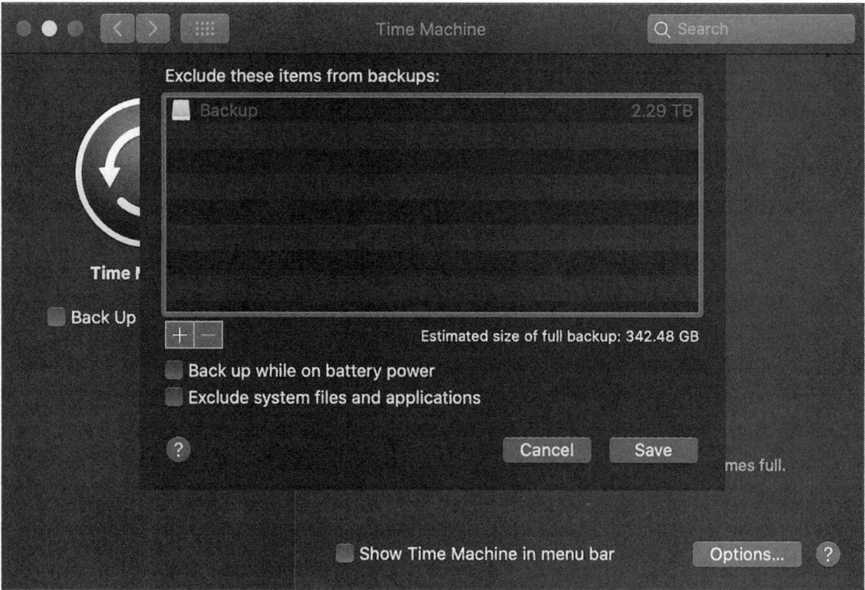

Figure 9-4: Time Machine backup options

Overall, Time Machine is a robust solution for backing up and restoring your Apple endpoints.

#34: Using Linux duplicity

In Ubuntu, several utilities are available for creating backups of your files. The easiest to use is *duplicity*, a command line utility that creates full and incremental backup archives to local storage, external hard drives, or network locations. Use the following command to install duplicity on your Ubuntu endpoints:

```
$ sudo apt install duplicity
```

Once the command completes, execute duplicity with the `-h` option to display its help file and confirm the installation was successful:

```
$ duplicity -h
Usage:
  duplicity [full|incremental] [options] source_dir target_url
  duplicity [restore] [options] source_url target_dir
  duplicity verify [options] source_url target_dir
  duplicity collection-status [options] target_url
  duplicity list-current-files [options] target_url
  duplicity cleanup [options] target_url
  duplicity remove-older-than time [options] target_url
  duplicity remove-all-but-n-full count [options] target_url
  duplicity remove-all-inc-of-but-n-full count [options] target_url
  duplicity replicate source_url target_url
--snip--
```

Read through the output to familiarize yourself with the available options and configurations. In the following sections, we'll discuss some of the most commonly used features.

Creating Local Backups with duplicity

The following example uses duplicity to create an initial full backup of a user's home directory, saving the output to the */tmp/* directory on the local system:

```
$ duplicity /home/user file:///tmp/
Last full backup date: none
GnuPG passphrase for decryption:
Retype passphrase for decryption to confirm:
--------------[ Backup Statistics ]--------------
StartTime 1634779305.32
EndTime 1634779305.94
ElapsedTime 0.62 (0.62 seconds)
SourceFiles 139
SourceFileSize 5793461 (5.53 MB)
NewFiles 139
NewFileSize 5793461 (5.53 MB)
DeletedFiles 0
ChangedFiles 0
ChangedFileSize 0 (0 bytes)
ChangedDeltaSize 0 (0 bytes)
DeltaEntries 139
RawDeltaSize 5465781 (5.21 MB)
TotalDestinationSizeChange 660694 (645 KB)
Errors 0
-------------------------------------------------
```

Note that the target directory (where the backup archive will be saved) must have the *file://* prefix. The */tmp/* directory is a holding location for the backup; you should either move the backup elsewhere once completed or save the backup somewhere else. The first time this command is run, duplicity will take a full backup of the source files or folders. Subsequent execution of the same command will create incremental backups of the source data. The command outputs statistics, as shown in the listing, including the start and end time of the backup operation, how many files were included, and the total size of the backup archive. Backups created with duplicity must be protected with a passphrase.

To create another full backup, specify the `full` option, like so:

```
$ duplicity full /home/user file:///tmp/
```

Doing so will force duplicity to create a full, rather than an incremental, backup of the data.

Creating Network Backups with duplicity

Saving backups to a network location is preferable to saving them to a local folder for several reasons. Saving backups locally is risky, because if you lose access to the endpoint or it becomes otherwise unavailable, you have no backups to restore from in other locations. Also, if an adversary gains access to the system, they've gained access to your (encrypted) backups as well. Therefore, it's safer to save to a remote location like a fileserver. This can be achieved using the rsync functionality built in to duplicity. The following command assumes you've followed the instructions in Chapter 1 to create SSH keys and use SSH key authentication instead of password authentication. If this is not the case, go back and do so now. SSH key authentication requires the use of a public/private key pair that's shared between the local and remote endpoints, enabling them to perform cryptographically secure communication that offers greater security than the use of password or passphrase authentication.

```
$ duplicity /home/user rsync://user@server_ip//path/to/folder/
```

Once you've decided which files and folders you want to back up, and the backup location, schedule duplicity to create regular backups of your files using Crontab, a built-in Linux job discussed in detail in Project 27 on page 122:

```
$ sudo crontab -e
--snip--
# m h  dom mon dow   command
0 0 * * 1 duplicity /home/user rsync://user@server_ip//path/to/folder/
0 2 1 * * duplicity full /home/user rsync://user@server_ip//path/to/folder/
```

The `-e` option of the Crontab application indicates that you will edit the cron file and the scheduled jobs maintained by cron. The commands shown in the Crontab in this example schedule duplicity to run at midnight every day, create an incremental backup, and force a full backup to be created on the first day of every month at 2 AM.

Restoring duplicity Backups

Use the command line to restore backups created with duplicity:

```
$ duplicity restore file:///tmp/ /home/user/backup_folder_name/
```

Entering the restore command with a source and target path restores all files from the backup set to the specified location.

There are various options to restore specific files and folders from a backup set if required. Here's an example:

```
$ duplicity -t 3D --file-to-restore /home/user/Documents/test.txt \
    file:///tmp/ /home/user/Documents/restored_file
```

In this command, we invoke duplicity, tell it to restore the version of the *test.txt* file (specified immediately after the `--file-to-restore` argument) from three days ago with the `-t 3D` parameters from the backup we created in the */tmp/* folder on the local system, and we then save the resulting file to the */home/user/Documents/* folder. For more information on restoring files and the options available, review duplicity's man page.

Additional duplicity Considerations

The duplicity utility has several other powerful options. You might want to exclude certain files or folders from your backups; for example, you'll often want to exclude system folders when creating backups of user data. Use the `--exclude` argument to exclude files and folders:

```
$ duplicity --exclude /proc --exclude /mnt / file:///tmp/
```

Once your backups have run to completion, use the `verify` parameter and swap the source and target locations from your original backup command to confirm they were created successfully:

```
$ duplicity verify file:///tmp/ /home/user/
Local and Remote metadata are synchronized, no sync needed.
--snip--
Verify complete: 325 files compared, 0 differences found.
```

If the output reveals no errors, your backups were successful.

There will be times when you want to delete older backups, either because they're no longer needed or to free up space for newer backups. First, review the available backups in your backup set using the `collection-status` parameter:

```
$ duplicity collection-status file:///tmp/
--snip--
Collection Status
-----------------
Connecting with backend: BackendWrapper
Archive dir: /home/user/.cache/duplicity/c2731c0788339744944161fd8afb74dd
```

```
Found 1 secondary backup chain.
Secondary chain 1 of 1:
-------------------------
Chain start time: Wed Oct 20 19:53:09 2022
Chain end time: Wed Oct 29 20:11:39 2022
Number of contained backup sets: 2
Total number of contained volumes: 2
 Type of backup set:                            Time:      Num volumes:
                Full         Wed Oct 20 19:53:09 2022                 1
         Incremental         Wed Oct 29 20:11:39 2022                 1
-------------------------

Found primary backup chain with matching signature chain:
-------------------------
Chain start time: Wed Oct 20 20:11:53 2022
Chain end time: Wed Oct 20 20:11:53 2022
Number of contained backup sets: 1
Total number of contained volumes: 1
 Type of backup set:                            Time:      Num volumes:
                Full         Wed Oct 20 20:11:53 2022                 1
-------------------------
No orphaned or incomplete backup sets found.
```

Once you know how many backups are in your backup set and how old they are, you can delete older backups based on age:

```
$ duplicity remove-older-than 3D file:///tmp/
```

The `3D` means older than three days.

You also can remove all but the desired number of full backups:

```
$ duplicity remove-all-but-n-full 1 file:///tmp/
```

Here the `1` indicates to duplicity that it should delete all but the most recent full backup from the backup set. Read duplicity's man page to become familiar with the available options for creating, restoring, or deleting backups.

Cloud Backup Solutions

Although cloud services like Google Drive and Dropbox are not true backups, they're capable of keeping a secondary copy of your local data in the cloud (akin to an offsite backup), keeping tertiary copies on your other systems, and maintaining a version history of each of your files—and they do all of this consistently and regularly. Most of these services come with some level of free storage as well, so you can try them out and upgrade to a paid plan if you decide they work for you.

Google Drive and Dropbox are generally designed for file sharing and online collaboration rather than for backing up data. Using a service geared explicitly toward backing up data, although not free, will generally provide more features, granular control, and storage at a lower cost. Backblaze and Carbonite are two reliable cloud backup services that encrypt your data locally and automatically back it up using a client application on your computer. Backblaze will back up your files, and Carbonite is capable of backing up your entire computer. In general, look for services that encrypt your data both at rest and in transit. Carbonite and Backblaze are currently available for Mac, Windows, and Linux.

Backblaze

Backblaze is a great option if you want a set-and-forget backup solution. Once downloaded and installed, it immediately begins backing up your files to the Backblaze cloud servers and will continuously do so unless set to do otherwise. Virtual machine files and folders are the only data automatically excluded, although you can remove those from the exclusions list. You'll be able to back up not only your computer's internal hard drive but any attached external drives as well. Backblaze maintains all versions of your files for the previous 30 days, which can be extended to one year or more with an additional fee. You can restore your files from the application (shown in Figure 9-5), the web UI, the mobile app, or by having Backblaze physically mail your files to you on a USB drive.

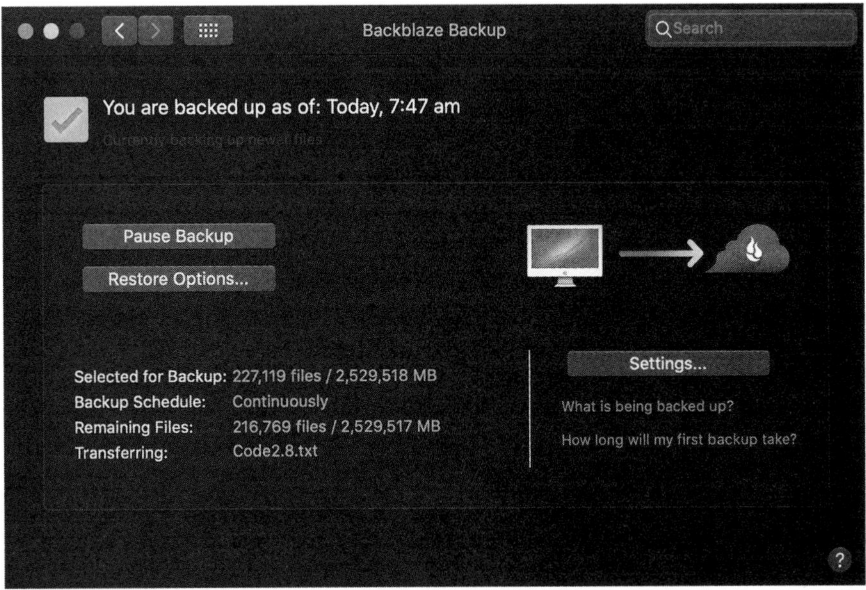

Figure 9-5: Backblaze GUI

The security features Backblaze offers are worth considering. Your files are first encrypted by the application, are transferred to the cloud using SSL (encrypted transmission), and are then stored, encrypted, on the Backblaze servers. Even better, you're able to configure your own decryption key, so Backblaze itself is unable to decrypt your data, which adds another layer of complexity for any adversary who might gain access to your encrypted data. You also can add two-factor authentication so that, in addition to your password, your decryption key, and your email address, anyone who wants to access your data, including yourself, requires a one-time password. With all of those features combined, any third party trying to access your data will have a lot of layers of defense to contend with. Additionally, Backblaze is one of the cheapest cloud backup solutions available.

Carbonite

If you need a backup provider capable of restoring your entire computer in the event of catastrophic failure, Carbonite is one possible solution. In extreme cases, like the event of ransomware, having the capability to restore your computer all the way down to the operating system settings and configuration in addition to your critical files is beneficial because you might find the entire operating system becomes corrupted or otherwise unusable. Carbonite has several plans at tiered price points so you can choose the level of cover for your specific needs. As with Backblaze, Carbonite locally encrypts all the data it backs up, which is sent to the cloud over SSL and encrypted on the Carbonite servers. Depending on the plan you choose, it's capable of backing up external hard drives and provides unlimited cloud storage (in some cases). Carbonite will also keep your backed-up files for an unlimited amount of time, and it won't delete file versions older than 30 days.

Once you've downloaded and installed the application (shown in Figure 9-6), it'll start uploading the first backup of your data automatically. You can tell it which files to include or exclude.

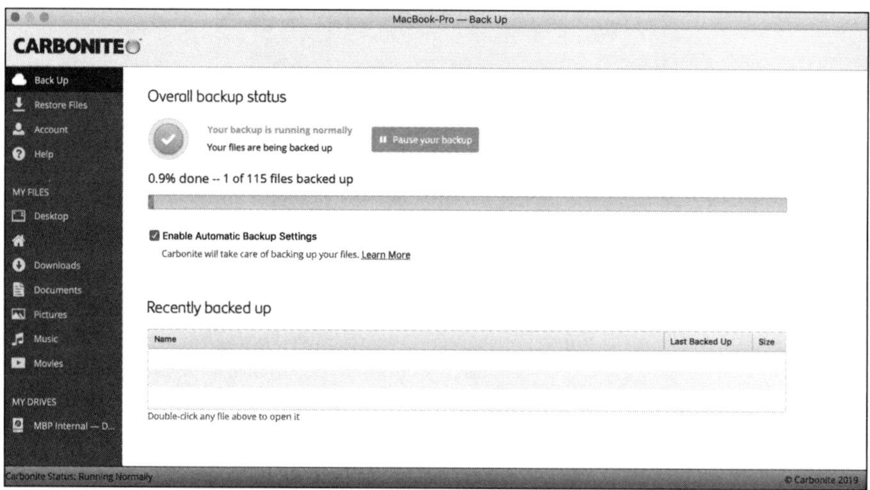

Figure 9-6: Carbonite GUI

Carbonite, like Backblaze, will run in the background, continuously backing up your data. When you want to restore a file from your backup, you can do so through the application. There is no web UI or mobile app available.

Virtual Machine Snapshots

Virtual machines provide a lot of benefits not seen in physical computers. They're able to share hardware (processors and RAM), are fast to start up or reboot, and can be created with just the right amount of resources for their specific purpose. One of the best things about them is the capability to create *snapshots*.

A virtual machine snapshot is a copy of that virtual machine at a given point in time. A snapshot generally includes all information related to a virtual machine at the time the snapshot is taken, including its power state (on, off, or paused/suspended), the contents of its virtual memory, and the contents of its virtual hard disk.

Whenever you're making significant changes to a virtual machine, it's wise to create a snapshot of that machine beforehand to protect yourself from the eventuality that your modifications will break your virtual machine. Having a snapshot just before the changes that rendered your virtual machine unusable allows you to revert to the known-good configuration as if the changes were never made in the first place. It's like a real-life undo button.

All major virtual machine software (such as VMware, VirtualBox, and Hyper-V) are capable of creating snapshots of the virtual machines they manage. Figure 9-7 shows an example of VMware's Snapshot Manager.

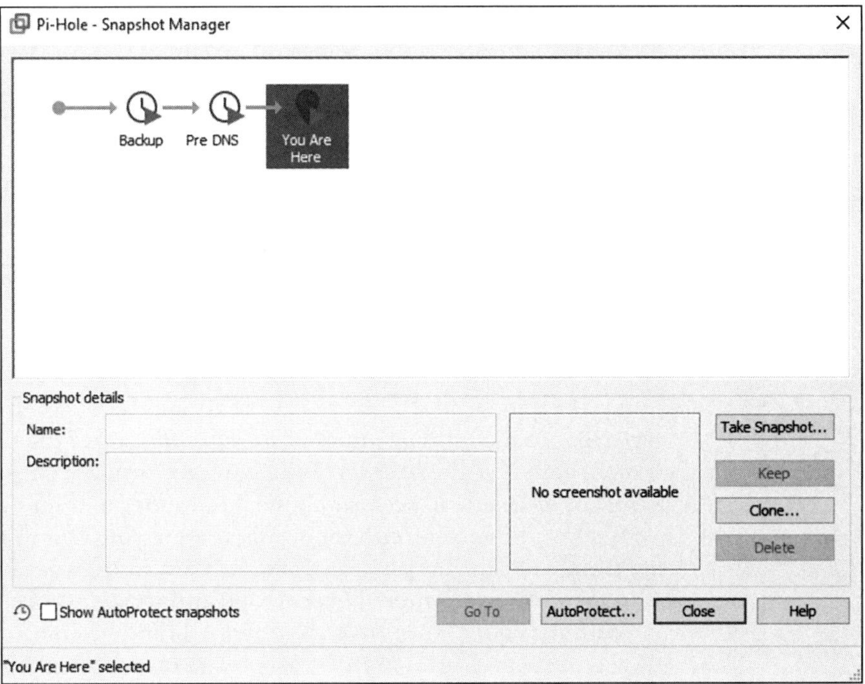

Figure 9-7: VMware Snapshot Manager

From within Snapshot Manager, you can create a new snapshot with the Take Snapshot button, go to a specific snapshot (that is, revert the virtual machine to the point in time a given snapshot was taken), delete or clone a snapshot, or enable AutoProtect, a feature that creates snapshots on a predefined schedule, allowing you to revert to a snapshot from multiple points in the past. Snapshots are available in most hypervisors, but the settings and options might differ slightly.

While snapshots aren't a backup in the literal sense, they are useful for restoring a working virtual machine configuration. You shouldn't use snapshots as your only means of backing up, but including them as part of your strategy is often handy. A sensible solution would be to include all the virtual machine files in your regular backup strategy.

Testing and Restoring Backups

Once you've created your backup strategy and your most important data is being regularly backed up onsite and offsite, it's important to test these backups at regular intervals. If you suffer a loss of data and try to restore it from your backup only to find out it has become corrupt, your backup strategy is providing no value.

To restore your files on Windows, open the **Backup and Restore** menu. Click **Restore My Files** or **Restore All Users' Files**. You can look through the contents of your backups by using the Browse for Files or Browse for Folders options. You can also search the contents of your backup via this menu.

To restore your files on a Mac using Time Machine, browse to the folder from which you want to restore files, such as your Documents or Downloads folder. Open Time Machine and then use the arrows and timeline to browse the available local snapshots and backups. Select one or more of the items you want to restore and then click **Restore**. This can include files, folders, or your entire disk. Restored items will return to their original location on your computer.

To restore files using Carbonite, Backblaze, or any other solution, open the web portal or the application GUI. Then, locate the files or folders you want to restore and follow the instructions provided.

When your first full backup of any system has been created, test a few files or folders at random to restore. It may be worth finding some larger files to include as part of this test, as the larger the file, the higher chance there is of the backup failing partway through. If you restore a sample of data and all seems well, set a reminder to do the same again in a week and then a month following. If all of your test restorations go smoothly, you can choose how often you want to test your backups from that point forward. Somewhere between one and six months is prudent.

With that done, your backup strategy should be complete and robust enough to recover from pretty much any data loss event or disaster.

Summary

The solutions discussed in this chapter will be adequate for most situations, but they aren't guaranteed to fit your needs. When looking for a backup solution, ensure that the one you choose is right for your operating system, allows for the creation of backups containing the data you want to back up (and nothing else), and is capable of the type of backups you want to create. It should also be capable of automatically creating backups on a schedule or creating a backup of your data constantly. Finally, make sure that, once backed up, you're able to restore your data within a reasonable timeframe and high confidence in the integrity of the restored data.

10

MONITORING YOUR NETWORK WITH DETECTION AND ALERTING

Network monitoring provides real-time visibility into your network activity, enabling you to stay ahead of potential threats and (ideally) stop adversaries before they've performed any disruptive action. Monitoring your network is a huge undertaking, so alerts are often a useful starting point for investigations. Without meaningful alerts, network monitoring is like finding a needle in a haystack—trying to identify malicious activity within a very large dataset.

Your firewalls, proxies, antivirus, and other solutions should be up and running for at least a month before you start trying to actively monitor your hosts and network traffic, just to ensure they're functioning correctly. Up until this point, everything has been relatively passive; once set up, no further input from you is required, unless you need to update or change the configuration.

Due to their nature, active monitoring and alerting can take considerable time and effort—not only to implement but to maintain, and that is especially true as a network expands. Not only will you need to check in regularly to see whether your network monitoring software has identified any threats or unusual behavior, but you'll also need to investigate this behavior and potentially work to mitigate the identified activity. Depending on the size of the network, monitoring it could be a full-time job for one or more people.

This chapter will arm you with the knowledge and tools required to monitor your network and alert you to suspicious behavior successfully. We'll discuss how, when, and where to implement network traffic access points (TAPs) and a switch port analyzer (SPAN) in your network to enable network traffic capture, monitoring, and analysis. Finally, we'll build a network monitoring appliance using Security Onion—a free suite of network security monitoring tools—and discuss how best to utilize its built-in capabilities.

Network Monitoring Methods

You can use several methods to monitor and capture network traffic for real-time or post-facto analysis and alerting. The method you choose depends mostly on your network's hardware, as each device has different capabilities. We'll discuss two of the most common methods in the following sections.

Network Traffic Access Points

In small networks without switches, you can install a network *traffic access point (TAP)* to monitor the data that passes through it. A TAP is an inline device, placed between two nodes on a network; it becomes an extension of the transmission medium (like an Ethernet cable) that already exists between those two devices. In Figure 10-1, the TAP is between the firewall and router.

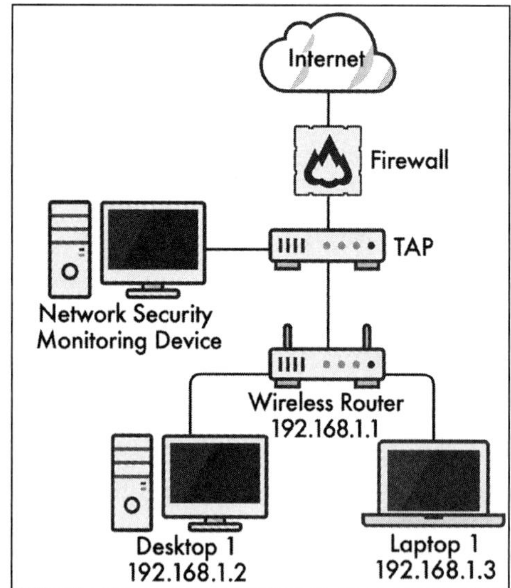

Figure 10-1: Placement of a network TAP

In this configuration, all traffic passing between the router and the firewall is sent by the TAP to a monitoring device, where it's stored for analysis.

> **TAPS AND INTRUSION DETECTION SYSTEMS**
>
> Coupling TAPs with an *intrusion detection system (IDS)* allows administrators to identify suspicious activity occurring across this ingress and egress point. An IDS is a software or hardware tool that uses a set of rules or signatures to identify known-bad behavior. When an IDS identifies something suspicious in your network traffic, it will generate an alert that you can investigate to decide whether it's actually malicious (a true positive) or benign (a false positive). You can then ignore the alert or take action to mitigate and remediate the problem, which we'll discuss at length later.

When placing a TAP, consider what you actually want to see and investigate. In a configuration like the one shown in Figure 10-1, you'd capture all the traffic between your endpoints and the firewall (the network's boundary). Monitoring your major egress point lets you investigate things like *data exfiltration*, where an adversary is trying to steal your data by sending it outside your network. However, with this configuration, you won't be able to see traffic between your endpoint devices, as that is handled by the wireless router and never reaches the TAP.

If you placed the TAP behind the firewall (as opposed to on the internet side), you wouldn't see any traffic from the internet attempting to reach the internal network that's blocked by the firewall. If the TAP is in front of the firewall, you wouldn't see the outbound traffic being blocked by the firewall; the security monitoring system also would lose the protection of that firewall and become an easy route into your network. Decide which of those scenarios you're comfortable with and place your TAP accordingly. In most cases, it's best to place the TAP behind the firewall (inside your network) and review the firewall logs for what the TAP doesn't see.

A TAP is an inline device. Be aware that if the TAP becomes unavailable or goes offline—if any of its limited network ports fail—your entire network will lose access to the internet. Your endpoint devices should still be able to communicate with each other via the router, but traffic will no longer pass through the TAP.

Several TAP devices are available at reasonable prices. One of the simplest is the *Dualcomm ETAP*. One possible configuration of such a TAP would be to connect the firewall in Figure 10-1 to the A inline port, connect the B inline port to the wireless router, and connect a separate cable to the monitoring port of your network security monitoring device (discussed in the next section). Such a configuration would allow traffic to flow through the TAP as if it wasn't there, except that it would be intercepted, monitored, and analyzed by the network security monitoring system.

Switch Port Analyzers

An alternative to a network TAP is the *switch port analyzer (SPAN)* or *mirror port* (interchangeable terms) functionality provided by a switch. A SPAN does the same thing as a TAP; it mirrors (or copies) all the data passing through a source port(s) to the destination SPAN port on the switch. Your network security monitoring system is then connected to the SPAN port to capture the network traffic for analysis and alerting. In most modern switches, it's possible to create a SPAN configuration with multiple source ports, so you can capture data from any port(s) on a switch.

A SPAN configuration in a small network might look like the one shown Figure 10-2, where the firewall or other system provides IP addresses to endpoints. Each host is connected by Ethernet to a port on the switch, and then the network security monitoring device is connected to the SPAN configured on the switch. Unlike TAPs, if a port on the switch fails, the rest of the network continues functioning, but if the entire switch goes offline due to a power failure, the entire network will go down with it.

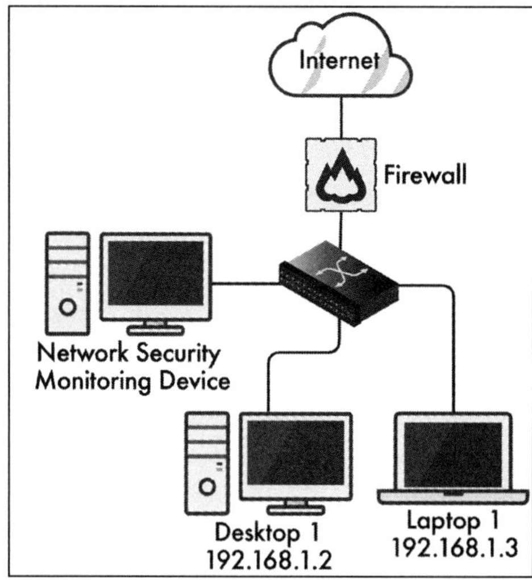

Figure 10-2: A small network with a switch and SPAN port

Unlike a TAP configuration, with a SPAN set up on a switch, you'll be able to capture and analyze computer-to-computer traffic in addition to inbound and outbound data. You'll still have the placement issue, though; when the switch is on the internal side of the firewall (as it should be), your security monitoring system won't have visibility over the traffic blocked by the firewall.

#35: Configuring a SPAN Port

To configure a SPAN port on a managed switch, like the Netgear switch that we used in Chapter 2, follow these steps:

1. Log in to the switch with administrator credentials.
2. Select **System ▸ Monitoring ▸ Mirroring**.
3. In the Port Mirroring Configuration table that appears, click the source ports from which you want to capture network traffic to select them. Selected ports will have a check mark.
4. In the Destination Port drop-down box, enter the port to use as the SPAN port you'll connect to your security monitoring system.
5. Finally, in the Mirroring drop-down menu, select **Enable ▸ Apply**.

Whether you choose to set up a TAP or a switch with a SPAN port, you'll need a network monitoring solution capable of aggregating collected data. The best solution currently available for small networks is Security Onion, which includes various components for capturing and aggregating network data and enables you to quickly analyze that data.

Security Onion

Security Onion is an open source platform for threat hunting, network security monitoring, and log management. It's an operating system, like Ubuntu, that includes several open source tools we'll utilize to monitor our network for security and configuration issues.

Security Onion's tools include suricata, an intrusion detection system, and zeek, a software framework for analyzing network traffic to identify anomalous behavior. Grafana is a set of visualizations and dashboards for monitoring the health of the Security Onion system, and osquery gathers data about the endpoints in your network and the operating systems they're running for analysis. Wazuh is similar to osquery; it's an agent-based tool that gathers analyzable data from your endpoints and is used for active endpoint detection and response (in the case of a security incident). Finally, Strelka is a real-time file-scanning utility that analyzes network traffic and scans any files traversing the network; it's useful for identifying malware or data exfiltration.

SECURITY ONION TOOLS FOR LARGER NETWORKS

Security Onion makes use of the ELK stack (which includes Elastic, Logstash, and Kibana) to create visualizations and dashboards. ELK is similar to Grafana, except where Grafana is used to display information about the system itself, ELK displays information about the network data being captured, allowing the user to view and analyze the data easily. ELK is a powerful tool but is outside the scope of this book as it is more advanced than the tools within Security Onion's security dashboard. However, many online resources discuss ELK and its use in great detail if you'd like to investigate it further.

Security Onion is designed to be scalable and is capable of monitoring very large networks, so it includes tools that aren't necessary on small networks, such as TheHive, an incident management system, and Playbook, a tool for creating incident management playbooks; those tools are primarily used in larger networks, so they aren't covered here.

In the following sections, we'll discuss creating your network security monitoring system using Security Onion and its built-in tools. We'll explore how to utilize these tools to start monitoring your network, and how to triage and investigate problems when they arise. It's up to you whether you'd like to buy or build your Security Onion appliance. Security Onion Solutions has preconfigured appliances ready to go out of the box.

#36: Building a Security Onion System

To build a Security Onion system, you'll need a device with a minimum of two network interfaces: a management interface and a capture interface (connected to the TAP or SPAN). We'll use an Intel NUC (a small form factor computing unit) with two Ethernet ports, which is very customizable and available at various price points depending on your budget and requirements. The following minimum hardware specifications are detailed in the Security Onion documentation:

- 12GB of RAM
- Four CPU cores
- 200GB of storage
- Two network interfaces

One additional consideration is how much storage you need. For reference, a NUC with an internal storage space of 2TB might be capable of storing around three weeks of data, depending on the number of devices, number of users, and amount of network traffic in your network. After that point, the data will be kept on a rolling cycle, where older data is deleted in favor of newer data. To enable better incident response capabilities in your network, the more data you keep, the better. If you discover an adversary in your network that has been there for 12 months but you have only one month of data, you'll never be able to determine root cause, making it difficult to kick them out and prevent the problem from recurring.

Once you have a NUC (or similar device), you'll install Security Onion. At this stage, it's also a good idea to connect the network port you plan to use for management (*not* the port you'll use for capturing network traffic) to your network so you can set up its configuration. It doesn't matter which of the two network ports you use for management and traffic capture. This device will need a static IP address, and while you could do that on the device itself, it's better to configure the static addressing on your router or whichever device is responsible for IP address leases in your environment (like your wireless router or pfSense device). Having the management port on your NUC (and only this port) connected will make it easier to identify when installing and configuring the rest of the software. After this process is complete, you can then configure the capture port independently. You should configure the static IP address for the management interface now, as some of the agents we'll install have requirements and dependencies based on this address, so changing it later can create challenges.

Installing Security Onion

You can install Security Onion from an ISO file (available directly from Security Onion Solutions at *https://securityonionsolutions.com/software/*) or manually using CentOS 7 as the base operating system and then installing the Security Onion package like any other application in a Linux environment (note that CentOS 7 is the only OS supported by Security Onion). Using the ISO file is a simpler and faster method of creating a Security Onion system, whereas manual installation requires slightly more effort. However, manual installation allows you to have more granular control over things like disk partitioning. If that is of interest to you, choose the manual installation method. If not, install Security Onion using the ISO file.

Installing Security Onion from the ISO File

Start by downloading the latest ISO from Security Onion Solutions, and follow the procedure outlined in Chapter 1's "Creating a Physical Linux System" to create a bootable USB drive from the ISO file. Plug your bootable USB into your NUC, turn on the NUC, and you'll be presented with the Security Onion installation wizard. Follow these steps to complete the installation:

1. The wizard will prompt you to install Security Onion, destroying all data and partitions. Type **yes** and press ENTER to accept this and begin the installation process.
2. Enter an administrator username when prompted; then press ENTER.

3. Enter a strong passphrase for the user; then press ENTER.
4. Repeat the passphrase to confirm it; then press ENTER to initiate the installation.
5. Once installation completes, the computer will reboot. Log in with your newly created credentials and the Security Onion setup wizard will pop up. Press ENTER to continue.
6. Using the arrow keys, select **Install** to run the standard Security Onion installation; then press ENTER.

   At this point, the process for completing the installation of Security Onion is the same for both the ISO file installation and the manual installation paths. Jump to the section "Completing the Security Onion Installation" on page 157.

Installing Security Onion Manually

You can install Security Onion entirely from scratch by installing CentOS 7 on your NUC and then installing the Security Onion packages and tools on top. To do this, follow these steps:

1. Download the most recent CentOS 7 ISO (the correct format is x86_64) from *https://www.centos.org/*.
2. Follow the procedure outlined in Chapter 1's "Creating a Physical Linux System" section to create a bootable USB drive from the ISO file.
3. Plug your bootable USB into your NUC and boot from the USB. You'll be presented with a few options; choose **Test this Media & Install CentOS 7**.
4. At this point, a graphical installation wizard appears. Select your desired language and click **Continue**.
5. Set the correct time zone and keyboard layout.
6. Under Software Selection, it's recommended to choose **Server with GUI** for ease of administration.
7. Under System ▸ Installation Destination, select the internal disk where you plan to install Security Onion and then choose **I Will Configure Partitioning**. Click **Done** to proceed to the partitioning wizard. Partitioning defines how the hard drive storage will be divided among the users and applications on the system.
8. Select **LVM Partitioning** and create the following partitions:
   a. */boot*: CentOS will boot from this partition; it should have at least 500MB of space available.
   b. */boot/efi*: Part of the boot partition; it should be at least 500MB.
   c. */*: The root of the filesystem; should be 300GB.
   d. */tmp*: For temporary files; should be 2GB.

   e. swap: For swap files; should be 8GB.
   f. */home*: A space for any user files; should be 40GB.
   g. */nsm*: For all the security tools and captured data; it should be assigned the remainder of drive space.
9. Click **Done ▸ Accept Changes** to write the changes to disk.
10. Click **Begin Installation** to install the operating system.
11. Set your root passphrase and create a non-root, administrative account on the following screen. If you want to connect to this system via SSH, ensure that your administrative account has a strong passphrase.
12. Once the installation is complete, reboot the machine and remove the installation USB. Then, boot to your CentOS operating system.
13. Accept the license information.
14. You might need to turn the network card on to enable the network. Click **Network & Host Name**, toggle the network button to **On**, and then click **Done**.
15. Click **Finish Configuration**.

With CentOS installed, next install Security Onion. First, connect to your server via SSH or log in directly. Change directory to the */nsm* partition you created during the initial setup:

```
$ cd /nsm
```

Use `sudo yum install` to install Git (an application for software management) and then `git clone` to download Security Onion:

```
$ sudo yum install git -y
$ sudo git clone \
      https://github.com/Security-Onion-Solutions/securityonion
```

(Whereas Ubuntu is based on Debian Linux and uses the `apt` utility to manage software packages, CentOS is based on Red Hat Linux and uses `yum`.)

Navigate to the newly created *securityonion* directory and run the setup script:

```
$ cd /nsm/securityonion/
$ sudo bash so-setup-network
```

Running this script starts an interactive installation wizard that leads you through the initial setup and configuration of your Security Onion server.

Completing the Security Onion Installation

Now that the basic configuration of the operating system has been completed, you'll start installing and configuring the tools you'll use to monitor and analyze the network traffic. Zeek is a security monitoring platform that will enable you to analyze network traffic more efficiently and alert on suspicious activity within your network automatically. It does this by utilizing rulesets containing information on suspicious or malicious activity, software, and network traffic, such as the ETOPEN ruleset you'll use here.

Regardless of how you've installed Security Onion, follow these steps to complete the process:

1. Press ENTER to continue past the welcome screen (and to progress to all other screens).
2. On the Installation Type page, navigate to STANDALONE with the arrow keys, and press the spacebar to select the option.
3. If you used the Security Onion ISO, select **Standard** on the next page to indicate that this machine has internet access.
4. If you performed the manual installation of Security Onion, type **AGREE** to accept the Elastic License on the next page.
5. On the next page, keep the default hostname for simplicity or change it if you like (in larger installations that have more than one server, changing the hostname will be beneficial). If prompted to change the hostname, choose to proceed anyway.
6. On the next page, enter a short description for this computer or leave it blank.
7. On the network card configuration page, shown in Figure 10-3, select the interface with the words *Link UP* next to it as the management interface. It should be the only interface plugged into the network at this point.

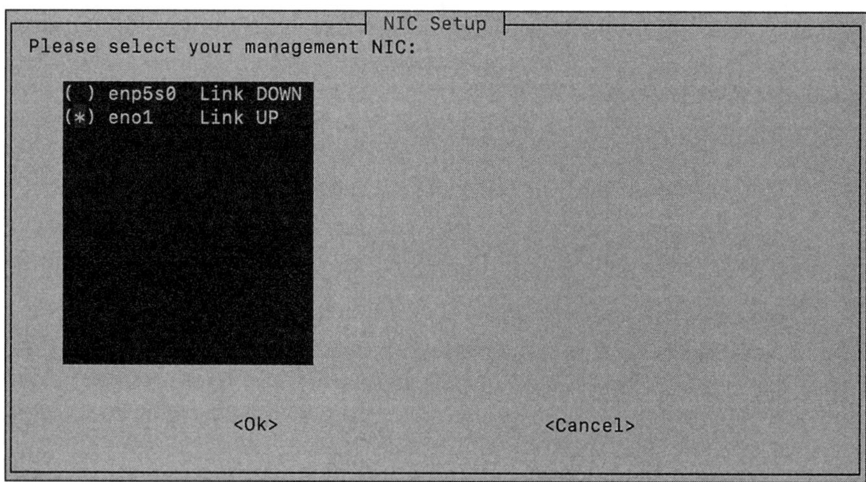

Figure 10-3: NIC setup wizard

8. Press the spacebar to set the monitor interface.

   On the management interface page, you may receive an informational error about using DHCP; as long as you've configured a static address for this device, you can ignore this message.

9. When asked how this computer should connect to the internet, select **Direct**.
10. Select **Automatic** on the OS Patch Schedule page to keep your operating system automatically up-to-date.
11. Specify your home network address range, identified in Chapter 1. If your network uses 10.0.0.0/8 addresses, leave that in the box provided and delete the other two subnets. If your network uses 192.168.0.0/16 addresses, keep that in the box and delete the other two, and so on.
12. When asked which type of manager to install, select **BASIC**.
13. Select **ZEEK** as the tool to use to generate metadata.
14. Select **ETOPEN** as the IDS ruleset to use to generate alerts.

NOTE *ETOPEN is an open source ruleset updated regularly with new and emerging threats and alerts. ETPRO and TALOS are similar to ETOPEN, but they require a subscription. For small networks, ETOPEN is sufficient.*

15. The wizard then asks which components of the Security Onion suite of tools you want to install. Select **Osquery**, **Wazuh**, and **Strelka**.
16. If asked if you'd like to keep the default Docker IP range, select **Yes**.
17. Enter your email address for the Security Onion administrator.
18. Enter and re-enter the password for your account.
19. When asked how you will access the web interface, select **IP**.
20. Set a strong passphrase for the *soremote* user account (for performing some administrative actions).
21. Choose **BASIC** to install the network security monitoring components with the recommended settings.
22. Type **2** for the number of Zeek and Suricata processes.

    The number of processes dictates how much network traffic your system can process. For small networks, two processes should be sufficient; you can change this later if necessary.

23. If asked if you'd like to configure NTP servers, choose **Yes**. Network Time Protocol (NTP) is used to keep endpoints synchronized. It's best to keep your monitoring server in sync with a time server to prevent time drift, which can cause issues when troubleshooting alerts. Browse to *https://www.ntppool.org/* and choose an NTP server in your region to keep your Security Onion server's time in sync.

24. Select **NODEBASIC** when asked.
25. Run **so-allow** by pressing ENTER when asked to correctly configure the firewall on the system to allow access to all the tools being installed.

When asked for an IP address to allow access to your network monitoring system, you can choose to allow access to the Security Onion web interfaces from a single computer or device or from any host in your network. For security purposes, you allow access only from a single IP address.

26. Enter the IP address you plan to use; then press ENTER.
27. Finally, accept the configuration you've just created by pressing TAB to select **Yes**; then press ENTER to finish the setup wizard and commit the changes.

NOTE *Security Onion and some of its tools, like Zeek, can run in a cluster configuration, where the agents are installed on multiple systems for enhanced data collection and processing. In small networks, a stand-alone system is sufficient. In larger networks with multiple network segments and switches, a cluster configuration might make more sense.*

At the end of the installation, the screen will display the URL to access the Security Onion web interface; write this down (it should be *http://<your_server_ip>/*). The system will reboot. Once it comes back up, you'll be able to log in via the URL using the email address and passphrase you entered earlier. To test the Security Onion configuration, run the following:

```
$ sudo so-status
```

This command lists the tools Security Onion is running and the status of each, which should appear as `OK` if everything worked.

If any services haven't started, wait a few minutes before running the status command again. If they still fail to start, try starting services manually using these commands:

```
$ sudo so-servicename-stop
$ sudo so-servicename-start
$ sudo so-servicename-restart
```

If you're still unable to get the services to start, reboot the computer. If all else fails, reinstall Security Onion.

Once you can access the Security Onion console, you'll see a menu on the left side that lists all the tools at your disposal (see Figure 10-4).

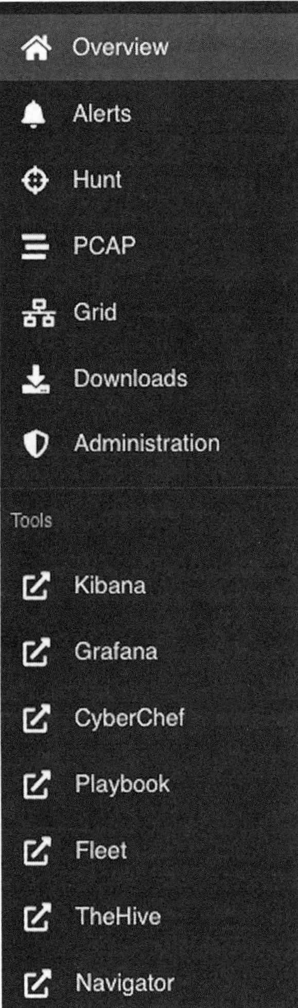

Figure 10-4: Security Onion tools

At this point, click **Kibana**, and a new tab will be launched in your browser. You should see a minimal number of records because you haven't plugged in the capture port on your device.

Connect this port to the SPAN or TAP you configured earlier. Once that's done, refresh the page after a few minutes to see Kibana populated with newly acquired data.

#37: Installing Wazuh

Security Onion's additional tools help you to understand what's happening in your network and take action to investigate, mitigate, and remediate issues when they arise. One of these packages is Wazuh.

Wazuh is an open source *endpoint detection and response (EDR)* platform that monitors your endpoints for malicious activity, alerts you within the Security Onion console, and provides the incident response capabilities of blocking network traffic, stopping malicious processes, and quarantining malware files.

Using agents like Wazuh can be controversial. In larger networks, oftentimes so much is going on that adding something new to the network, especially across all the systems, can cause stability issues or create/exacerbate challenges around limited resources like bandwidth. This is usually less of an issue in smaller networks because capacity isn't shared between so many devices, users, or processes, and there generally aren't as many solutions competing for resources.

Installing Wazuh won't have a meaningful impact on the daily operations of your small network. Conversely, the value you receive from the additional monitoring and security uplift far outweighs any potential negative consequences of using multiple agents. Ultimately, it's your decision whether to install these agents on one, some, or all of the endpoints in your network. The more complete your coverage and network monitoring, the more secure your network is likely to be.

This section provides instructions for installing the Wazuh agent on Windows, macOS, and Linux.

Installing Wazuh on Windows

To install the Wazuh agent on your Windows endpoint(s), follow these steps:

1. Log in to your Security Onion console and click **Downloads** in the left menu.
2. Click the **MSI** installer agent option to download the correct installer; then run the downloaded executable on your Windows computer.
3. Accept the license agreement and click **Install**.
4. Once the installation completes, tick the **Run Agent Configuration Interface** checkbox and click **Finish**.
5. To add this new system to your Security Onion, log in to Security Onion via SSH and run the `manage_agents` script. Following the prompts, add an agent with **`A`**, list agents with **`L`** to confirm the addition was successful, and extract the authentication key for your new agent with **`E`**:

```
$ sudo docker exec -it so-wazuh /var/ossec/bin/manage_agents
--snip--
Choose your action: A,E,L,R or Q: A
- Adding a new agent (use '\q' to return to the main menu).
  Please provide the following:
❶ * A name for the new agent: Test
   * The IP Address of the new agent: 192.168.1.50
Confirm adding it?(y/n): y
Agent added with ID 002.
--snip--
Choose your action: A,E,L,R or Q: L
```

```
Available agents:
   ID: 001, Name: securityonion, IP: 192.168.1.49
❷ ID: 002, Name: Test, IP: 192.168.1.50
** Press ENTER to return to the main menu.
--snip--
Choose your action: A,E,L,R or Q: E
Available agents:
   ID: 001, Name: securityonion, IP: 192.168.1.49
   ID: 002, Name: Test, IP: 192.168.1.50
Provide the ID of the agent to extract the key (or '\q' to quit): 002
Agent key information for '002' is:
❸ MDAyIFJvcnkgMTkyLjE2OC4xL . . .
** Press ENTER to return to the main menu.
--snip--
Choose your action: A,E,L,R or Q: Q
manage_agents: Exiting.
```

You'll have to provide a name and IP address when you add an agent ❶. For the name, use the hostname of the computer being added. Run the `hostname` command to find the name:

```
$ hostname
Test
```

Find your IP address (see Project 8 in Chapter 1) or consult the asset list or network map you've been maintaining. When you list the agents, verify that an agent with that name and IP address is present ❷. Use the agent's ID number to get its authentication key ❸. Return to the main menu with ENTER and use the `Q` option to quit.

6. Open the **Wazuh Agent Manager** on your Windows computer (see Figure 10-5) and enter the IP address of your Security Onion system and the agent authentication key; click **Save**.

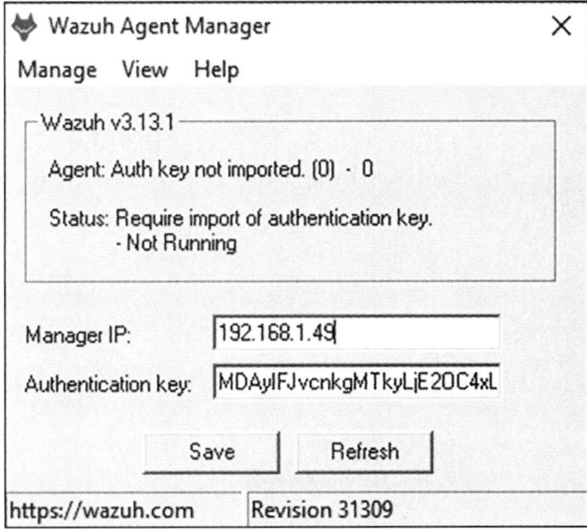

Figure 10-5: Wazuh agent configuration

7. Click **Manage ▸ Start** to start the agent.
8. Every time you add an agent or make a change to Security Onion or the systems that communicate with it, run the **so-allow** script to enable communication between the devices (otherwise, the host firewall on Security Onion will block it). You should do this at the terminal, logged in to the Security Onion system via SSH:

```
$ sudo so-allow
```

9. When prompted, enter **w** to add a firewall rule for a Wazuh agent; then enter the agent's IP address.

Wazuh will now manage this PC. Repeat the process for all other devices (computers, laptops, virtual machines, and so on) in your network that you want to manage in this way. System event logs will then start showing up in your Kibana dashboard, so expect to see new data and alerts in Security Onion.

Installing Wazuh on macOS

To install the Wazuh agent on your macOS endpoint(s), follow these steps:

1. Log in to your Security Onion console, click **Downloads**, and download the macOS package.
2. Run the installation wizard on your Mac.
3. Once complete, log in to your Security Onion system and run **sudo so-allow** to allow your Mac access through the firewall (this must be done before agent registration; otherwise, the agent won't be able to connect to the management server).
4. Following the prompts, choose the Wazuh registration service with **r** and enter the IP address of your endpoint.
5. Now, register the agent with the Security Onion server:

```
$ sudo /Library/Ossec/bin/agent-auth -m security_onion_IP
```

Next, you'll add the Security Onion's IP address to the agent configuration file on your Mac so the agent can communicate with the Security Onion server.

6. Open */Library/Ossec/etc/ossec.conf* with a text editor.
7. Find the following lines and change *MANAGER_IP* to your Security Onion server's IP address:

```
<client>
  <server>
    <address>MANAGER_IP</address>
```

8. Restart the Wazuh agent:

```
$ sudo /Library/Ossec/bin/ossec-control restart
```

9. Confirm the agent has been successfully configured by listing the agents on the Security Onion server; run the *manage_agents* script and enter `L` when prompted for an action:

```
$ sudo docker exec -it so-wazuh /var/ossec/bin/manage_agents
--snip--
Choose your action: A,E,L,R or Q: L
Available agents:
   ID: 001, Name: securityonion, IP: 192.168.1.49
   ID: 002, Name: Computer1, IP: 192.168.1.50
   ID: 003, Name: MacBook-Pro.local, IP: 192.168.1.51
** Press ENTER to return to the main menu.
--snip--
Choose your action: A,E,L,R or Q: Q
manage_agents: Exiting.
```

If you see the hostname and IP address of the Mac, the agent is active. Return to the main menu with ENTER and use the `Q` option to quit.

Installing Wazuh on Linux

To install the Wazuh agent on your Linux endpoint(s), follow these steps:

1. Log in to your Security Onion console, click **Downloads**, and download the relevant package. For Ubuntu, this will be the DEB package (it'll be the RPM package for CentOS and Fedora).

   You can download the package directly from your Ubuntu system, or you can download the package to your Windows or Mac computer and transfer it to your Ubuntu system:

   ```
   $ rsync -ruhP wazuh-agent.deb user@linux_ip:/home/user
   ```

   When installing packages directly from package files (like *.deb* files), use the dpkg utility instead of the APT package manager (dpkg is the Debian package manager and is used similarly to APT).

2. To install the Wazuh agent, run the following:

   ```
   $ sudo dpkg -i wazuh-agent_3.13.1-1_amd64.deb
   ```

   Your package's version number may be different.

3. Next, log in to your Security Onion system via SSH and run `sudo so-allow` to allow your Linux system access through the firewall.
4. Following the prompts, choose the Wazuh registration service with `r` and enter your endpoint's IP address.
5. Register the Linux agent and connect it to the Wazuh management server (that is, the Security Onion server):

```
$ sudo /var/ossec/bin/agent-auth -m security_onion_IP
```

6. Then, modify the configuration file on your Linux system to allow it to communicate with the management server by changing the `MANAGER_IP` placeholder in the *ossec.conf* file to the IP address of your Security Onion server:

```
$ sudo nano /var/ossec/etc/ossec.conf
--snip--
<client>
  <server>
    <address>security_onion_IP</address>
--snip--
```

7. Restart the Wazuh agent to start sending data to Security Onion with this:

```
$ sudo systemctl restart wazuh-agent
```

8. Finally, confirm the agent has been successfully configured by listing the agents on the Security Onion server; run the **manage_agents** script and enter **L** when prompted for an action:

```
$ sudo docker exec -it so-wazuh /var/ossec/bin/manage_agents
--snip--
Choose your action: A,E,L,R or Q: L
Available agents:
   ID: 001, Name: securityonion, IP: 192.168.1.49
   ID: 002, Name: Computer1, IP: 192.168.1.50
   ID: 003, Name: MacBook-Pro.local, IP: 192.168.1.51
   ID: 004, Name: Linux1, IP: 192.168.1.52
** Press ENTER to return to the main menu.
--snip--
Choose your action: A,E,L,R or Q: Q
manage_agents: Exiting.
```

9. If you see the Linux computer's hostname and IP address, the agent should be active. Press ENTER to return to the main menu, and enter **Q** to quit.

You can now manage all types of computers in your network with Wazuh.

#38: Installing osquery

osquery provides improved visibility within your network. It gathers endpoint data such as the operating system details, installed software, command-line history, and details of running processes; you can then query this data to identify suspicious activity or devices not in compliance with your security policies or configurations. When used together with Wazuh, these tools provide a detailed view of the systems in your network and what each of them is doing or being used for, legitimately or not. Once installed, osquery uses a user interface called Fleet to display and manage the details of your monitored endpoints.

Installing osquery on Windows

To install the osquery agent on your Windows endpoint(s), follow these steps:

1. Log in to your Security Onion console, click **Downloads**, and download the osquery package for Windows (the MSI file).
2. Execute this file on your Windows system and complete the installation wizard.

   Once osquery is installed, it'll be invisible and run in the background; there's no user interface to deal with.
3. Next, log in to your Security Onion system via SSH and run **`sudo so-allow`** to allow your computer and osquery access through the firewall. Enter **`o`** (for osquery) and the IP address of your Windows system when prompted.
4. To view and manage systems with osquery, log in to your Security Onion console. In the left menu, click the **Fleet** link to open the Fleet Manager Dashboard.

When you install osquery on an endpoint and after you run **`so-allow`** to enable communication between the osquery agent and the Security Onion server, your managed hosts should show up here as cards; it can take a few minutes for communication to begin.

Installing osquery on macOS

To install the osquery agent on your macOS endpoint(s), follow these steps:

1. Log in to your Security Onion console, click **Downloads**, and download the osquery package for Mac (the PKG file).
2. Run **`sudo so-allow`** on your Security Onion server and add your Mac to the list of allowed agents for osquery. Enter **`o`** (for osquery) and the IP address of your Mac when prompted.
3. Execute the file you downloaded and complete the installation wizard on your Mac.
4. Log in to the Fleet Manager Dashboard and click **Add New Host** to find your Fleet Secret.
5. Add your Fleet Secret to the */etc/so-launcher/secret* file using any text editor.
6. Update */etc/so-launcher/launcher.flags* so the hostname value is ***`security_onion_IP`*`:8090`** and the root directory value is **`/var/so-launcher/`*`security_onion_IP`*`-8090`**:

```
autoupdate
hostname 192.168.1.200:8090
root_directory /var/so-launcher/192.168.1.200-8090
osqueryd_path /usr/local/so-launcher/bin/osqueryd
enroll_secret_path /etc/so-launcher/secret
update_channel stable
root_pem /etc/so-launcher/roots.pem
```

7. Copy the contents of the */etc/ssl/certs/intca.crt* file on your Security Onion server into the */etc/so-launcher/roots.pem* file on your Mac.

After a few minutes, your Mac should show up as a new card in the Fleet Manager Dashboard.

Installing osquery on Linux

To install the osquery agent on your Linux endpoint(s), follow these steps:

1. Log in to your Security Onion console, click **Downloads**, and download the osquery package for Linux (the DEB file for Ubuntu, RPM for CentOS, and so on).
2. Run **sudo so-allow** on your Security Onion server to add your Linux system to the list of allowed agents for osquery. Enter **o** (for osquery) and the IP address of your Linux system when prompted.
3. Install the downloaded file on your Linux system; here's an example using dpkg on Ubuntu:

```
$ sudo dpkg -i deb-launcher.deb
```

Your Linux system should automatically show up as a new card in your Fleet Manager dashboard.

A Network Security Monitoring Crash Course

You've now installed the necessary hardware and software to monitor your network for suspicious and malicious activity. You need to be able to identify issues, respond to incidents when they occur, and keep your network, users, and data secure. In this section, we'll cover the fundamentals of how to configure and make use of osquery, Wazuh, and the Security Onion Alerts Dashboard.

Using osquery

If you're familiar with *relational databases* and *Structured Query Language (SQL)*, using osquery will be reasonably easy for you. If not, here are the basics. You can view all the data for the devices in your network that osquery manages in the Fleet Manager Dashboard. To reach the dashboard, log in to your Security Onion console at *https://<security_onion_IP>/* and click **Fleet** in the administrator menu on the left.

Data is stored in a series of *data tables*, wherein each table contains two or more columns (also called *tuples*) that include information such as hostname, IP address, MAC address, uptime, last shutdown time, and so on, for each device. Each row in the table relates to a specific entity, such as a computer or laptop, or something more atomic, like a specific user account on a device. For example, the *users* table looks similar to Table 10-1.

Table 10-1: The osquery Users Table

UID	GID	UID_Signed	GID_Signed	Username	Description
0	0	0	0	testuser	A test user account

The Username column's first row of data pertains to the *testuser* account on a device. Each of these tables is related to one or more of the other tables in the database (of which there are more than 200). These tables and their relationships allow you to perform powerful queries about the details and status of each managed device.

We can ask questions of this data using a query language called SQL, a high-level language for accessing and manipulating databases. A SQL query looks like this:

```
SELECT c1,c2 FROM tablename
```

In this query, the uppercase commands, `SELECT` and `FROM`, indicate the action you want to perform—in this case, asking for the data in columns 1 and 2, represented by the `c1` and `c2` parameters, from the table called `tablename`.

In practice, that query would look like this:

```
SELECT username FROM users
SELECT * FROM users
```

The first command returns (displays to the user running the query) all the usernames that exist in the `users` table and no other columns. The second command returns all (*) of the columns and rows from the `users` table.

NOTE *Several SQL commands are available for retrieving data in different ways; see the SQL cheat sheet at* https://www.sqltutorial.org/sql-cheat-sheet/ *for more details. See also the osquery documentation at* https://osquery.io/ *for a listing of all available tables and their data.*

Fleet stores a lot of queries in your Fleet dashboard. Click the **Query** menu on the left of the page (see Figure 10-6).

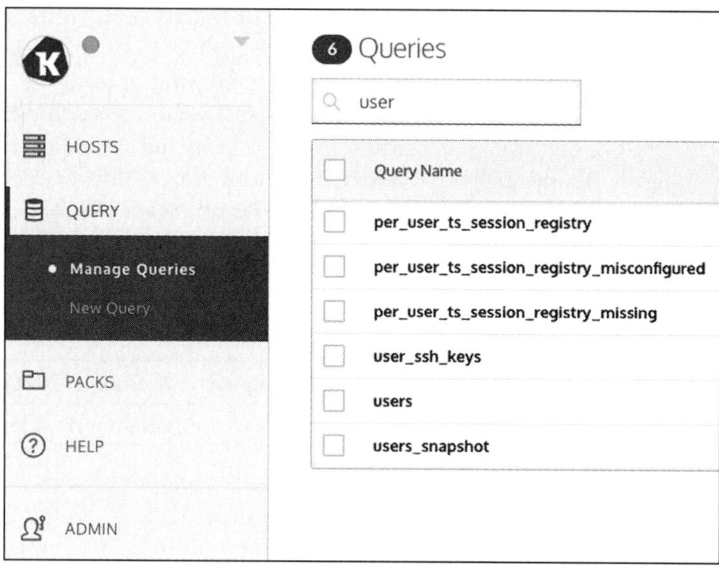

Figure 10-6: Stored SQL queries in Fleet Manager

From this menu, you can scroll through the available queries or search for a specific query using the search bar at the top of the page. Once you've identified a query you want to run, click to select it, and then click the **EDIT/RUN QUERY** button on the right side. Before you're able to execute the query, you need to select the devices you want to query for this information. Select the relevant device(s) from the Select Targets drop-down menu and then click **Run**. When the query completes, Fleet will present you with the results of the query at the bottom of the screen; you can filter the results using the column filters provided.

It's up to you which queries you run, and it depends on what kinds of problems or examples of noncompliance are most concerning to your network. However, these are a few good places to start:

`users` Useful for identifying user accounts that should or should not exist on given endpoints

`browser_plugins` Shows all browser plug-ins on a device(s); useful if your users install potentially malicious browser plug-ins

`chrome_extension` As previously, specifically looking for Chrome plug-ins

`crontab` Identifies scheduled tasks on Linux systems performing suspicious or malicious activity

`disk_free_space_pct` Identifies devices with low disk space

`installed_applications` Identifies malicious or potentially unwanted applications installed on devices

The Hosts dashboard in Fleet shows the details for each managed device at a glance in the form of cards (see Figure 10-7).

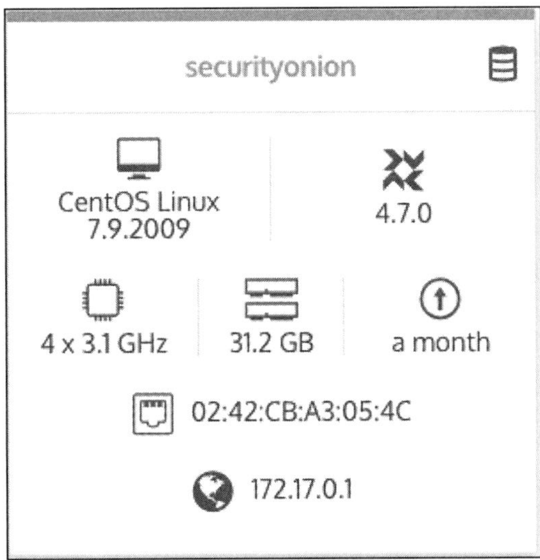

Figure 10-7: Fleet Host dashboard view

Here you can see the hostname, operating system, osquery version, processor details, amount of RAM, uptime, MAC address, and IP address of this host. Clicking the blue query button (the stacked cylinders) at the top right will allow you to easily query this device.

Spend some time familiarizing yourself with the available queries and do some online research to find other potentially useful queries. Try reviewing some of the saved queries and edit or copy them to get the queries you want.

Using Wazuh

We installed the Wazuh agent in Project 35, and we'll configure it in this section. Wazuh allows us to review the logs and alerts in Security Onion, which we'll explore in the next section.

The primary Wazuh config file is located at */opt/so/conf/wazuh/ossec.conf* on the Security Onion system. Each section of this configuration file is separate and identified with a line like the following:

```
<!-- Files/directories to ignore -->
```

You can revise the settings in this file to change the way Wazuh behaves, which can be useful if, for example, Wazuh reacts to a false positive detection and stops you from doing something benign. Review this file to get an understanding of the types of things Wazuh monitors for.

The section shown in the following snippet specifies files that contain lists of files that are known or expected to be malicious based on identified adversary behaviors, followed by files that are expected to contain trojans (a type of virus) and then files and folders to audit for various vulnerabilities:

```
--snip--
<rootkit_files>/var/ossec/etc/shared/rootkit_files.txt</rootkit_files>
    <rootkit_trojans>/var/ossec/etc/shared/rootkit_trojans.txt</rootkit_trojans>
    <system_audit>/var/ossec/etc/shared/system_audit_rcl.txt</system_audit>
    <system_audit>/var/ossec/etc/shared/system_audit_ssh.txt</system_audit>
    <system_audit>/var/ossec/etc/shared/cis_rhel7_linux_rcl.txt</system_audit>
--snip--
```

Each of these files contains a list of things Wazuh will monitor. If the agent detects a file or configuration on a device that matches a behavior or setting in the *rootkit_files.txt* file, it will take action to remediate that threat. If you don't want it to take that action, delete or comment out that line in the configuration file with a #.

When you update Wazuh as part of your efforts to consistently update and patch your Security Onion and other systems, the configuration files such as *rootkit_files.txt* may also receive updates. This ensures that as new threats are identified and indicators of compromise are made publicly available, your network stays protected. To avoid losing any changes you make to these files, consider creating new, custom configuration files (such as *my_custom_trojans.txt*) and adding a reference to this file in the *ossec.conf* file, such as the following example:

```
--snip--
<rootkit_files>/var/ossec/etc/shared/rootkit_files.txt</rootkit_files>
    <rootkit_trojans>/var/ossec/etc/shared/rootkit_trojans.txt</rootkit_trojans>
    <rootkit_trojans>/var/ossec/etc/shared/my_custom_trojans.txt</rootkit_trojans>
--snip--
```

Adding files to the *ossec.conf* file will result in Wazuh referring to those files for its configuration and settings, in addition to its default configuration files. Using custom files is a good way to add custom configurations that you might have.

If you want Wazuh to ignore a directory or list of directories on any of the endpoints on which it's installed, add that information in the relevant section. You can also tell the agent to ignore specific files or file types, to exclude certain devices from active response (if you want the agent to never block activity on a specific device that might impact your network), and to set various other options. Familiarize yourself with these configuration files so you can tailor them to your environment.

Using Security Onion as a SIEM Tool

Security Onion, in addition to the other useful capabilities it provides, acts as a *security information and event management (SIEM)* tool. Several SIEMs are available on the market, including Splunk, SolarWinds, or ManageEngine, all of which are commercial solutions and can be very expensive. Security Onion, on the other hand, is open source and free.

A SIEM is designed to aggregate data from devices in a network and act as a central repository for logs and other data. Implementing a SIEM like Security Onion centralizes your logs, making it harder for an adversary to hide their tracks by deleting the logs on any one system. It also enables you to query your logs and other system data in one location so you don't have to check every system or device individually, streamlining the process. Security Onion then analyzes this data and alerts you to potentially malicious activity. Figure 10-8 shows a list of alerts, found by logging in to the Security Onion console and clicking the Alerts option in the menu on the left.

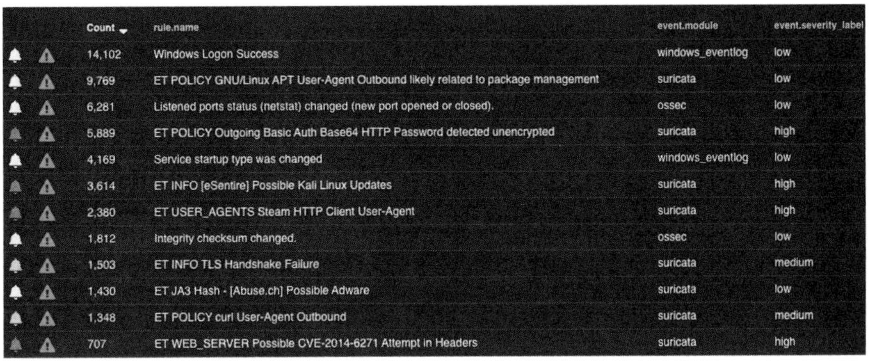

Count	rule.name	event.module	event.severity_label
14,102	Windows Logon Success	windows_eventlog	low
9,769	ET POLICY GNU/Linux APT User-Agent Outbound likely related to package management	suricata	low
6,281	Listened ports status (netstat) changed (new port opened or closed).	ossec	low
5,889	ET POLICY Outgoing Basic Auth Base64 HTTP Password detected unencrypted	suricata	high
4,169	Service startup type was changed	windows_eventlog	low
3,614	ET INFO [eSentire] Possible Kali Linux Updates	suricata	high
2,380	ET USER_AGENTS Steam HTTP Client User-Agent	suricata	high
1,812	Integrity checksum changed.	ossec	low
1,503	ET INFO TLS Handshake Failure	suricata	medium
1,430	ET JA3 Hash - [Abuse.ch] Possible Adware	suricata	low
1,348	ET POLICY curl User-Agent Outbound	suricata	medium
707	ET WEB_SERVER Possible CVE-2014-6271 Attempt in Headers	suricata	high

Figure 10-8: Security Onion alerts

When you click an alert, a context menu is displayed with filtering options; you can include, exclude, show only, or group by the alert you've selected. You can also drill down into an alert to show every instance of the alert in the timeframe you're filtering for. By expanding any of these alerts, you can see all of its information, including metadata (see Figure 10-9) such as the alert's timestamp, the source and destination IP address of the network traffic, the full message associated with the alert, the actual decoded network data that caused the rule or alert to fire, the rule itself, and often a reference so that you can learn more about the alert, including potential remediation steps or other solutions.

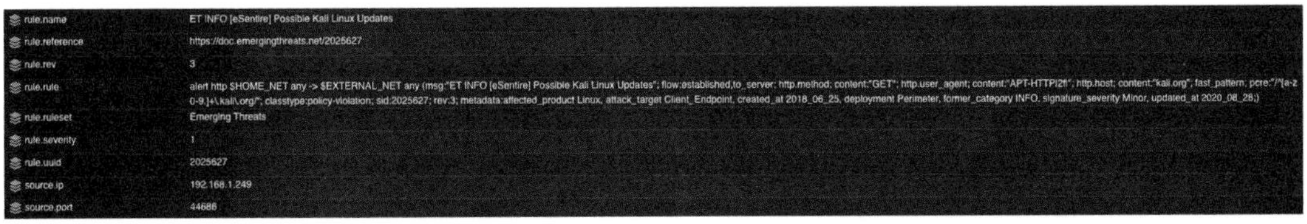

rule.name	ET INFO [eSentire] Possible Kali Linux Updates
rule.reference	https://doc.emergingthreats.net/2025627
rule.rev	3
rule.rule	alert http $HOME_NET any -> $EXTERNAL_NET any (msg:"ET INFO [eSentire] Possible Kali Linux Updates"; flow:established,to_server; http.method; content:"GET"; http.user_agent; content:"APT-HTTP|2f|"; http.host; content:"kali.org"; fast_pattern; pcre:"/^[a-z0-9.]+\.kali\.org/"; classtype:policy-violation; sid:2025627; rev:3; metadata:affected_product Linux, attack_target Client_Endpoint, created_at 2018_06_25, deployment Perimeter, former_category INFO, signature_severity Minor, updated_at 2020_08_28;)
rule.ruleset	Emerging Threats
rule.severity	1
rule.uuid	2025627
source.ip	192.168.1.249
source.port	44686

Figure 10-9: Security Onion alert metadata

In practice, the alerts dashboard will show a lot of different categories and types of activity; you'll almost always see alerts that require further investigation. Let's discuss a few to help get you started.

Table 10-2: Examples of Potentially Unwanted Software in an Environment

Rule name	Event module	Severity
ET INFO [eSentire] Possible Kali Linux Updates	suricata	high
ET USER_AGENTS Steam HTTP Client User-Agent	suricata	high
ET POLICY curl User-Agent Outbound	suricata	medium
ET POLICY Dropbox.com Offsite File Backup in Use	suricata	high
ET SCAN Possible Nmap User-Agent Observed	suricata	high
ET TFTP Outbound TFTP Read Request	suricata	high
ET P2P eMule KAD Network Connection Request	suricata	high

Table 10-2 shows several examples of software that is potentially vulnerable, could lead to or be used for malicious activity, or shouldn't be on your network in the first place. Kali Linux, for example, is typically used for penetration testing, but attackers can also use it to compromise your network. If you receive this alert, investigate it, identify the system responsible, and remove it from the network. Security Onion provides all of the information you need to do this. You could choose to take the source IP address in the alert and add firewall rules (on your hosts as well as your border firewall) to block all traffic to and from that address, as an example of one mitigation strategy.

Looking at the other alerts in Table 10-2, several pieces of software have been identified that might not be allowed or necessary in your network. Steam is a game client. Curl is a utility for transferring data to or from a server and can be used to exfiltrate data from your network or download malware. Dropbox is a cloud storage solution that can likewise be used to exfiltrate or steal data. Nmap is a network mapping tool that attackers can use to identify potential targets and vulnerabilities within your network. Trivial File Transfer Protocol (TFPT) is a vulnerable protocol used for transferring files, and eMule is a peer-to-peer application typically used for file sharing.

Generally, if you aren't using a tool or application, you should uninstall or otherwise remove it to prevent attackers from using it and make your network more secure. If you don't use curl, for example, track down the client responsible for this alert using the hostname, source and destination IP address, or other metadata in the alert itself, and uninstall or remove the offending software. If you use Dropbox, you can safely ignore the alert. Otherwise, investigate and remove it from your network. Do this for all software-related alerts.

Then, use the same process to investigate and remediate all the alerts related to potential malware activity; Table 10-3 shows an example. Drill down into each alert, identify the device(s) related to the alert, look at the references for the rule behind the alert, and identify and resolve the root cause. If you get stuck, an internet search is usually the best tool to solve a lot of problems.

Table 10-3: Possible Malware Alerts in Security Onion

Rule name	Event module	Severity
ET JA3 Hash - [Abuse.ch] Possible Adware	suricata	Low
ET JA3 Hash - Possible Malware - Neutrino	suricata	Low
ET INFO Packed Executable Download	suricata	Low
ET INFO EXE IsDebuggerPresent (Used in Malware Anti-Debugging)	suricata	Low
ET EXPLOIT Possible OpenSSL HeartBleed Large HeartBeat Response (Client Init Vuln Server)	suricata	Medium
ET EXPLOIT Possible OpenSSL HeartBleed Large HeartBeat Response (Server Init Vuln Client)	suricata	Medium

Other alerts of interest are those related to account login or log-off actions and elevation of privileges, such as Successful sudo to ROOT executed, as shown in Table 10-4.

Table 10-4: Successful and Failed Login Alerts in Security Onion

Rule name	Event module	Severity
Windows Logon Success	windows_eventlog	Low
PAM: Login session closed.	ossec	Low
PAM: Login session opened.	ossec	Low
Successful sudo to ROOT executed.	ossec	Low
Logon Failure - Unknown user or bad password	windows_eventlog	Low

While successful logon attempts alert you to accounts that may already be compromised, failed logon attempts can alert you to an attacker trying to break in. In both cases, investigate those alerts to determine whether it's legitimate activity. If, for example, you see an account increasing their privileges to root on a Linux system, determine whether it was you or another trusted user in your network. If it wasn't you or another administrator in your network, change your passwords and investigate any related activity that occurred around the same time.

Summary

Security Onion's alerts provide a starting point for you to identify and chase down suspicious activity; use them to your advantage when securing your network. Use every tool you have at your disposal, as you can be sure that adversaries are doing the same. Simply increasing the visibility of activity on your network enables you to better protect it. With the instructions and tools described in this chapter, you'll soon find a multitude of potential activity to investigate and remediate. Expect this investigation activity to be ongoing and try to keep up with the alerts in Security Onion as your network continues to grow and evolve over time.

11

TIPS FOR MANAGING USER SECURITY ON YOUR NETWORK

Being responsible for a network containing more than one user is challenging. You can't reasonably expect to manage other users' activity within your network, especially when they use their own devices. However, there are some strategies that you can use to mitigate the risks associated with multiple users.

This chapter discusses the value of strong passphrases versus passwords, password managers, multifactor authentication, and privacy-protecting browser plug-ins. It should provide the information you need to have productive discussions about security with your users.

Passwords

Having strong passwords and using different credentials for every website are the best first steps to remaining safe online. Passphrases and password managers make it harder for adversaries to guess your passwords and easier for you to manage them. *Passphrases* consist of several words, such as *libertyextremecluecustodyjerky*. You can make them more challenging to guess by adding uppercase letters, numbers, and special characters, but generally speaking, it's better to have longer passphrases that are easy to remember than complex passwords that aren't. The same rules for typical password security still apply. Don't use personally identifiable information, such as birthdays, pets' or relatives' names, or the schools you've attended. Refrain from including words that relate to the current month or season or the name of the company you work for. Basically, avoid constructing a passphrase from easy-to-guess elements.

Passphrases are longer than passwords, making them more resilient against the brute-force attacks adversaries use to crack them. In a *brute-force attack*, the attacker tries every possible combination of characters until they find the right one. They can do this programmatically, allowing for millions (or *billions*) of password guesses per second. The shorter the password and the smaller the *keyspace* (the number of character types—letters, numbers, and symbols—available), the less time it takes to crack. For example, an eight-character password consisting of lowercase letters and numbers would take less than two hours to crack on today's computing hardware. Adding one character increases that time to more than two days, and every additional character grows the time it takes to crack the password exponentially—a 30-character passphrase's cracking time approaches infinity with the computing power available today.

NOTE *Be sure to change any default passwords for your accounts and devices. Default passwords for devices such as routers and switches (such as username: admin, password: admin) are well-known and documented, so if you don't change those in your network, you're leaving the door wide open for adversaries to infiltrate your environment. Even if they aren't well known, they're easy to guess.*

Password Managers

Use a *password manager* (also called a *password safe* or *vault*) to securely store your passwords. A password manager can store hundreds of unique passphrases that are accessed by one master passphrase. This practice removes the temptation to write passphrases down, which is never a good idea. Several password managers are available, such as 1Password (*https://1password.com/*) or LastPass (*https://www.lastpass.com/*).

The best way to convey the value of a password manager is to discuss *credential stuffing*, an attack that exploits the fact that most people still use the same password across multiple services. When adversaries obtain a list of passwords and email addresses during or after a data breach, they try logging in with those credentials on various well-known sites and services, and they're often successful because a significant percentage of the password and email address combinations are reused on other sites. Users can prevent credential stuffing by using a different passphrase for every account and storing those passphrases in a password manager.

Password Breach Detection

The free service Have I Been Pwned (*https://haveibeenpwned.com/*) lets you enter your email address and immediately find out whether it's been identified in any data leaks or breaches. Figure 11-1 shows an example of a report for a compromised email account.

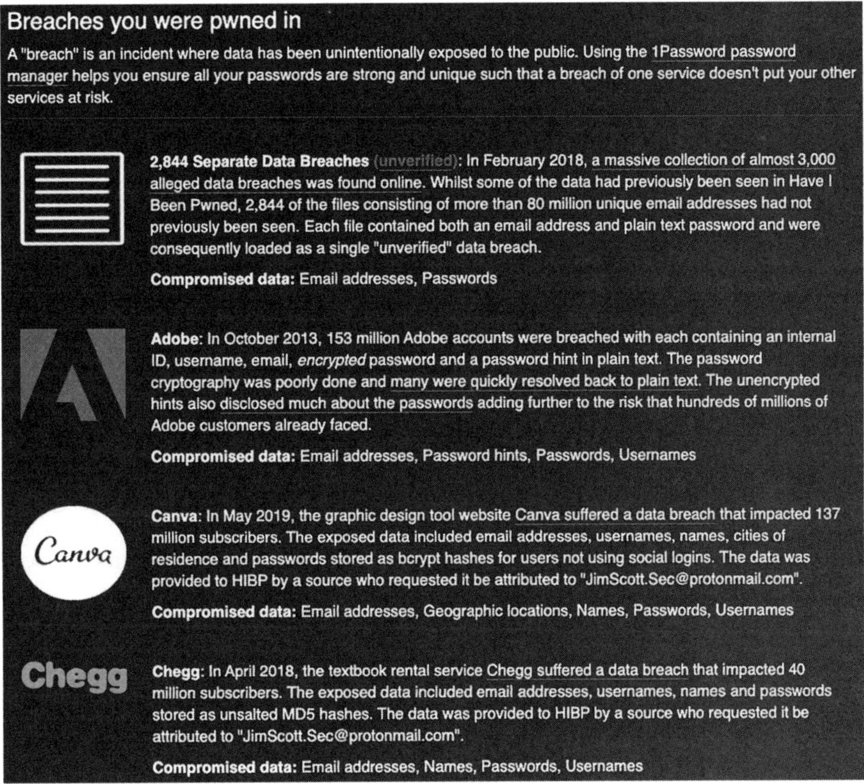

Breaches you were pwned in
A "breach" is an incident where data has been unintentionally exposed to the public. Using the 1Password password manager helps you ensure all your passwords are strong and unique such that a breach of one service doesn't put your other services at risk.
2,844 Separate Data Breaches (unverified): In February 2018, a massive collection of almost 3,000 alleged data breaches was found online. Whilst some of the data had previously been seen in Have I Been Pwned, 2,844 of the files consisting of more than 80 million unique email addresses had not previously been seen. Each file contained both an email address and plain text password and were consequently loaded as a single "unverified" data breach.
Compromised data: Email addresses, Passwords
Adobe: In October 2013, 153 million Adobe accounts were breached with each containing an internal ID, username, email, encrypted password and a password hint in plain text. The password cryptography was poorly done and many were quickly resolved back to plain text. The unencrypted hints also disclosed much about the passwords adding further to the risk that hundreds of millions of Adobe customers already faced.
Compromised data: Email addresses, Password hints, Passwords, Usernames
Canva
Canva: In May 2019, the graphic design tool website Canva suffered a data breach that impacted 137 million subscribers. The exposed data included email addresses, usernames, names, cities of residence and passwords stored as bcrypt hashes for users not using social logins. The data was provided to HIBP by a source who requested it be attributed to "JimScott.Sec@protonmail.com".
Compromised data: Email addresses, Geographic locations, Names, Passwords, Usernames
Chegg
Chegg: In April 2018, the textbook rental service Chegg suffered a data breach that impacted 40 million subscribers. The exposed data included email addresses, usernames, names and passwords stored as unsalted MD5 hashes. The data was provided to HIBP by a source who requested it be attributed to "JimScott.Sec@protonmail.com".
Compromised data: Email addresses, Names, Passwords, Usernames

Figure 11-1: Example report of a compromised email account

The service also provides ongoing updates and monitoring; you can opt to receive a notification to change your password(s) if your email address is identified in future data breaches.

Multifactor Authentication

Once you've created strong passphrases, you should implement *multifactor authentication* (sometimes called *two-factor authentication*, *2FA*, or *MFA*) on all accounts and services that offer it. While *single-factor authentication* typically requires a combination of only two things—your email address or username plus your passphrase—MFA requires two or more factors of authentication. Usually, the first factor is something you *know*, and the second is either something you *have*, like a hardware or software token, or something you *are*, like a fingerprint or other biometric. By requiring a second or third authentication factor, adversaries will have an exponentially more difficult task when trying to gain access to your accounts and systems. Adding a second factor may introduce a minor inconvenience to you or your users, but you'll be much more secure.

One of the most common MFA solutions uses SMS as a second factor, sending the user a text message containing a code or one-time password; they then use this code to log in to their account or perform certain types of transactions, particularly if it's from a new or unknown device or location. Everyone can receive text messages regardless of their phone model or service provider, it's free or cheap, it's more or less instant, and it alerts you to suspicious activity if you aren't actively trying to log in. The main drawback is that SMS isn't a secure technology, and it's relatively trivial for an attacker to gain access to someone's phone number and text messages.

Next, there are software solutions, including Google Authenticator, Authy, Microsoft Authenticator, and even password vaults like 1Password that offer MFA tokens. Typically, you'll download the app to your smartphone and scan or type in a code from your service provider (such as your bank or social media) to set up the app. When you want to log in, you'll check the app for an authentication token that you'll use along with your passphrase. The tokens change every 60 seconds. This is a significant improvement on SMS as a second factor, as an adversary would have to physically access and unlock your mobile device to retrieve the token. The rolling tokens also mean the access window is minimal, unlike SMS where access windows can be a few minutes long. Software tokens such as these are the most convenient and secure MFA option for many users.

Finally, there are hardware tokens, like Yubikey and Google Titan Key. If the key isn't plugged in to your computer, you can't access the encrypted or protected data. Hardware tokens are considered the most hardcore of the MFA solutions because losing your hardware key means you can't access your data. They offer the same or better protection as a software token, as an adversary needs physical access, but they are the least convenient; most people carry their phones with them, but it's easy to leave a hardware token at home when you need it at the office. Additionally, hardware tokens can't be phished; while SMS and other similar MFA tokens can be drawn out of a potential victim via social engineering and phishing attacks, an adversary can't access your hardware key remotely.

WEBCAM COVERS

An important aside when discussing computer security is the necessity of webcam covers. Adversaries can gain access to the webcam on your laptop or computer and surreptitiously monitor whatever may be happening in front of the computer without alerting you that the camera is on. To protect your own privacy and that of those around you, invest in some low-tech, opaque tape or a webcam cover (available inexpensively from many online stores).

Browser Plug-ins

All major internet browsers, such as Google Chrome, Mozilla Firefox, and Microsoft Edge, have several browser plug-ins or add-ons to block ads and trackers (see Chapter 7 for more on trackers) and more generally improve user privacy. The plug-ins mentioned here have been vetted and are known to be legitimate or are created and maintained by well-known and trusted sources. Browser plug-ins are designed to provide additional functionality to a standard browser, and users can choose from a wide range of available plug-ins to improve their browsing experience. It's beneficial to discuss the pros and cons of these browser add-ons with your users to enable them to make educated decisions about which plug-ins to use and which to avoid.

Adblock Plus

Adblock Plus removes "unacceptable" or disruptive ads from websites. To install this plug-in, navigate to *https://adblockplus.org/en/download* and download the appropriate version for your browser or device. Once it's installed, go to the **Settings** page for the plug-in (shown in Figure 11-2) and select **Block Additional Tracking**, **Block Social Media Icons Tracking**, and **Disallow Acceptable Ads**. You can also choose to allowlist specific websites if you choose.

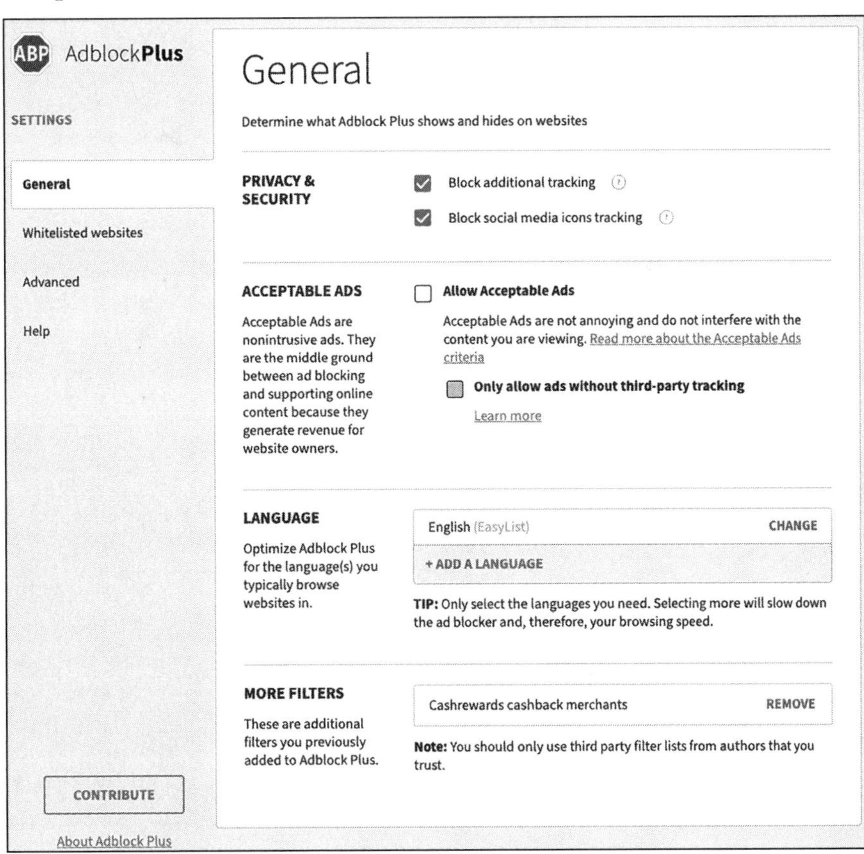

Figure 11-2: Adblock Plus settings

Additional Tracking includes methods such as websites gathering your browsing habits. Blocking Social Media Icons Tracking keeps you from being tracked by social media buttons across the websites you visit. Finally, Disallow Acceptable Ads removes all ads from websites (as much as possible anyway). All of this results in a cleaner, faster web-browsing experience.

Ghostery

Similar to Adblock Plus, Ghostery's mission is to improve user privacy by removing many user tracking capabilities on websites. To install Ghostery, browse to *https://www.ghostery.com/* and sign up for an account. Download and install the plug-in for your browser; once it's installed, the plug-in will function out of the box, but you can modify the settings from the plug-in menu if you so choose, as shown in Figure 11-3.

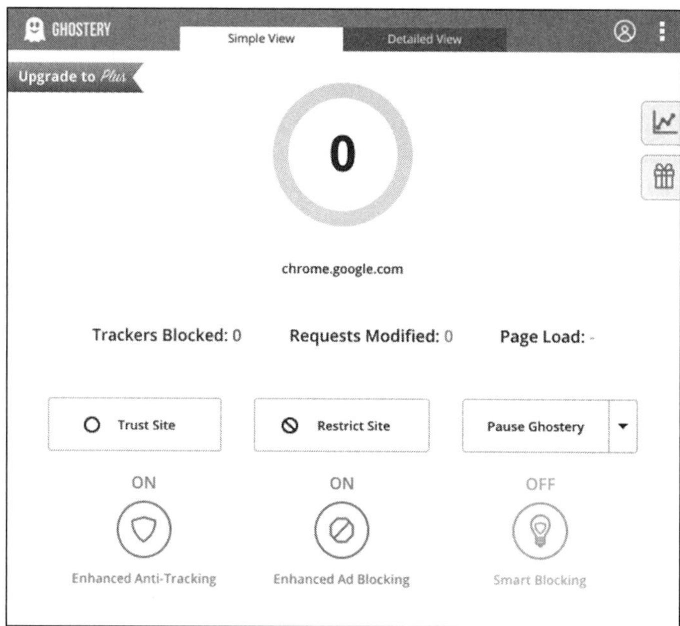

Figure 11-3: Ghostery settings

If you want to manually allow or disable a specific website and pause or resume Ghostery, you can do so from this menu.

HTTPS Everywhere

HTTPS is the secure internet protocol preceded by the insecure HTTP protocol. HTTPS uses SSL/TLS to secure your internet traffic while you browse the internet. Using encryption protects your traffic so adversaries can't intercept it and decrypt it. Unfortunately, not all websites provide encryption for their users. This is where a plug-in like HTTPS Everywhere comes in handy; it provides the encryption layer for you, keeping you secure no matter what you're doing in your browser.

To install this plug-in, browse to *https://www.eff.org/https-everywhere/* and download and install it. From here, the options are simple: on or off (as shown in Figure 11-4).

Figure 11-4: HTTPS Everywhere settings

With this plug-in installed and running, you can feel safe knowing all of your browser traffic is being encrypted.

Internet of Things Considerations

We discussed internet of things devices like Google Home and Amazon Alexa and the methods by which you can mitigate the risks of smart devices using network segmentation in detail in Chapter 2. However, there are still risks associated with devices with always-on cameras and/or microphones that need to be considered.

Whether it's a laptop of desktop computer, a gaming console, or a smart home device, many modern endpoints have a microphone or camera (or both) built in. For a determined adversary, these devices can be used to spy on you and those around you. Therefore, wherever possible, it's best to invest in smart home devices that have a physical off switch or button for these features. If that isn't possible, consider using a webcam cover (available cheaply from many online stores) or even a piece of opaque tape to cover your web cameras when not in use. Doing so is one of the best ways to protect your privacy.

Besides covering any cameras, consider where you place and use smart home devices. In the case of smart speakers, you might choose to use them only in common areas, away from private areas like bedrooms or private offices. Consider the activities and conversations that might take place in range of the microphone and place devices accordingly.

Additional Resources

This book has been an introduction to the fundamentals of cybersecurity and ideally has enabled you to think more deeply about the security of your network and users and implement solutions to help protect your privacy. However, there are so many more resources available that delve further into these topics than could be covered here. The first I'd like to mention is *https://chrissanders.org/*. Chris has written several books and online courses covering topics such as network security monitoring, intrusion detection, and advanced use of the ELK stack, which we briefly discussed in Chapter 10. If you'd like more information on any of these topics, this is a great place to start.

Another fantastic resource for anyone interested in cybersecurity, digital forensics, or incident response is *https://dfir.training/*. This website contains a wealth of information related to tools, training courses (free and commercial), practice materials, and other resources to add to your knowledgebase and improve your security maturity.

Finally, SANS is a research and training organization with a focus on cybersecurity. At *https://www.sans.org/*, you can find more information on their training courses, but also several resources and research papers related to tools and techniques for securing networks and endpoints, from both a defensive and offensive viewpoint.

Summary

Ultimately, your online privacy and security can be as well-protected as you like. The trade-off for being secure on the internet is one of compromising privacy, security, or both, for convenience. At the cost of slightly less convenience, you'll receive a better overall experience on the internet and enjoy a higher level of security and privacy, whether it's yours alone or shared with your users. The benefits of being secure far outweigh the inconvenience of implementing these solutions.

INDEX

Symbols

A

B

C

D

E

F

J

K

L

M

P

R

T

U

V

W

X

Y

Z

RESOURCES

Visit *https://nostarch.com/cybersecurity-small-networks/* for errata and more information.